THE END OF
PROTESTANTISM

THE END OF PROTESTANTISM

Pursuing Unity in a Fragmented Church

PETER J. LEITHART

Brazos Press

a division of Baker Publishing Group
Grand Rapids, Michigan

Published by Brazos Press
a division of Baker Publishing Group
P.O. Box 6287, Grand Rapids, MI 49516-6287
www.brazospress.com

Printed in the United States of America

Library of Congress Cataloging-in-Publication Data
Names: Leithart, Peter J., author.
Title: The end of Protestantism : pursuing unity in a fragmented Church / Peter J. Leithart.
Description: Grand Rapids, MI : Brazos Press, 2016. | Includes bibliographical references and index.
Identifiers: LCCN 2016022624 | ISBN 9781587433771 (cloth)
Subjects: LCSH: Protestantism. | Protestant churches. | Christian union. | Protestant churches—United States.
Classification: LCC BX4817 .L45 2016 | DDC 280/.4—dc23
LC record available at https://lccn.loc.gov/2016022624

Chapter 9 was originally published in a slightly modified form in Michael Bird and Brian Rosner, eds., *Mending a Fractured Church: How to Seek Unity with Integrity* (Bellingham, WA: Lexham, 2015). Used by permission.

Portions of this text have been revised from the author's blog posts at *First Things* (http://www.firstthings.com/blogs/leithart/) and are used here by permission.

16   17   18   19   20   21   22   7   6   5   4   3   2   1

To my unborn grandchild,
who may, or may not,
be another grandson

Contents

Acknowledgments   ix

1. An Interim Ecclesiology   1

MOVEMENT ONE: **CHURCH UNITED**

2. Evangelical Unity   11
3. A Reformed Church   25
4. The End of Protestantism   37

MOVEMENT TWO: **CHURCH DIVIDED**

5. The Case for Denominationalism   55
6. The Case against Denominationalism   71
7. Denominationalism's Dividing Walls   89

INTERMEZZO

8. From Glory to Glory: The Pattern of History   101

MOVEMENT THREE: **DIVIDED CHURCH DISSOLVING**

9. The Restructuring of Global Christianity   119
10. American Denominationalism and the Global Church   133

11. American Denominationalism in the Twenty-First
    Century   149

MOVEMENT FOUR: **UNITED CHURCH REBORN**

12. A Way Forward: From Present to Future   165

    Notes   193
    Index   223

Acknowledgments

I have been thinking and writing about Protestant catholicity for more than two decades, but this book had a more immediate catalyst in the energetic response I received to several essays published in *First Things* magazine during 2013. *First Things* later teamed up with the Torrey Honors Institute at Biola University to sponsor a public forum at Biola in the spring of 2014 on the future of Protestantism. I am grateful to the organizers of that event and to my interlocutors, Carl Trueman, Fred Sanders, and Peter Escalante, for helping me refine my thoughts about these issues. During a spring teaching session at New St. Andrews College in 2015, I had the privilege of debating these issues again with Douglas Wilson. My practical suggestions, such as they are, were inspired by the examples of Rev. Richard Bledsoe of Boulder, Colorado, and the late Pastor Tom Clark of Somerset, New Hampshire, both of whom embody local catholicity.

Over the past several years, I have been part of ecumenical dialogues sponsored by Evangelicals and Catholics Together, the Center for Catholic-Evangelical Dialogue, and the Paradosis Center at John Brown University. I am grateful for the friendships I have formed in these settings—with Matthew Levering, Hans Boersma, Chad Raith, Timothy George, Tom Guarino, Francesca Murphy, Rusty Reno, Robert Wilken, and many others—and grateful too for the opportunity to learn much from theologians outside my own tiny sector of Protestantism.

At Brazos, Dave Nelson and his team provided steady guidance as this book took shape. My thanks to all these, and to the many who have contributed to this book in ways that I have failed to mention here.

This book is dedicated to my forthcoming, as yet unnamed grandchild, reputed to be a grandson—by the time the book is published, we'll know for sure. I would be glad to see the grandsons evening the score with the granddaughters, though I hasten to add that it's *not a competition.* My prayer is that he will grow up in a world where the broken church is being put together again, and I even entertain fond hopes that he will play some small role in that reunion. Regardless of what lies ahead in that regard, I have no doubt that his life will be full of challenge, and also trust that our faithful Lord will prepare him to meet these challenges and triumph through them all.

Though I do not yet know you, Noni and I love you and can't wait to see you.

1

An Interim Ecclesiology

Jesus prayed that his disciples would be united as he is united with his Father (John 17:21). Jesus is in the Father, and the Father in Jesus. Each finds a home in the other. Each dwells in the other in love.

Jesus prayed that the church would exhibit *this* kind of unity: Each disciple should hospitably receive every other disciple, as the Father receives the Son. Each church should dwell in every other church, as the Son dwells in the Father.

This is what Jesus *wants* for his church. It is *not* what his church is.

The church is divided. It is *not* that the church has remained united while groups falsely calling themselves churches have split off. It is *not* that we are spiritually united while empirically divided.

The church is a unique society, the body of Christ and the temple of the Spirit. But it is a visible society that exists among other societies.

That visible society is divided, and that means the *church* is divided. This is not as it should be. This is not the church that Jesus desires. So long as we remain divided, we grieve the Spirit of Jesus, who is the living Passion of the Father and Son.

Some will object that I am exaggerating. Some will object that we are united in many ways. All churches confess common doctrines, celebrate common rituals, have some form of pastoral care and leadership. There is unity in doctrine, sacrament, and office.

In reality, every apparent point of unity is also a point of conflict and division. We are united in confession of the God who is Father, Son, and Spirit, in confessing Jesus as the incarnate Son who died and rose again. Most churches can affirm most of the *contents* of the Apostles' Creed, even if they do not adopt the creed.

Yet we are doctrinally divided. Virtually every church has added to the early creeds and made those additions fundamental to the church. Presbyterian pastors must affirm not only the early creeds but also the elaborate system of the Westminster Confession. Lutheran churches define themselves doctrinally by the Formula of Concord, a doctrinal statement used by no one but Lutherans.

Even when we affirm the same doctrine, we affirm it differently. Protestants and Catholics both confess "justification," but they mean very different things by it. Even on something as central to Christian faith as Jesus's resurrection from the dead, churches diverge. Some deny that the resurrection actually happened. Others, rightly, insist on Paul's claim that without the resurrection we are not saved.

To say that we agree on fundamentals assumes that we agree on what the fundamentals are. But we do not agree. For some, it is fundamental dogma to believe that the pope can speak infallibly and that Mary was immaculately conceived and assumed into heaven. For others, those are not only nonfundamental; they are not even true.

The church is as doctrinally divided as it is doctrinally unified, if not more so.

We celebrate the same sacraments of baptism and the Lord's Supper. To that degree we are united. But it is a low degree of union.

We cannot agree on how many sacraments there are. We do not agree on what those sacraments do, how essential they are, whether we should call them sacraments. We cannot agree on how to perform them. We differ on how much water is needed to baptize and how much of the baptized person's body needs to get wet. We disagree about whether a baptism with only a little water is a baptism at all.

Our liturgies are wildly diverse. Some churches have formal, repetitive liturgies that change little from week to week. Other churches follow no apparent liturgy at all. In some churches the sermon is the high point of worship; in others the sermon is reduced to a brief scriptural meditation.

We disagree on whether to sit or stand or kneel at the Lord's Supper and how often we should have it. We disagree about what happens to the bread and wine and about whether we should reserve a consecrated host for veneration. The largest church in the world will not admit millions of other believers to its eucharistic celebrations. The tiniest sects of Christianity likewise refuse to commune with any but their own.

Some believe that veneration of icons is a spiritual discipline; others call it liturgical idolatry. Some believe we should offer prayers to the Mother of God and the saints; others decry it as necromancy.

The church is sacramentally and liturgically divided.

We are not united by visible authority. Most (not all) churches have pastors, but we are not united in our understanding of what pastors do. We do not agree about what makes a pastor a pastor. Pastors of some churches regard pastors of other churches as nonpastors because their ordinations are defective. We do not agree about whether bishops are necessary to the church, or what form of church polity is best.

Catholics claim that the pope is the universal bishop, which is hotly disputed by everyone else. Free churches acknowledge no authority beyond the congregation.

When it is exercised, church discipline is not respected by other churches. Excommunicated Christians can easily find another church to receive them, no questions asked.

The church is governmentally divided.

Every mark of unity is also a sign and site of division. Jesus wants his church to be one. But we are not.

How can Christians live with this contradiction? Why do we not grieve with the grieving Spirit? Should we not join Jesus in praying that the church be one as the Father and Son are one? And, having so prayed, should we not so live?

We can live with ourselves because we have created a system to salve our conscience and to deflect the Spirit's grief. We have found a way of being church that lets us be at peace with division. Denominationalism allows us to be friendly to one another while refusing to join one another. It allows us to be cordial while refusing to commune together at the Lord's table. It permits us to be civil while refusing to acknowledge that another's baptism is truly baptism, or another's ordination truly ordination. It makes us forgetful of our divisions and our defiance of Jesus.

Churches and Christians have fellowship across denominational lines. Denominational churches serve and evangelize and witness together. American Christianity has been marked by a lively interdenominational spirit of mission. God uses denominational churches and Christians to accomplish his ends.

But denominationalism is not what Jesus desires for his church. It does not fulfill his prayer. Denominationalism does not produce a church that is united as the Father is united with the Son and the Son with the Father. Denominational churches do not dwell in, nor are they indwelt by, one another. Methodist churches dwell in other Methodist churches; Lutheran churches are indwelt by other Lutheran churches. In the nature of the case, being a Methodist church means *not* dwelling in a Lutheran church. Being a Methodist church means *not* exhibiting the unity of the Father and the Son.

Denominationalism is not union. It is the opposite. It is the institutionalization of division. Our friendliness is part of the problem. It enables us to be complacent about defining ourselves not by union with our brothers but by our divisions.

Once there were no denominations. Once the church was *not* mappable into three great "families" of churches—Catholic, Protestant, and Orthodox.

Once there was just "the church," then East and West, and then, over centuries, the crazy quilt of churches we know today. As the Great Schism created "Catholicism" and "Orthodoxy," so the Protestant Reformation not only produced Lutheran and Reformed and Anglican churches but also founded the Catholic Church as a distinct Christian body. Each division gave Christians new names.

Denominationalism was not lurking under the surface, waiting for a Luther to midwife it into the world. The three "families" did not exist in seminal form prior to the various fissures that produced them. The distinctions and groupings, the territorial boundaries, the liturgical and doctrinal differences, all the topographical clues and cues by which we map the Christian world today had to be *created*.

Whatever was *once* true but is *not* true any longer is contingent, by definition. "Once" is a signal that whatever is under consideration is not a design feature. Our mapping of the church into three clusters of churches has emerged over the course of a thousand years of church history. It is in no way essential to the church, as Jesus and the Spirit, the Scriptures and sacraments, are of the essence of the church. As Ephraim Radner has put it, the historical formations of the church have *no ontological weight*. We are what we will be, and what we will be is *one* body united by the Spirit to the Son in communion with the heavenly Father. *That* is the essence of the church.

Ecclesial maps have changed in the past. They will change again. The church as we know it had to be mapped, and so it is *re*mappable.

Edit that: it is not remapp*able*; it *is being* remapped before our eyes, if we open our eyes to see it. Or, edit again: it *has been* remapped, while many of us had our heads down and our eyes fixed obsessively on the frequently petty travails of our own denominations.

The church is being rearranged, and that opens up fresh opportunities for reunion, fresh opportunities to repent of our divisions and to seek once again to please our Lord Jesus. We are seeing God answer Jesus's prayer before our eyes, and that encourages us to pray and work more fervently.

This will require nothing less than death. To please Jesus, we must share his cross by dying to our unfaithful forms of church and churchmanship. We must die to the names we now bear, in hopes of receiving new ones. Reunion demands death because death in union with Jesus is the only path toward resurrection.

■ ■ ■

This book is an exhortation in the interim. I speak from within denominational Christianity to call Christians to strive in the Spirit toward a new way of being church. This is an interim ecclesiology and an interim agenda aimed specifically at theologically conservative evangelical Protestant churches. I am not addressing other churches, except tangentially. I have suggestions for Catholic and Orthodox churches, but I have a faint suspicion they do not care much what I have to say. Protestants may not care much either, but at least in addressing Protestants I can address my own tribe and appeal to them to abandon their tribalism.

I propose an ecclesiological program for the present. If it were enacted, it would move Protestant churches *toward* full reunion, toward obedience to Jesus.

Protestants should adopt a different stance toward one another, toward Catholics and Orthodox and Pentecostals and other new movements in

Christianity. I propose that Protestants pursue internal reforms that, I argue, will bring their churches more in line with Scripture as well as with Christian tradition. My agenda will make Protestant churches more catholic, but that is because it will make them more evangelical. The two go together because catholicity is inherent in the gospel.

I call this ecclesiology and this agenda "Reformational Catholicism," which I have composed in four movements. The first movement lays out a vision for the Reformational Catholic church of the future, arguing that it expresses a biblical and a Reformational paradigm for the church. The second movement focuses on denominational Christianity in the United States. While acknowledging that God has used denominationalism to extend his kingdom, I argue that it suffers from fundamental flaws and inhibits us from manifesting the unity Jesus desires.

We *know* we are not condemned to denominational Christianity in perpetuity. In a biblical intermezzo, I show how the Creator God regularly tears down the world and reassembles it in new ways.

The third movement argues that God is remapping the global church and that the American denominational system is collapsing in the process. I argue that this opens an opportunity for Reformational Catholicism.

In the fourth movement, I offer some guidelines to theologians, pastors, and lay Christians who want to enact this interim ecclesiology in the hope of ultimate reunion.

■ ■ ■

This amounts to a call for the end of Protestantism. Insofar as opposition to Catholicism is constitutive of Protestant identity; insofar as Protestants, whatever their theology, have acted as if they are members of a different church from Roman Catholics and Orthodox; insofar as Protestants define themselves over against other Protestants, as Lutherans are *not*-Reformed and Baptists are *not*-Methodist—in all these respects, Jesus bids Protestantism to come and die. And he calls us to exhibit the unity that the Father has with the Son in the Spirit.

To persist in a provisional Protestant-versus-Catholic or Protestant-versus-Protestant self-identification is a defection from the gospel. If the gospel is true, we are who we are by union with Jesus in his Spirit with his people. It then *cannot* be the case that we are who we are by differentiation from other believers.

The Father loves the Son and will give him what he asks. He does not give a stone when Jesus asks for bread. When Jesus asks that his disciples be one, the Father will not give him bits and fragments. The Father will give the Son a unified church, and the Son will unify the church by his Spirit. That is what the church will be. It is what the Son and Spirit will make of us as we follow, worship, and pray. It is what we will be, and we are called by our crucified Lord to die to what we are *now* so that we may become what we will be.

CHURCH UNITED

2

Evangelical Unity

When Jesus prays that his disciples would be one as the Father and Son are one, he is not introducing a new theme into the Bible. From its opening chapters, the Bible tells the story of a human race unified, divided, and then reunified.

First there was Adam, the father of humanity. Then there was Noah, a new Adam, father of a new, postdiluvian humanity. Many of the major peoples and cities of the Bible first appear in Genesis 10, in a list of descendants from Shem, Ham, and Japheth. Mizraim—Egypt—is one of the sons of Ham, as is Canaan (Gen. 10:6). Nimrod, a son of Cush, founds the cities of Babel and Nineveh (vv. 10–11). The Pathrusim and Casluhim—"from which came the Philistines"—were children of Mizraim, Egypt (v. 14). All of them came from a single man who had sons and whose sons had sons. All traced their heritage back to the Adam whom God formed from the ground, to Noah who passed through the waters into a new creation.

Humanity was created one but was divided by sin. Sin disrupted, and it resulted in division. After Adam sinned, he and Eve covered their vulnerable nakedness. When Yahweh confronted them, Adam turned on his wife, accusing her and implicitly accusing God. Created to become one flesh, Adam and Eve were estranged from one another. In the next generation, the division caused by sin ended with murder: Cain killed his brother. In the garden and the field, division was the result of disobedience and false worship. Adam and Eve listened to the serpent and so disobeyed God in their garden sanctuary. Before Cain became the first murderer, he was the first to offer unacceptable sacrifice.

The third "fall" had to do with the unity of humanity, but from the opposite direction. Adam's and Cain's sins led to division, husband against wife and brother against brother. The sin of the sons of God (Gen. 6:1–4) was a sin of false union. Because they intermarried with the daughters of men, the world was corrupted and filled with violence.[1]

Division and false union come together in the tower of Babel episode, the great biblical story of false unification and final dispersal (Gen. 11:1–9). A human race unified in speech and confession tried to build a city and a tower, but Yahweh intervened to stop the construction and scatter the rebels. He confused their languages and lip (religious confession), so that they would never be able to unite their energies in the same way again. Though God made humanity to be one, he scattered a humanity unified in opposition to him, a humanity unified by coercion, fear, or slavery, all efforts at unity that impose uniformity on the human race.[2] Babelic powers reappear at various times throughout Scripture—in Egypt (Exodus), at certain phases of the neo-Babylonian Empire (Daniel), in the Roman beast who demands that all peoples and nations worship him (Rev. 13). Each of these Babels suffers the same fate as the original Babel: God overthrows them and liberates their slaves.

Babel was a perversion of God's own intention for humanity, and in the aftermath of Babel God embarked on his own plan for reconciliation and reunion. God chose Abram and called him to be the bearer of his promises. As many have noted, the Abrahamic promises match the aspirations of the people of Babel. God promised Abram blessings that Babel sought but could not reach. The Babelites strove to make a name; God promised to make Abram's name great (Gen. 12:2). They built a city, but Abram looked for the city built by God. They wanted to unite the nations, but God promised to make Abram an agent of blessing to all the families of the earth (v. 3).[3]

In calling Abram, Yahweh chose to separate one people from all the others. Israel received the oracles of God, enjoyed the covenants and the temple and the glory and the promises (Rom. 9:2–4). But separation was never God's final aim. If sin brings disruption and division, overcoming sin means reuniting the race. God planned to crush the head of the serpent whose temptation divided the one human race at the beginning. The separation of Abraham and Israel was always overshadowed by the promise that the one God would one day bless humanity as *one* humanity. As he did during the creation week, God separated in order ultimately to reunite. He dug a rib out of Adam to make Eve, so that the two could become one flesh. He dug Abraham out of the flesh of humanity to make Israel, so that ultimately he could knit the human race back together again.

In Psalms and the Prophets, the Abrahamic promise is reiterated again and again. The nations will stream to Zion and worship the God of Israel, beating their swords to plowshares and their spears to pruning hooks (Isa. 2:2–4). It will be impossible to distinguish the homeborn children from the adopted. Egypt and Babylon, Philistia, Tyre, and Ethiopia will be registered as if they were Zion's own children (Ps. 87:4–6).

One New Man

Jesus came to fulfill this promise of reunification. He was the son of Abraham (Matt. 1:1) come to fulfill the promises to Abraham. He came with a sword. His teaching and actions provoked opposition and forced people in Israel to choose sides. He divided fathers from sons, mothers from daughters, brothers from brothers. But division was not an end in itself. At the heart of Jesus's ministry was his work to realize the promise of the "one." Jesus died and rose to repair the breach in the human race, to gather the scattered, to form one new man.

Prior to his death, Jesus prayed that his disciples would be one, and he specified the kind of unity he and his Father desire: "that they may all be one; even as You, Father, are in Me and I in You, that they also may be in Us" (John 17:21). The unity of the church is rooted in the unity of the Father and Son, and because of that the unity of the church manifests the sort of unity that exists between Father and Son. Jesus died and rose again to make the church one, that is to say, so that one believer will be in another, so that one church will indwell another, so that each community of believers will make hospitable room for other believers and communities. The unity of the church is to be an image of God's triunity.

This is how Paul describes in Galatians 3 the Abrahamic promise and Jesus's work.[4] Paul was fighting Judaizers. Under pressure from Jerusalem, the Galatian church had reverted to the divisions that characterized the old world. Peter refused to eat with gentiles, an act that Paul saw as an abandonment of the gospel and a threat to justification by faith (Gal. 2:11–17). For Paul, the gospel must be enacted in practice, in the union of Jews and gentiles, slave and free, male and female at a common table. As Paul explains his rebuke of Peter, he goes back to Genesis 15, which says that Abraham believed God's reverse-Babel promise, "all the nations will be blessed in you" (Gal. 3:8). God himself pre-evangelizes Abraham with the promise of blessing to the nations.

Paul emphasizes that Torah is a temporary arrangement and Moses at best a penultimate mediator, because he is not the mediator of "the one" seed of Abraham that is Christ. But God *is* one (Gal. 3:20). If God is one but Moses is *not* the mediator of the one, then Moses cannot be mediator of the final order of the people of God. The one God must have one people, and insofar as Torah divides Jew from gentile, it must be a temporary arrangement, ordered to the realization of the promise to Abraham. As N. T. Wright puts it, Paul uses the Shema, the confession that the God of Israel is one God, to "relativize the Torah."[5] For Paul, the gospel announces the fulfillment of the one God's one plan for the one human race: the plan to unify all tribes, tongues, nations, and peoples in Christ.[6]

Paul emphasizes that this promise is given to a singular seed rather than to many seeds (Gal. 3:16). Christ is the single recipient of the promise, and all those who trust in Jesus and follow him are members of "Christ."[7] The law enters after the promise but does not nullify or qualify it. Even when Jew and gentile were distinct because of Torah, God's purpose in the promise to Abraham stood. God still intended to bring the human race into unity. The one God still intended to gather the scattered into one humanity.

This came as news to the pagan world. And it was good news.

"Christianity," writes Eugen Rosenstock-Huessy, "came into a world of divided loyalties." Each race, tribe, class, nation, and empire lived to itself. Peoples had different gods, different customs, different political structures. Each pagan history "begins somewhere within time," with the founding of Rome or the Olympic games, and each history is therefore the history of a single people. Pagans had no single history because paganism did not conceive of the human race as the kind of thing that might have a single history. Paganism meant "disunity, dividedness of mankind." Christianity did not "simply erase these loyalties," which would have been nihilism. Jesus came not to abolish but to fulfill, and "by its gift of a real future, Christianity implanted in the very midst of men's loyalties a power which, reaching back from the end of time, drew them step by step into unity."[8] This is what salvation means, "the advance of the singular against the plural." Salvation enters a world of "many gods, many lands, many peoples," many histories, and it proclaims instead a set of singularities: "one God, one world, one humankind."[9]

Rosenstock-Huessy is right: "One God = one humanity" is axiomatic for Paul. The reunion of humanity in Christ *is* the gospel, the revelation of the one God against his many rivals. The unity of the church is an "evangelical" unity, a unity proclaimed in the good news of Jesus, a unity that must be realized among those who believe it.

Sevenfold Unity

Ephesians 2 lays out seven dimensions of the unity of the new humanity in the church. Gentiles, Paul writes, were once "separate from Christ, excluded from the commonwealth of Israel, and strangers to the covenants of promise, having no hope and without God in the world" (v. 12). Through Jesus's blood, they are brought near. According to Paul, the death of Jesus does not merely establish intimacy between God and the gentile world. Precisely because Jesus brings the gentiles near, as he had brought the Jews near, he unites Jews and gentiles together as a single people. The cross breaks down not only the barriers between God and humanity; it breaks down the wall dividing the human race, abolishing the enmity of the Torah that divided them, "that in Himself He might make the two into one new man, thus establishing peace" (v. 15). Once strangers and aliens among the Jews, gentiles are now fully members of the household of God, fellow citizens with the holy ones (*sympolitai ton hagion*, v. 19). Once distant from the temple of God, now they *are* that temple, built up as a dwelling place in the Spirit (vv. 21–22), a unified house of prayer for all nations.

Scattered throughout this stirring passage are references to the work of the Spirit. By the Spirit, Jews and gentiles together have access to the

Father. The Spirit who brings everyone near is a singular Spirit, the "one Spirit" of God (v. 18). The same Spirit dwells in Jew and gentile, consecrating this new people as a holy temple in the Spirit (v. 22). Paul placed a similar emphasis on the Spirit in Galatians 3–4, where he calls the gift of the Spirit the blessing of Abraham (3:14). It is the advent of the Son and the Spirit of the Son that makes Jews and gentiles cry out "Abba" to a common Father (4:4–6). The Spirit shared by the Father and Son, the Spirit who is the unifying Love of the Father and Son, is the Spirit poured out on the church to make one new man.

Jesus breaks down barriers at the cross. The Spirit continues that work at Pentecost. After his ascension, Jesus pours out his Spirit on the disciples, who preach the good news to an assembly of every tribe and nation under heaven (Acts 2). Pentecost is a chiastic reversal of Babel:

A   Table of nations (Gen. 10)
   B   Scattering at Babel (Gen. 11)
      C   Call of Abraham (Gen. 12)
         . . .
      C′ Gift of the Spirit (Acts 2:1–4)
   B′ Nations hear the good news together (Acts 2:5–7)
A′ Table of nations (Acts 2:8–11)

Through the Son of Abraham who unleashes the blessing of Abraham—the Spirit—the one God at long last fulfills his promise to make one humanity in a new Adam.[10]

The Spirit is the source of the church's diversity as well as of her unity. One and the same Spirit gives gifts of wisdom, knowledge, faith, healing, miracles, tongues, interpretation, prophecy, service, administration (Rom. 12; 1 Cor. 12). This diversity is not division, since one and the same Spirit harmonizes these gifts so that they all contribute to the common good, to the edification of the body. Through the diverse gifts of the Spirit, the church grows up to the full stature of what she is, the fullness of Christ (Eph. 4:13).

We can put this in trinitarian terms: The Father sent the Son to become the seed of Abraham to fulfill the promises to Abraham. Exalted to heaven, the Son sends the Spirit who calls together and knits together people from all nations. Divided humanity is reunited as the family of the heavenly Father, in the body of the Son, as the temple of the Spirit.

The church is reunited humanity, the social manifestation of the gospel of Jesus. The church is salvation itself in social form. Humanity was created to be one. Sin divided and scattered, but God was determined to overcome sin and reunite humanity by the Spirit in the seed of Abraham. Sin has not been entirely overcome. Death remains as the last enemy. The human race will be more unified at the end than it is in the present. But Jesus has overcome the world and crushed the head of the ruler of this world. He has triumphed over Satan. If the reunion of humanity has not taken place, Jesus's death and resurrection had no effect. Unless the gospel comes into social reality as the church, there *is* no salvation and we are still in our sins.

The gospel is the good news of reunion, a reunion of God with man and of humans with one another that takes public, historical form in the church. No wonder Paul was beside himself when the Corinthians divided along party lines. "Is Christ divided?" (1 Cor. 1:13 KJV).

Be What You Will Be

Ephesians 4 offers the most succinct summary of the unity to which Christians are called, the unity that Jesus died and sent his Spirit to achieve: "There is one body and one Spirit, just as you were called in one hope of your calling; one Lord, one faith, one baptism, one God and Father of all who is over all and through all and in all" (vv. 4–6). It is a thoroughly trinitarian formula. The one Spirit is associated with the one body and the one hope; the one Lord Jesus with the one calling, the one faith, the one baptism; God the Father over all. One God—the one *Triune* God—will have one people. Spirit, Lord, and Father create and sustain a people in sevenfold unity, a unity that is the new creation in Christ.

The church is to be unified in hope, eagerly expecting the fuller and final fulfillment of God's promises. Elsewhere, Paul emphasizes that the church is to be unified in mind, spirit, and confession. He rejoices when the Philippians are "of the same mind, maintaining the same love, united in spirit, intent on one purpose" (Phil. 2:2). Unity in faith includes holding to a unified set of beliefs, a unified confession of truth, but includes a common purpose and intention. It encompasses a union in prayer, including prayer for the unity that is the direct social effect of the gospel.

The reference to baptism highlights the ritual dimensions of this unity. Baptism and the Supper both express the evangelical unity of the body of Christ. Baptism in the one name of Jesus calls us away from allegiances to favorite teachers and leaders, from loyalties to tribe or nation or family (1 Cor. 1:10–17). Baptism in the name of Jesus calls us from schism, division, and heresy to love and harmony with one another. By one Spirit we "were all baptized into one body," whatever our ethno-religious origin, our social status, or our sex (1 Cor. 12:13; cf. Gal. 3:28). The one loaf of the Lord's Supper not only signifies but also forms us into the one body of Christ (1 Cor. 10:17). As we participate in the body and blood through the loaf and the cup, we are bound together into a single people. As we eat and drink, we are called to discern the corporate body, renouncing greed and selfishness. As we eat and drink, we show forth the meaning of Jesus's wall-demolishing death.

The church's unity is a *fact*, rooted in Christ himself, the work of the one Spirit who animates the many members of the body, and the promise of God the Father to gather the nations in Abraham's seed. Jesus prayed that his disciples would be one as the Father is one with the Son, and the Father does not ignore his Son's prayers. We join with Jesus in prayer, and the Father is our Father too, a Father who does not give serpents when we ask for fish.

It is essential to correctly understand the factuality of the church's unity. It is common to say the church is *spiritually* one, even when it is institutionally divided. For many, this implies that the church's institutional, practical, or ritual divisions are irrelevant. The fact that Lutherans and Presbyterians and Methodists have distinct churches is irrelevant, because our unity exists on another plane. The true church, it is said, is an invisible reality that can coexist with visible conflict, division, estrangement, and mutual hatred.

That certainly was not Paul's perspective. Paul rejoiced whenever the gospel was preached and by whomever, even if they preached from greed and envy (Phil. 1:15–18), but he was hardly indifferent to visible, bloody battles in the church. When the Corinthians divided their loyalties among their preferred apostles, Paul did not excuse them by saying that, despite it all, the church is still one. He was *outraged* that the Corinthians had divided Christ. When Peter withdrew from table fellowship with gentiles, Paul did not excuse him with the assurance that spiritual unity was more important than table fellowship. Paul expected—*demanded*—that the church's unity be visible in table fellowship, in loyalties and allegiances, in the *names* Christians adopt for themselves.

The unity of the church is not an invisible reality that renders visible things irrelevant. It is a *future* reality that gives present actions their orientation and meaning. Things are what they are as anticipations of what they will be. Individual Christians are not who we are because of our present condition of weakness and sin; we are who we are in Christ, in anticipation of what he will make us in the end. So too the church's unity is a fact because God has promised that one humanity will share his life forever. God *will* form humanity into one new man. He began that work with Abraham, fulfilled it in the incarnation, cross, and resurrection, breathed life into dead humanity when he poured out the Spirit at Pentecost. In the Son and Spirit, God's future became present, and when we share in the Son and Spirit we are caught up toward that future. We can realize that future by submitting to the Son and following the Spirit, or we can grieve the Spirit and become an obstacle to that future. God will keep his promises in any case, with or without us. But the call and demand of the gospel is to keep in step with the Spirit who makes present the future of God.

Paul's ethics is sometimes, "Be what you are. Practice the unity that you have." It is also, more deeply, "Be *now* what you *will be*. Practice the future in the present." That is what it means to live by faith, the substance of things hoped for, the reality of things not yet seen.

Emphasizing the eschatological dimension of unity keeps us from unrealistic expectations. The reunion of humanity is salvation, and as such it is as much a gift as is our individual deliverance from sin. God has promised to unite humanity, and so we can be confident he will do so. At the same time, we know that this promise is yet to be fully realized in the new Jerusalem. We strive for future unity now, prayerfully trusting God to achieve it both now and more perfectly at the end of all things. We must die to what we are now, so that we might become more and more what we will be.

We develop unrealistic expectations when we "overrealize" our eschatology, when we act as if we have already arrived at the end, when we claim a unity that we have not yet reached, when we think that we need no longer pray for unity because the prayer has been entirely fulfilled. That is an error. But the church has suffered just as much from an "underrealized" eschatology, from a quietist complacency that has learned to live with division and waits passively for unity to come. An underrealized eschatology is a failure of faith, a failure to trust and act on God's promise that he has and is reuniting humanity in the Son and Spirit, a failure to believe that God's promise is already yes and amen in Jesus. The future determines the present, and if we are going to be unified, we should prayerfully strive for unity here and now.

Living as One New Man

We live the future now when we receive and cultivate the fruits of the Spirit that preserve and deepen the unity of the church. The strong are not to flaunt their strength but to accept the weak in love (Rom. 14:1). Having been liberated by the Spirit given by the seed of Abraham, the Galatians are to use their freedom to serve one another (Gal. 5:13), each loving others as himself (v. 14). Killing the flesh means resisting the temptation to bite and devour one another (v. 15) and renouncing boastfulness, challenge, competition, and envy (v. 26). Christians extend the unity of the church by correcting one another in gentleness and humility, aware of their own temptations. In this way, they bear one another's burdens, fulfilling the Torah of Christ by imitating his burden-bearing (6:1–2). Christians walk according to our calling to be the one new man, the holy household of God, by cultivating humility, gentleness, patience, forbearance. In these ways, we "preserve the unity of the Spirit in the bond of peace" (Eph. 4:2–3). We are called to "lay aside falsehood" and speak "truth each one of you with his neighbor, for we are members of one another" (v. 25). Believers are to be "tender-hearted" as each imitates the free forgiveness of God in Christ (v. 32). Bitterness, anger, clamor, and wrath grieve the Spirit who binds us together (vv. 30–31). Retaining resentful anger gives the devil an opening (v. 27). Paul commends the Philippians for standing in "one spirit, with one mind striving together for the faith of the gospel" (Phil. 1:27). He rejoices as they maintain "the same love, united in spirit, intent on one purpose" (2:2). We can approach a unity of mind only when we take on the mind of Christ, only when we "do nothing from selfishness or empty conceit, but with humility of mind regard one another as more important than yourselves" (v. 3). By the Spirit, we imitate Jesus's humility.

Christians should refrain from judging one another over "food or drink or in respect to a festival or a new moon or a Sabbath day" (Col. 2:16), since each believer is accountable to one Master, Jesus. We are to put on the new man, "bearing with one another, forgiving each other, whoever has a complaint against anyone; just as the Lord forgave you, so also should you" (3:13). The peace of Christ is to rule the heart, and this is closely linked with gratitude (v. 15). Unity is not achieved through easy toleration. Rather, each is responsible to correct and admonish each, not least in "psalms and hymns and spiritual songs" (v. 16). We are to "encourage one another and build up one another" (1 Thess. 5:11) and never to repay "another evil with evil, but always seek after that which is good for one another and for all people" (v. 15). Christians are to "malign no one, to be peaceable, gentle, showing every consideration for all men" (Titus 3:2).

Unity should be evident in the way Christians talk to and about one another, in forbearance and forgiveness, in fellowship of psalms, hymns, and spiritual songs. It involves a recognition of our brotherhood in baptism and a practice of table fellowship. It is a unity in faith, in life, in practice, in water and bread. An invisible unity is not a biblical unity. Visible division is incompatible with the New Testament's portrayal of the church.

Conclusion

The church is called to be one and catholic. The two are not identical, but they go together. The church is one body with one Head, enlivened by one Spirit. Though the church exists in millions of local communions of believers, it is one church. That unity exists in a church that encompasses the entire world, a church that is "catholic" or "universal." Though it has existed in different times and in different forms, it is one church; though churches are found on every continent of our sizable planet, it is one church. It is one now because it *will be* one in the consummation, at the last day. We are what we will be. And we strive to be what we will be. What the church *will* be is one catholic church. Catholicism is our future.

That catholicism must take visible form in various dimensions. As the World Council of Churches Assembly at New Delhi (1961) put it, fully committed communion must include

- mutual recognition of baptism
- common confession of apostolic faith and common proclamation of the gospel
- common celebration of the Lord's Supper

- common devotional worship, petition, intercession, and thanksgiving
- common life in witness (mission) and service in the world
- mutual recognition of ministries and members
- ability to act and speak together in view of concrete tasks and challenges[11]

Unity in these ways does not preclude diversity of language, culture, and history. But it does preclude division, including the division evident when churches define themselves over against one another.

For various reasons, conservative Protestants have regarded such talk and such aspirations with a great deal of suspicion.[12] While acknowledging the good of unity among believers, evangelicals have charged that the ecumenical movement displaced Christ from the center of the church, watered down doctrine, formed alliances with barely believing liberals and unbelievers, and erected global bureaucracies that resemble the tower of Babel more than the church of the New Testament. The defection of the National and World Council of Churches from faithfulness into trendy leftism has not aided their reputations among evangelicals. Evangelical Protestants have often balanced the biblical demand for unity with their hostility to ecumenism by distinguishing between a unified spiritual church and a fragmentary visible church, a unified organism that exists despite the shattered state of the organization.

Some of this critique of the ecumenical movement is based on prejudices and lies. Some of it hits home and echoes critiques from within the ecumenical churches.[13] At bottom, though, we must utterly reject ecclesiologies, whether Protestant or Catholic or Orthodox or otherwise, that treat the church as an ethereal, invisible, spiritual entity. The New Testament church is a visible communion of men and women, united in the Son of the Father by the Spirit, marked by confession of Jesus as Lord, by baptism and the table, living a particular way of life in the world. That visible communion is the present social form of the future saved humanity.

And that means that the *dis*unity of the church is a disease in Christ's body, a shattering of the Spirit's temple. We must utterly reject ecclesiologies that imply indifference to visible division. We cannot exonerate the church by treating division as *extra*-ecclesial, ecclesiologies that imply that "the 'Church as such' is never divided."[14] Protestants excuse division by separating the true, united invisible church from its visibly divided husk. Catholics claim that the church as such is figured by immaculate Mary, untouched by the sins of her children. Orthodox think that the church is the Orthodox Church and therefore any division is happening to something *other* than the church.

We should have no patience for such cheap solace, which only makes us complacent in the face of disunity. Painful as it is to acknowledge, the church *as such* is a historical community and thus *as such* is both sinful and divided.[15] And that means that the church as such is not living in the gospel. To the extent we are divided, we are not evangelical. Jesus is the evangel in person, and he prays for our unity and calls us to peace.

Separation and reunion is the story of the Bible. It is the story of human history. Unity of the many members in the one Christ *is* the evangel.[16]

3

A Reformed Church

Every proposal for the reunion of the church is necessarily also a proposal for the reformation of the church. As soon as we suggest that the church become one, we must also explain what that reunified church will look like. What will this newly reunited church teach? How will it worship? How will it be governed, and what institutional form will it take? What kind of ecclesiology will govern the church? Jesus prayed for unity, but he did not only pray for unity. He also taught his disciples how they were to live and worship before him.

The ecumenical movement in the early part of the twentieth century was intertwined with the liturgical movement and the renewal of biblical theology. When Anglicans, Methodists, and Presbyterians in India stripped away their denominational identities to become the Church of South India, they adopted a eucharistic liturgy, a unified doctrinal statement, and a process for unifying the clergy of the different churches. At the same time that the Roman Catholic Church opened its doors for ecumenical engagement, it issued a decree on the liturgy and *Lumen Gentium*, Vatican II's dogmatic decree on the church.[1]

Some Christians will claim that reunion will occur when all the schismatics come back home to the mother ship. Everyone should become Orthodox, or Roman Catholic, or Anglican, or Lutheran. I do not believe

that is a viable option, either practically or theologically. History matters.[2]
The status quo constrains us. Today's churches are not blank slates. Our
history of division is real, and we have to journey *through* it to reach a
destination *past* it. Divided, we share in the agony of the cross, and future
reunion is a promise of resurrection *after* the cross. What is needed is not
a return to one or the other existing churches but faith to walk in a way
of being church that does not yet exist. We must walk by faith to be what
we will be. What is needed is a death to our present divisions so that we
may rise reconciled.

   This book offers an "interim ecclesiology." It proposes an agenda for
conservative Protestant churches *on the way* toward full reunion. Yet this
interim ecclesiology is oriented to a more ultimate ecclesiology, a vision
of what a more fully reunited church will look like. That vision is the
product of speculation and imagination, rooted, I trust, in Scripture and,
to a lesser degree, in the church's tradition. I acknowledge that I cannot
know in detail what the future church will be, nor how we will get there.
One thing we *can* know is that it will not be a mere continuation of any
of today's churches. We can also know that God will keep his promise to
make his people one as he is one with his Son. Somehow, someday, reunion
will happen, because the Father gave his Son to make it happen.

   Uncertain as we must be, provisional as all our imaginations and propos-
als must be, it is useful to speculate on the future toward which we aspire.
So long as we hold humbly, loosely to our agendas, we may find it edifying
to ask, What should future church look like? What will the church look
like in five hundred years, or a thousand, or ten thousand?[3]

One and Catholic

Future church is one and catholic, that above all. When unity is realized,
individual congregations and groups of congregations will no longer
identify themselves by denomination. There will be no Roman Catholic,
Orthodox, Presbyterian, Reformed, Methodist, Baptist, Lutheran, or
other churches. Churches will erase theologically exclusive names from
their signs. First Baptist will have become Second Street Church, and
the United Methodist Church on the next block will be identified by its
location or a saint rather than by a theological distinction. Presbyterians

and Episcopalians will not symbolize themselves by their polity, because the church will be united in polity as well as in faith and sacrament. Each congregation will view itself as a congregation of a single, global communion of congregations. Each congregation will pray for the others that it knows, and will pray continuously for even deeper and broader unity among Christians.

This may sound utopian. It may seem that this church will exist only at the last day. But it is not utopian. It is essentially what the church *was* for the first several centuries, what the Western church was before the Reformation. It is what happened in South India in the mid-twentieth century, as formerly Methodist and Reformed and Anglican churches died to their old names and rose to become the united Church of South India.

Can we say more?

A Biblical Church

The reformed, united church of the future will be a biblical church. It will *not* ignore the riches of Christian history. Pastors and theologians of the future church will draw on the *whole* tradition of biblical commentary and theology, all the tradition's wealth of pastoral wisdom and liturgical beauty, as they go about their work. Former Lutherans will discover fresh insights in the writings of former Mennonites and Calvinists; former Baptists will study encyclicals from Rome with appreciation; former Methodists will deepen their insight into the liturgy by studying Eastern Christian writers. Everyone will accept the whole of the tradition, East and West and beyond, past and present, as a treasure entrusted by the Spirit to the church. Origen and Augustine and Aquinas and Luther and Barth will be remembered and honored. A millennium from now, everyone will be studying the Latin American and African "church fathers" of the twenty-first century.

Confessions and creeds will remain in play. Churches will unite around the early creeds and will continue to use the treasures of the great confessions of the Reformation, of Trent and the Catholic Catechism, and of the hundreds of creeds and confessions that the global South will produce between now and then. Confessions, however, will cease to serve as wedges to pry one set of Christians from another. Confessions will be used for edification rather than as a set of shibboleths for excluding those who mispronounce.

No confession or creed can settle all questions for all time. No confession or creed can be trusted as a permanent prophylactic against heresy. Reformed by the Word, Catholic churches will have a future, and an open one. The church will be unified in the Truth that is Jesus and by the Scriptures in which the Spirit speaks of the Son and his Father. The churches of the future will not be able to rest lazily on the achievements of the past. They will acknowledge that the Creator God who reassembles the church will not be finished when he has finished that reassembly. They will confess the God who does new things and prayerfully strive to keep in step with him.

The future church will revel in the gifts of the Spirit to the church, but the future church will subject all teaching and preaching, every theological formulation, to the judgment of the Bible, the *whole* Bible.[4] The united churches of the future will acknowledge that their confessions and creeds, no matter how faithful to the Scriptures, are no substitute for the Scriptures. They will acknowledge that, however patiently and painstakingly composed, confessions and creeds may be distorted by the pressure of polemic or the limitations of the writers. They will leave every creed and confession open to correction by the Word of God.

The reformed Catholic church of the future will teach the whole Bible. Leviticus, Proverbs, and the Epistle of James will loom as large as the Epistles of Paul. School children will learn the sacrificial system and the varieties of impurity, knowing that these things will instruct them in the way of holiness without which no one will see the Lord. No one will shy away from the death penalties of the Torah or be embarrassed by Joshua's extermination of the Canaanites. Christians will believe everything the Bible claims, strive to obey every command, trust in every promise, tremble at every threat, sing every hymn. Members will be awed by the beauty, wonder, and breadth of the Scriptures.

In the reformed Catholicism of the future, "faith without works is dead" will be heard as frequently as "justification by faith." Seminary professors and theologians will follow Scripture wherever it leads. Theologians trained in what used to be the Reformed tradition will acknowledge the stress the Bible places on human choice and will not try to sidestep the many passages of the New Testament that speak about apostasy. Theologians who have cut their teeth on Arminius will acknowledge that the Bible teaches predestination and that Paul did write, "I will have mercy on whom I have mercy" (Rom. 9:15) and "He hardens whom He desires" (v. 18). Pacifists will not try to explain away Israel's *herem* warfare, and just warriors and crusaders will acknowledge that nations, like individuals, must be willing to turn the other cheek rather than seek revenge. Formerly Lutheran pastors will teach obedience (as Luther did!). Formerly Anglicans churches will exercise discipline. Jolly former Presbyterians will develop a reputation for levity, former Pentecostals will be attuned to the Christian tradition, and former Baptists will acknowledge hierarchy. The best theologians will be willing to admit that they do not know how to resolve apparent tensions and contradictions in Scripture or Christian dogmatics, and they will study prayerfully and patiently, waiting for further light. Bad theologians, impatient and prayerless, will strive to make a name for themselves. In the best cases, the church will limit the damage by exercising doctrinal discipline. There will be failures, and heresies will break out and gain a following, perhaps a significant one.

Pastors, theologians, and members of the church of the future will *not* hold to absolutely uniform beliefs. No church *ever* has been a place of absolutely uniform beliefs. Even in the most rigidly dogmatic church, there is much that is *not* defined, where there is freedom for debate and refinement and speculation. There will be more freedom for speculation in the church of the future, because the difference between dogmatic decision and speculation will be clearer. No one in the reformed Catholic church will claim to have mastered and comprehended everything in Scripture. Church members will disagree on a range of significant theological questions, and the differences of opinion will not always be handled charitably or wisely. Fights will break out. There will be *more* theological battles in the reunited church than there are today, because in a reunited church believers will be reluctant to relieve pressure by breaking from the church and because Christians of different views will have to learn to live together, dwelling in each other as the Son dwells in the Father.

Guided by Scripture above all and by the Christian tradition, the church will issue binding judgments about which deviations are tolerable and which are intolerable. Some opinions and teachers will be judged a threat to the gospel itself, and impenitent teachers will be expelled from the church. It will get ugly. Tempers will flare; insults will be cast. In the united church of the patristic era, fistfights and beatings sometimes occurred at church councils. A reunited church will restore those good old days. But the reunited church will have one advantage over the churches of today: expulsion from the reunited church will be plausibly seen as expulsion from *the church*. It will not be expulsion from one denomination that leaves the expelled with the option of going down the road to start his or her own denomination. It will be clear—at least, it will be much *clearer*—that starting a new church is an act of schism.[5]

Churches will be Bible-saturated. Preachers will teach the Bible from their pulpits and lecterns. Churches will provide a variety of venues for deeper Bible study. Scripture will become the pop culture of the church, as instinctive to young people as movie and pop music quotations are today. As the Bible becomes the pop culture of the church, it will fire the imagination of poets, screenwriters, and novelists. The beautiful symmetries of the Bible and its multilayered imagery will inspire painters and visual artists, filmmakers and composers. Politicians will look to Torah and the political dramas of Samuel and Kings and the scathing polemics of the prophets when forming their platforms and policy agendas. Because the reformed Catholic church will be Bible-centered, it will be culturally formational and transformational.

A Sacramental and Liturgical Church

The future reformed Catholic church will be sacramental and liturgical.[6] By "liturgy" I mean a formalized pattern of worship with a double focus on the Word and the sacrament of Communion, the Eucharist. In worship, Christians present ourselves in God's house, where he declares his forgiveness, speaks to us in his Word, and invites us to share in his table. He is present to hear our prayers and to receive our praises.

In the reformed Catholic church, every worship service will begin with a confession of sin and absolution.[7] Declared clean, worshipers will begin their ascent to the heavenly Zion, where the Lord will speak to them and where they will feast together in his presence. Cleansed, they will enter the temple of God, the temple that is constituted by the very people who have been cleansed, where the Lord is enthroned above the cherubim. At every stage, the Bible will be read and heard, sung and taught. Scripture will saturate worship, determining not only the forms of our worship but the content of praise and instruction. Scripture will shape the common prayers, said in unison by all the assembly, and the pastoral prayers, spoken by the liturgical leader on behalf of the people.

In the churches of the future, the Lord's Supper will be a weekly event, the climax of *every* worship service. It will become so habitual that a worship service without the Supper will feel unfinished and worshipers will feel cheated. Every member of the church will be allowed to come to the table, no matter how old, young, or mentally infirm. Christians in the future church will develop a eucharistic form of piety. They will recognize that they commune most deeply with Jesus through the Spirit at the Lord's table, and they will come to see the table as the center of their communion with one another as well. Eucharistic piety will spread out in daily eucharistic practice, in lives of joy and thanksgiving, in lives of hospitality and sharing.[8]

Reformational Catholic churches will not be "high church" in any simple sense. High churches can turn liturgy into what my colleague James Jordan calls "panoply." Instead of the work of the people, worship becomes the work of the priests *observed* by the people. In a strange convergence, both low-church Bible churches and high-church Anglo-Catholic churches reduce a congregation to an assembly of subdued spectators. In the future church, the minister, as a living icon of the Lord's presence among his people, will lead the service, declaring absolution, offering prayer, teaching, and sharing the body and blood at the Lord's table. He will be the leader among a company of priests, all offering living sacrifices in Christ to the Father.

Here as elsewhere, the church of the future will be infused with a Pentecostal energy, a spiritual liveliness. Liturgy will not be passionless ritual. Liturgically structured worship will be from the heart and will be energetic and joyful. Reformational Catholic churches will not believe that "spiritual" worship means "nonphysical" worship. Worshipers will clap their hands and sway to the music; they will raise hands in prayer. Confessing their sins, they will kneel or, more biblically, fall prostrate on their faces. The living Spirit of Jesus will be evident to everyone. Music will be energetic, accompanied by strings, horns, and drums. Psalms will dominate the repertoire, and church members will come to know the psalms as well as any medieval monk. Hymns and prayers and other praises will be infused with the cadences of the Psalter. The churches of the future will have made enough enemies to make imprecatory psalms meaningful. Liturgical music will draw on the whole tradition of church music—medieval chant, sung with energetic rhythm, as it was composed; Reformation hymns and metrical psalms; Wesleyan communion hymns; and contemporary hymns from the global South. The church's musical culture will draw its inspiration more from the tradition of church music than from the sounds of commercialized pop music. Congregations will sing together, rather than watching professionals or semiprofessionals onstage.

Mary will be honored as God-bearer. Saints will be celebrated. Church buildings will be bright and colorful. But in the reformed Catholic church, there will be no prayers to Mary, no appeals to the saints, no veneration of icons. Places of worship will be colorful and beautiful, resembling the temple and tabernacle more than a Quaker meeting hall. Formerly Presbyterian and Baptist churches will paint their walls and put in stained glass. Ministers will be dressed for the heavenly ministry that they truly perform—in white robes. Everyone will have a white robe hanging on a rack at the church so that they can join the heavenly chorus, with extra robes for visitors. All churches will follow a unified festival calendar, so that Jesus's birth, death, resurrection, ascension, and gift of the Spirit will be celebrated simultaneously throughout the earth.

Outside the formal assemblies, the churches will devote themselves to prayer. Businesspeople will gather for prayer before they head to the office. Mothers will bring their children to prayer meetings at noon. Prayer meetings will go late into the night, and in times of intense need, prayer vigils will last for days. The churches will pray because they will know their utter need. They will pray with Jesus that the church would be one, would remain one, will become more deeply unified. They will pray with Jesus that the church will become more and more what she will be.

A Metropolitan Church

When modern Christians imagine a united church, they imagine a united organizational structure, a head office, and a global bureaucracy. That is understandable, because some of the most visible ecumenical institutions of the twentieth century produced such organizations. The UN liaison office of the World Council of Churches (WCC) is in a large building just across from the UN building on Manhattan's First Avenue, and the Ecumenical Center in Geneva houses not only the WCC but also the Lutheran World Federation, the World Student Christian Federation, the Conference of European Churches, and other international Christian organizations. That sort of organizational unity is not at all central to the Reformational Catholicism I advocate here. It is a twentieth-century denominational vision of church unity, a church unified by having a centralized bureaucratic structure. The Catholic church of the future will be visibly united, and that visibility will have organizational elements. It will not be the unity of a faceless bureaucracy, but a unity of human faces. The organizational unity will be visible as a local and global communion of pastors and overseers.[9]

Scripture will shape not only the church's doctrine and worship but also the church's polity and organizational structures. In Reformational Catholic churches, pastors will lead the church by teaching the Word of God to the people of God and by leading worship. Within each congregation, the pastors, along with other leaders, will exercise diligent discipline of the members of the church. They will encourage them in private counseling and visitation and will rebuke and correct them when necessary. Pastors will hear confession and offer forgiveness and advise sinners on how to "sin no more." People will sin, and there will be conflicts. Through the complex and arduous process of rebuke and correction, those who sin flagrantly and impenitently will be subject to public rebuke and, at the extreme, excommunication. Pastors will use the tools of discipline with all love, gentleness, kindness, and patience; they will make errors of judgment, sometimes being overly gentle, sometimes being overly harsh. But pastors will *use* the keys they have to open and shut, rather than using love and gentleness as excuses for cowardice and lethargy.

Reformational Catholic churches will take their cues from Exodus 18 and Deuteronomy 1, where Jethro suggests to Moses an organization that builds up from groups of ten to fifties to hundreds to thousands. Over each group of families is a single ruler, a head, and the whole structure climaxes in Moses, before whom the most difficult cases are presented. Under this system, most cases would arise and be resolved at the lowest levels. Decentralized as it is, at each level a single leader has authority. This is not rule-by-committee, much less a bureaucratic structure. Rule is personal, with responsibility lodged in individuals who meet the qualifications that Moses lays out. From the hints that the New Testament provides, it appears that the structure of the early church largely replicates the structure of Israel, now spread out to the entire *oikoumene*. There is no individual Moses at the top of the hierarchy, unless it is Jesus himself. For the rest, the structure is similar. Timothy appoints *presbyteroi* in each church. Each congregation is overseen, led, fed, and guided by a single shepherd, a *pastor*, while others share responsibility for the care of the flock.

The New Testament church is organized as a metropolitan church. Paul meets with the elders of the city of Ephesus. Though there are many cells of Christians, the elders act together as a body of rulers. Paul can exhort the elders of the city's church to shepherd the flock of God by protecting it against the wolves who will descend to devour the sheep. More strikingly, Jesus addresses letters to an "angel" in each of the churches of Asia Minor.[10] Each of the cities has a single angel who is held responsible for the condition of the church in that city.

In the Catholic church of the future, there will continue to be many local congregations meeting each Lord's day, but the pastors of these churches will form a unified body of leaders, with one among them identified as *the* angel of the local church in that city. These angels will form an interlocking network of overseers around the world. The angels of the most prominent cities will naturally take on more authority.

Each congregation will function as an assembly of a single church.[11] All pastors will recognize the ordination and authority of all others. Every scandal and challenge will be taken on as a scandal and challenge for the whole church. Congregations and members will recognize that if one suffers, all the members suffer. Pastors of the future church will know one another and meet together often for prayer, worship, and Bible study. They will pray for each other during Sunday worship. They will offer an example to their congregations of mutual respect and deference, treating one another as more important than themselves. When necessary, the church leaders of the city will adjudicate moral and doctrinal lapses of other clergy in the city and when necessary will take the step of excommunicating them. Churches that, for instance, abandon biblical sexual morality will be rebuked and excluded from the fellowship. Fights will break out. It will get ugly.

Together with lay leaders, the ministers will coordinate the church's mission to the city and beyond. Instead of competing for membership, churches will cooperate to provide the best possible pastoral care for as many people as they can. Together, pastors will minister to the needs of the city and its civil leaders. Pastors will meet and befriend the mayor, the city manager, the police and fire chiefs, the city attorney, and others in authority. Churches will join forces with police departments and social services to address gang violence in the city, or to care for the poor and homeless. Churches will, as Jeremiah has stressed, seek the peace and the good of the cities in which they live (Jer. 29).

Congregations will strive for ever-deeper communion with one another. A congregation's members will not see each other only on Sunday morning. They will share life together, pray together, and their communion with one another will attract others to join in the communion of the body of Christ. Strangers, immigrants, the lonely, and the outcast will find in the church a new form of family life. They will be welcomed as brothers and sisters and knit together into a communion in Christ and his Spirit. Each church will strive to be a community of brothers, striving together for the gospel. The entire church will be organized for mission, and every member will view his or her vocation as the vocation of a priest-king who is united to Christ. Members will be trained to pursue their vocations with intelligence, creativity, and energy, ready at all times for the witness that may lead to exclusion, expulsion, and martyrdom. Every believer will enter his or her vocation with an openness to the possibility of martyrdom.

The Reformational Catholic church will be prophetic as well as pastoral. Because it will speak with a united voice (or a *more* united voice), it will be able to speak decisively (or *more* decisively) to the powers of the city. Its witness to Scripture will not be diffused into a "he said, she said." Because the church will be involved pastorally with the leadership of the city, its prophetic call will be recognizably an act of pastoral love and correction rather than a brickbat thrown from afar. The future Catholic church will be a thoroughly public church, declaring the gospel as public truth, truth that is true for everyone. It will be a deeply political church, but not because it takes one side or another on the myriad political disputes of our time. In some cases, it will take a strong, biblically based stand on some political issue of the moment—on the murder of unborn children in abortion, on biblical standards of sexual conduct, on the abuse of the poor, on the racial hatreds that infect public life, on the irrationalities that infect public discourse, on the justice of war. But it will not be political primarily because it takes a stand on political issues. It will be political because it will be formed as an alternative public within the public sphere. It will be the concrete form of civil society.

The Reformational Catholic church of the future will be able to maintain critical distance from the self-interests of nations. With that critical distance, the reunited church will be better positioned to bring the actions of nations under the judgment of the Word of God. A reunited church will be less susceptible to the passions of nationalism. A reunited church will recognize that each congregation is part of a global network of churches, that the "angels" of each city form an angelic host that covers the earth. Members of the reunited global church will refuse to take up arms against brothers and sisters on the other side of the world, even if their nation tells them that these brothers and sisters are a mortal threat.

Conclusion

The vision outlined here is neatly summarized by the World Council of Churches 1961 New Delhi statement on unity, still a touchstone of much ecumenical discussion.

> We believe that the unity which is both God's will and his gift to his church is being made visible as all in each place who are baptized into Jesus Christ and confess him as Lord and Saviour are brought by the Holy Spirit into one fully committed fellowship, holding the one apostolic faith, preaching the one Gospel, breaking the one bread, joining in common prayer, and having a corporate life reaching out in witness and service to all and who at the same time are united with the whole Christian fellowship in all places and all ages in such wise that ministry and members are accepted by all, and that all can act and speak as occasion requires for the tasks to which God calls his people.[12]

To achieve anything resembling this vision, every church will have to die, often to good things, often to some of the things they hold most dear. Protestant churches will have to become more catholic, and Catholic and Orthodox churches will have to become more biblical. We will all have to die in order to follow the Lord Jesus who prays that we all may be one.

4

The End of Protestantism

Protestantism is a loose family of churches, distinct from Catholics and Orthodox (at least), with each church distinguished from the others. Protestantism has a positive content and mission, but Protestantism is Protestant only over against other families of churches. It is what it is by being *not*-Catholic and *not*-Orthodox. Protestant churches have their own doctrinal and practical commitments, but they identify themselves by their differences from other Protestants. To be Presbyterian is to affirm certain doctrines, to operate according to certain rules of polity, to adopt certain liturgical practices. To be Presbyterian is also to *not* be Lutheran, Methodist, Episcopalian, Baptist, or Pentecostal.

If Protestants were to become Catholics (not Roman), churches that once identified with one or the other variety of Protestantism would cease to identify themselves in this way. Presbyterian churches would no longer be not-Lutheran, nor the Lutheran a not-Presbyterian. Methodists would no longer identify themselves as not-Catholic. All would be congregations of the church, local outposts of one global communion.

In short, if Protestants were to become Catholics, it would be the end of Presbyterianism, Lutheranism, Methodism, Baptist churches, and the whole range of other churches. It would be the end of Protestantism.

Reunion would also be the end of Roman Catholicism and Orthodoxy. Despite claims to the contrary, Roman Catholicism and Orthodoxy, as much as Protestantism, are defined by their differences from one another and from other parts of the church. In the ecclesial world as it actually exists, the *church* is divided into various camps defined by their differences from others. To suggest otherwise is a form of ecclesial idealism that easily becomes a form of ecclesial bullying.

Talk about the "end of Protestantism" will sound pretentious. But we must take the risk. If the Father listens to Jesus, if the church is the one new humanity, if Christ is not divided, then the communion to which we aspire *cannot* be a communion internally divided among various denominations or churches, each defined by its differences from fellow believers. Corinthian Christians who were pro-Cephas and contra-Apollos divided Christ. So do Presbyterians and Baptists who wear the badge of not-Methodist and not-Orthodox. No matter how nice they are to each other, they rend Christ. If God is faithful to his promise to Abraham, there will be one church in the end, and we should strive now to approximate that unity before the end. God *is* faithful to his promise to Abraham, faithful enough to send his Son to the cross to fulfill it. He has given his Spirit so that we can become what we will be.

Talk about the end of Protestantism is also alarming. Christians whose identity is bound up with being Lutheran or Methodist or Reformed are disoriented by the prospect of erasing those titles from the signs in the churchyard. My name is myself; change my name, and I cease to be and must die or become something new or both. Christians who are determined to *not* be Catholic will be frightened at the prospect of reunion with Rome. The World Council of Churches spoke wisely in the New Delhi report on unity: "The achievement of unity will involve nothing less than a death and rebirth of many forms of church life as we have known them. . . . Nothing less costly can finally suffice."[1] We can achieve unity only by faith in the God who raised Jesus and so liberated us from the old world into the new creation, the God who is able to break us out of old ways to walk in paths that are ever new.

It may seem little reassurance to say that this "end" of Protestantism is the "end" the Reformers had in mind from the beginning, but that is the consolation this chapter offers to the disoriented. The Reformers did *not* intend to form a new church. They did *not* wish to divide the church. They hoped to reform the one Catholic Church, and their catholic reforms were motivated by a catholic spirit. They longed to see Jesus's prayer answered, that the church would be one as all the disciples were united in the truth that is the Word of God. They aimed for a reformed Catholicism, and they would be the first to rejoice at the end of Protestantism if that meant that Protestantism had achieved its end—a church reformed according to the Word of God. The Catholicism I advocate is a Reformational Catholicism that draws its inspiration from the catholic vision of the earliest Reformers.

The Catholic Reformation

Everyone who knows anything about the Reformation knows that it divided the Western church. Protestants left Rome or were forced out. They started their own churches or continued existing churches outside papal oversight. The Reformation itself splintered. Martin Luther and Ulrich Zwingli clashed over the question of the real presence at the Colloquy of Marburg in 1529. The rift between the Magisterial Reformation and the "churches of the disinherited," the latter often lumped together as branches of the Anabaptist movement, was earlier and has been nearly as long-lasting. The latter may be more significant, in part because it is less obvious. Protestantism's difficulty in dealing with the radical offshoot movements it throws up has been one of its enduring weaknesses.[2]

The Reformation era ended in the bloodiest and most brutal wars Europe had witnessed to that time,[3] which destroyed the order of medieval Christendom[4] and unleashed a flood of unintended consequences.[5] The inability of Christians to agree on basic dogmas of Christian faith opened space for skepticism and atheism. Economic and political life was "disembedded" from ethics, facilitating the formation of "secular" political and economic spheres. When the dust of war settled in the middle of the seventeenth century, Europe was in almost every respect a very different place than it was in 1500. It is not surprising that many thought the apocalypse was at hand. It was not *the* end, but it was certainly *an* end.

These results were often tragic, breathtakingly so. The greatest tragedy was the division of the Western church, because that involves the rending of the body of the Son of God. Like Elijah and Elisha, the Reformers left the corrupt establishment to form communities of the "sons of the prophets." Yet it is crucial to recognize that these divisions were *unintended* consequences of a Reformation that began as a catholic movement to restore the church. Contrary to the mythology that one sometimes hears from Roman Catholic apologists, the Reformation was not individualistic but catholic. It was an effort not to destroy Catholicism but to restore it.

Making Communion Visible

All the Reformers affirmed the creedal claim that the church is one and catholic. Martin Bucer, a leading reformer in Germany who ended his days as an advisor to Edward VI of England, was a major ecumenical force throughout his life. His efforts to maintain and restore unity were driven by his conviction that the church is one body: "The church is the congregation and society of those who are thus in our Lord Jesus Christ gathered out of the world and associated together, that they may be one body and members one of another; each one of whom has an office and work for the common edification of the whole body and of all the members."[6] Children in Geneva were taught in catechism class that the word "catholic" means that "as there is but one Head of the faithful, so they ought all to be united in one body. Thus there are not several churches, but only one, which is extended throughout the world."[7] In this, the catechism reflected the views of Calvin, who stated that "the true stability of the church, the restoration of the world, consists in this, that the elect be gathered into the unity of the faith, so that with one consent all may lift their hearts to God." Calvin was horrified by the "frightful mutilation of Christ's body" and stated that "such is the value which the Lord sets upon the communion of his church that all who contumaciously alienate themselves from any Christian society in which the true ministry of the word and sacraments is maintained, he regards as deserters of religion."[8]

Some of the Reformers spoke of an "invisible church," but that did not undermine concern for visible reform and visible unity. On the contrary, they spoke of an invisible church out of an interest in reforming the visible. Their aim was to restore the visibility of the church *as church*, as a *communio* of saints. According to John T. McNeill, the Reformers "interpreted the creedal tenet of 'the Holy Catholic Church' in terms of the *communio sanctorum*, and identified the latter both with the invisible communion of the saved and with the true visible church in the world which they felt themselves called to restore." *Communio* "involved a high degree of corporate consciousness, a group solidarity, and the recognition of an obligation mutually to bestow religious benefits and render social services." It was a sacramental communion, "associated with the mystery of the Eucharist, and its values were impressed under the idea of the priesthood of every Christian, an office conceived of not in an individualistic but in a social sense as obligation to aid his fellow Christian and 'be a Christ' to him." The invisible church "functioned in the cause of practical church reform," as the ideal by which the visible church was to be judged and the *telos* toward which the visible church was moving.[9]

From the perspective of the Reformers, the Roman Catholic Church was not *too* visible; rather, its character as *communio* was barely visible at all. As McNeill puts it, "The spiritual qualities, which in the contemporary state of decline had seemingly passed out of the external and could be posited only of the unseen church, were to be given visibility again as the renovated visible society took on the character of the invisible model."[10] For the Reformers, "A reformation or revival of the church . . . means the glorious increase of her visibility, the prosperity of the earthly counterpart to the heavenly model."[11] What was visible in the Roman Catholic Church was not the *communio* of the church, which only peeked out here and there in the corners of an overly juridical and monarchical organization.[12] The Reformation was an effort to *restore* the visibility of a social form that had been nearly buried under what the Reformers considered the rubble of Roman error. The Reformation was a *retrieval*, not a rejection, of catholicity.

The communion that is the church needed to be made visible especially in the rite of Communion. Instead of offering holy things to the holy people, the medieval Mass reserved the holy things for the holy priesthood. When they did commune, laypeople typically communed only in one kind, eating bread but not drinking wine. Roman communion did not manifest the church's *communio* but falsified it. This was one of the central complaints in Luther's early work: because all the baptized are priests, all should share in the communion of the Lord's table, in bread and wine.

It was a universal trope of Reformation rhetoric that the *Reformers* were defending orthodoxy and catholicity against the sectarianism of Rome. Luther vehemently disputed the Catholic idea that catholicity would be defined by obedience to Rome, and he disputed it on the basis of the universal (catholic) testimony of the church.[13] Calvin defended the Reformers against the charge that they were schismatics: "Verily the wolves complain against the lambs."[14] The 1559 French Confession distinguished the true church from "all other sects who call themselves the church,"[15] a thinly veiled allusion to Rome. McNeill writes, "The Reformation was a revolt, not against the principle of unity and catholicity, but against the privileged and oppressive monarchy of Rome—an uprising not merely of national, but of catholic feeling, against what had become a localized and overcentralized imperialism in Christianity, which made true catholicity impossible."[16]

War against the Idols

The Reformation was also a revolt against the idols.

In 1533 Hugh Latimer, already well known in the city of Bristol, preached a series of sermons attacking "pylgremages, worshyppying of seyntes, wurshypyng off ymages, off purgatory, &c. yn the whyche he dyd vehemently perswade towarde the contrary." According to the understated account of this writer, "the people ware nott a lyttle offendyd." Bristol's priests organized a series of counter-sermons, and there were efforts to silence Latimer. Catholic authorities set up a commission to investigate his case. Though the commission's decisions were inconclusive, the events at Bristol were critical to the early development of the English Reformation. Through this incident, Latimer established himself as a leading advocate of reform and was soon assisting Thomas Cromwell in spreading the Reformation throughout England.[17]

Over the following years, the English reformers systematically dismantled the liturgical idolatry of the late medieval English church. Protestants removed and catalogued relics from all over England, either destroying them or sending them off into private hands. Someone at Bury St. Edmunds discovered "the coles that Sant Laurence was toasted withall, the paring of S. Edmundes naylles, S. Thomas of Canterbury's penneknyff and his bootes," and from Bath came "St Mary Magdalen's comb, and St Dorothy's and St Margaret's combs." An anonymous anti-Reformation poet lamented the silence of the "wracks of Walsingham," complaining that "toads and serpents hold their dens / Where the palmers did throng" and

"Sin is where Our Lady sat."[18] In the Swiss cantons, reformation produced outbreaks of iconoclasm and emptying of reliquaries, spreading from Bern to Basel to Neuchâtel and Geneva.[19]

Like the great biblical reformations of Hezekiah and Josiah, the Reformation was a purgation of idolatry, a stripping of the altars. The Reformers broke down the idols because they believed that idolatry prevented the Catholic Church from flourishing. Idolatry divided the church and obscured the *communio sanctorum* that was the essence of the church.

The Reformers' assault on idolatry was spurred by catholic motivations. Luther was as concerned about idolatry as his iconoclastic comrades in England and Switzerland. In place of the medieval, and especially Thomist, notion that God is the Supreme Being or Being in general, Luther developed the late medieval insight into the personal character of God and his covenantal relations with humanity. Without the earlier shift, "the Reformation breakthrough would be inconceivable," but this does not mean that there is "unbroken continuity between the discovery of God as Person-acting-in-history and Luther's discovery of the God of covenant and promise." His distinctive contribution was a theology of the cross: "The God who acts has become the God who acts in Christ, the God who is unpredictable and foils any systematic search, who contrary to reason and against expectation carries the cross from Christmas to Easter."[20] Following Luther, the other Reformers renounced the God of the philosophers, the idol of onto-theology, a theology proper taken captive to Aristotle or some other philosophical system. They insisted that the Christian God was the living, moving, acting, covenant-making Triune God.

Anxiety over idolatry was also one of the deep sources of Luther's Reformation turn. In a profound essay, Lutheran theologian David Yeago argues that the key question that drove Luther was not "How can I find a gracious God?" but "How can I find the true God?"[21] Yeago writes, "If one looks carefully at what Luther actually wrote in the period up to 1517–1518 (as distinguished from his reminiscences twenty or twenty-five years later), one discovers that the celebrated question 'How can I get a gracious God?' is rather conspicuous by its absence. . . . All the evidence in the texts suggests that it was the threat of *idolatry*, not a craving for assurance of forgiveness, that troubled Luther's conscience if anything did."[22] Above all, Luther wanted to root out the subtle spiritual idolatry of treating God as a means to one's own spiritual satisfaction.

Operating with an Augustinian distinction between the "useful" (*uti*) and the "enjoyable" (*frui*),[23] Luther worried that in his sin he would treat God as if he were in the category of the useful instead of the enjoyable. When a sinner falls into this idolatry, even his legitimate devotional practices become idolatrous, an expression of his tendency to "curve in on himself" (*incurvatus in se*): "Our nature, by the corruption of the first sin, is so deeply curved in on itself that it not only bends the best gifts of God toward itself and enjoys them (as is plain in the works-righteous and hypocrites), or rather even uses God himself in order to attain those gifts, but it also fails to realize that it so wickedly and viciously seeks all things, even God, for its own sake."[24]

Anyone who "uses God" is clearly not dealing with the true God, who always remains the sovereign Lord.

> By the same steps [of idolatry] people even today arrive at a spiritual and more subtle idolatry, which is now quite common, by which God is worshiped, not as he is, but as he is imagined and reckoned to be. For ingratitude and love of vanity (that is, one's sense of oneself and of one's own righteousness, or, as they say, one's good intention) violently blind people, so that they are incorrigible, and unable to believe otherwise than that they are acting splendidly and pleasing God. And in this way they form a God favorable to themselves, even though he really is not so. And so they more truly worship their fantasy than the true God, whom they believe to be like that fantasy.[25]

For Luther, there is no difference in principle between bowing to a carved statue and constructing a god from, or in, our own fantasy.

Luther initially develops his theology of the cross as a way of addressing these concerns. To the question, "How can I know that I am actually having contact with the true and living God?" he answers, "The excellent God, after he has justified and given his spiritual gifts, lest that ungodly nature rush upon them to enjoy them (for they are very lovely and powerfully incite to enjoyment), immediately brings tribulation, exercises, and examines, lest that person perish eternally by such ignorance. For thus a person learns to love and worship God purely, when one worships God not for the sake of his grace and gifts, but for himself alone."[26] Yeago glosses Luther's point: "The problem is that we don't want to come into God's presence for God's sake, but for the sake of all the good things he can do for us: we want to *use* God. Luther answers: If it's really God, then he will crucify and torture you, and thus leave you no reason to cling to him except for his own sweet sake."[27]

Ultimately, Luther addressed the problem of idolatry in a way that "anchored [him] more deeply than ever before in the traditions of catholic dogma, catholic sacramentalism, and catholic mysticism."[28] Luther's shift in 1518 hinged on his struggle to formulate a coherent sacramental theology, and Luther resolved the theological problem of idolatry through a christologically shaped sacramental theology. God can be known to be God because he has made himself known in Jesus:

> Since the terms "trusting God" and "serving God" must suffer being stretched to such lengths that everyone draws them out to fit his own ideas, one interpreting them one way, another in another way—therefore God has placed himself and fixed himself at a definite place and a definite person where he wants to be found and encountered, so that one may not go astray. Now this is none other than the person of Christ himself in whom the whole fullness of deity dwells bodily. . . . Therefore Christ wants to say "You have heard that you are to trust God; but I want also to show you where you will genuinely meet him, so that you don't make yourselves an idol according to your own ideas under his name. This means: If you want to believe in God, then believe in me. If you want to orient your faith and trust rightly, that they may not be out of place or false, then orient them to me, for in me the entire deity is and dwells in fullness."[29]

For Luther, the incarnation—God coming near to offer himself to and for us—*is* the doctrine of justification:

> You have heard already that he calls himself "the Son of Man." In this way he wants to show that he is our true flesh and blood, which he took to himself from the Virgin Mary, in which eternal life are to be found. *This is the article of justification*: the Holy Spirit wills that one under no circumstances learn, know, imagine, hear, or accept another God besides this God whose flesh and blood we imprint and grasp in our hearts if we want to be saved. We are not to let ourselves be taught by a God who sits up above in heaven in his throne room, who is therefore to be sought only in the divinity. For thus you will be led astray; but if you want to escape death and to be saved, let no God come to you besides the Son of Man. In his flesh and blood you will find God; that is where he has located himself, there you will meet him, where the Son of Man is.[30]

The Reformation teaching on justification should be understood as part of this same iconoclast project. To say that we are justified by grace alone through faith alone is to say that God alone justifies *solo Christo*. To be justified by faith is to trust God's gracious word of forgiveness, graciously given in the body and blood of the Lord's table. Justification by faith cuts through the jungle of the penitential system and the distracting cloud of mediators to the heart of the matter. This is the article of justification: God gives himself in his Son by his Spirit. He gives himself in Word and sacrament. Take and hear; take and eat; take and trust.

Luther's answer to the questions "Who is the true God?" and "How can I know that I have the true God?" was christological: I know the true God because he has revealed himself; the true God is the one incarnate in the womb of Mary and born at Bethlehem, risen and ascended into heaven. Along similar lines, the answer to the practical question of true worship was sacramental: I have access to and contact with the true God revealed in Jesus when I seek him where he has promised to be found. He has promised to make himself available in specific concrete places and practices, in Word and sacrament.[31] The Protestant war against the idols was driven not by sectarian or anti-sacramental instincts but by a catholic desire to restore God's promise to the center of Christian worship and Christian experience.

True Church?

The Reformers' *communio* ecclesiology expressed itself in practical action to restore unity in the church as a whole and to unify the Protestant movement. Luther repeatedly appealed for a free council to decide disputed questions. At the Wittenberg Concord of 1536, Melanchthon and Bucer attempted unsuccessfully to heal the breach between Lutherans and Reformed. Melanchthon continued to seek union with the Roman Catholics into the 1530s, and Calvin's successor Theodore Beza was involved in a Reformed-Catholic colloquy at Poissy as late as 1561.[32]

More than a half century later, some Protestant theologians in England were still musing on the possibility of reunion. These theologians and pastors had no hesitation charging the Roman church with making illegitimate additions to the church's worship, with idolatry, and with grievous error concerning transubstantiation and the Mass.[33] Yet some expressed their continued hope for unity with Rome. Godfrey Goodman, bishop of Gloucester, argued that it was illegitimate "to make such a difference between these two Churches, as is between damnation and salvation." All churches have "blemishes and imperfections," but "as long as the foundation is sound, that we believe in Christ crucified, and that we believe the three creeds, so long there is hope of Salvation."[34] Richard Montagu pressed even further, suggesting that there should be intercommunion between Protestants and Catholics.[35]

This conciliar, catholic orientation implied a certain view of the Roman Catholic Church. Today some Protestants persist in denying that the Roman Catholic Church is a church at all, but that was not the view of the Reformers or of most of their heirs. They regarded the papal church as deeply flawed, sectarian, oppressive, but they accepted the sacrament of baptism practiced by the Catholic Church as valid. The Catholic Church was churchly enough to possess baptism.

Anglican theologians of the seventeenth century were still sorting through the churchiness of the Roman Catholic Church.[36] It was tricky. If Anglican divines were too hard on the Catholic Church, they provided ammunition for dissenting groups who suggested that what they saw as the semi-reformed Church of England might not be a true church either. It was tricky too because Anglicans were on the whole devoted to an Augustinian sacramental theology and accepted the Reformers' view that Catholic baptism was valid. That would argue for acceptance of the Catholic Church as a true church, but then it became difficult to explain what was so wrong with Catholicism.

Part of the trickiness came from slippage in the usage of the term "true church." In some contexts and theological treatises, "true church" refers to the whole assembly of genuine believers who will be saved at the last day. In that sense, nearly everyone agreed that there were members of the true church in Rome. For some, "the difference between the Church of Rome and the Protestant Churches was expressed in terms of an absolute division, corresponding with the distinction between the true church and the false."[37] Yet "most divines worked on the practical assumption that Rome was a church, though unsound."[38] In taking these positions with regard to Rome, Anglican theologians did not believe they were departing from the Reformation. On the contrary, their treatises were liberally sprinkled with quotations from the Reformers as well as from Scripture and the church fathers.[39]

Almost invariably, statements about the "true church" were qualified with a *secundum quid*, "in some sense." And immediately after acknowledging the Church of Rome in this qualified way as a true church, the writer would launch into polemics against Roman heresies and apostasy. Those like Joseph Hall who failed to qualify their affirmation of the churchiness of Rome sparked vehement controversy.[40]

Yet a century and a half after the Reformation, some Protestants still held out hope for communion with Rome. They still hoped for the eventual end of Protestantism.

From Catholicity to Confessionalization

This catholic agenda for reformation was not realized. The Reformation did not reach its end, and so Protestantism has not yet ended.

There were many reasons for that: the intransigence of the Roman Catholic Church, the divisiveness of Protestantism, the meddling of politicians who used the religious clash for their own purposes, the crash and thunder of bombastic personalities. For my purposes, the most important factor is what recent historians have come to call "confessionalization."[41] This refers to a complex movement of consolidation during the generations after the Reformation, as each church attempted to clarify doctrine by formulating detailed confessions of faith. From one angle, confession-writing unified belief. The late Middle Ages was a crazy quilt of heresy; after the Reformation, the collection of official beliefs had been reduced to a handful. John McNeill states, with some hyperbole, that "it is not improbable that there was less actual sectarianism in Western Christianity in the seventeenth than in the fourteenth century."[42] Lutherans had only the Augsburg Confession and the Formula of Concord, and the proliferation of Reformed confessions disguises the fact that they were largely variations on a theme.

Yet confessionalization also made hope for union among Protestants and between Protestants and Catholics more distant. Each church formulated its theology in response to controversies with other branches of the Reformation. Preachers and writers identified themselves through oppositions and contrasts. Even the big-tent Church of England, home to everyone from Perkins to Laud, was united by "a pervasive and virulent anti-Catholicism." Anglicans could live together with their liturgical, governmental, and doctrinal divergences because they were united against common enemies—"the bloodthirsty inquisitor, the Jesuit spy, the tyrannical prince, the traitor who gave his allegiance to Rome."[43] After the crypto-Calvinist struggles in Lutheran churches, Lutherans adopted a *via negativa* toward the Reformed and toward one another: "Out of the crypto-Calvinist controversy . . . emerged a more precise and rigid definition of Lutheran orthodoxy. Those who did not concur with it were disciplined into conformity or expelled from the Lutheran churches, while within those churches beliefs and practices grew more uniform." Reformed churches, aiming to "abolish everything that smacked of Catholicism," made their specific practices "markers of confessional identity." Practices that were originally regarded as adiaphora became fixed points of reference and identification.[44]

That such anti-Catholic fantasies could be exploited by state-building monarchs and cunning Machiavellians was not incidental, and "confessionalization" refers to the political consolidation as well as to the doctrinal. Following the Thirty Years' War (1618–48), each principality determined its own religion on the Westphalian principle of *cuius regio, eius religio* ("whose realm, his religion"), using not only confessions but oaths of subscription, propaganda and censorship, education, ritual markers of confessional difference, and unification of language to create a national ethos distinguished from the religio-national ethos of surrounding principalities.[45]

Confessional consolidation proved "a fruitful instrument in explaining the transformation of medieval feudal monarchies into modern states, in particular how the new states changed their inhabitants into disciplined, obedient and united subjects." Religious uniformity formed a people whose ethnic identity merged with its identity as Catholic, Lutheran, or Calvinist. "This distinguished 'us' as a religious and political community from 'other,' often neighboring, religious-political societies. The ruler was sacralized as the defender and—in Protestant lands—leader of the church, rightfully overseeing the church of his land. These state-led churches also aided state development by imposing moral discipline on the communities."[46] Political uses of confessions sacralized national differences and raised political conflicts to the level of spiritual warfare.

Similar dynamics were at work as the Reformation was consolidated in Geneva. The office of pastor became more regimented:

> Church life became more carefully regulated, supervised, and documented through the codification of confessions, catechisms, and church ordinances; the establishment of ecclesiastical bureaucracies; and the creation of disciplinary courts. . . . Likewise, the clerical office was increasingly professionalized with the establishment of formal educational requirements and more detailed guidelines for examination and ordination. In this process of modernization . . . clergymen emerged as quasi-agents of the state, serving as a crucial link for communication between political leaders and their subjects; supervising public discipline; and providing administrative resources for the state (such as maintaining baptismal, marriage, and death registers).[47]

The campaign of Geneva's Small Council "to gain control over clerical recruitment and election was indicative of a broader strategy to bring the city's pastors in line with the political objectives of the governing authorities. The ministers were gradually transformed into quasi-agents of the state who were not only paid out of the state coffers but were also hired, supervised, and dismissed with significant involvement of the magistrates."[48] Against the hopes of Calvin and other pastors, the Genevan church lost its independence and became a department of metropolitan governance.

Thus the catholic Reformation was co-opted by a powerful sweep of early modern state formation.[49] Despite its catholic impulse and origination, the Reformation's heirs created a religious system that institutionalized church division, reinforced by ethnic and national divisions. Along the way, the character of religion itself was substantially changed. Confessions taught people what to believe. In a departure from the original catholic vision of the Reformers, confessionalization left the impression that *belief* was the important—perhaps the *only* important—thing about Christianity: "Religion became further consolidated around what people 'believed,' detached from the religious observances they performed."[50]

This was one of the crucial changes from the Latin medieval system. Some popes cowered before emperors, but medieval popes and bishops knew that they represented a church that was not confined to national borders, a church that operated with a certain degree of contested independence from the state. By the middle of the seventeenth century, that was no longer true of Protestant churches. As we shall see, this continues to be a fundamental dilemma for Protestant ecclesiology.

Conclusion

Reformational Catholicism is inimical to certain *forms* of Protestantism. That is certainly true. It is hostile to the politics of confessionalized Protestantism. If Protestants are going to obey the gospel imperative to be at peace with brothers and sisters, to love them as members of the one body, we have to renounce tics and habits, beliefs and practices that have become second nature to Protestantism. We have to repent of the ways we have denied the gospel by our divisions and undermined our beloved doctrine of justification by faith. We need to repent of our failure to follow the Lord Jesus, who prays that we would be one, as well as our failure to pray for unity in and with him.

Reformational Catholicism aims to bring an end to Protestantism as a family of churches defined over against Rome and Orthodoxy, a collection of churches defined over against one another. But Reformational Catholicism also sees this as a consummation the Reformers devoutly wished for. When reunion comes, Protestantism will end, and in that end Protestantism will reach its end.

CHURCH DIVIDED

5

The Case for Denominationalism

In the first movement, I laid out a "Reformational Catholic" ecclesiology. A Reformational Catholic church is a unified church, a church reformed by the Word of God, a church in continuity with the original catholic vision of the Reformation. I have speculated, fondly no doubt, that Reformational Catholicism will characterize the church of the future.

It is *not* the church of the present. Emphatically not.

In the United States,[1] the present church is a denominational church.[2] I concede in this chapter that denominational Christianity has strengths and virtues and a record of impressive accomplishments. As a matter of faith, I confess that God providentially established denominationalism as the order of the church at a particular place and time. It is in some mysterious way the creation of God, as was the church of the patristic age, the church of the Western Middle Ages, the church of Byzantium, the divided state churches of early modern Europe, the forgotten churches of the Middle and Far East, and as *is* the burgeoning church of the global South. I have been and will be severely critical of denominationalism, but I must give it its due. It is God's good gift, and we should show proper gratitude. It is not a concession to say that God has worked among American denominational churches. It is an act of thanksgiving.

Yet denominational churches are not Reformational Catholic churches, and denominational Christianity is not Reformational Catholicism. If I am right that Reformational Catholicism expresses a biblical vision for the church's unity, then denominational Christianity is flawed. While I am thankful for denominationalism, it remains the case that denominationalism institutionalizes division and thus displeases Jesus, who prays for unity.

There is no contradiction in affirming that denominationalism is from God while denouncing the damage it has done to the church. Constantine was an instrument of God, just as he thought he was; but he was hardly above criticism. Athanasius was a hero of the faith, but he could be thuggish. I admire Benedictines, but monasticism has sometimes gone to seed. The missionary movement of the nineteenth century was a tremendous move of the Holy Spirit, yet it had some damaging effects. Pentecostalism is one of the great successes of the modern church, but I have deep reservations about some basic Pentecostal claims.

For a time, denominational Christianity has been God's tool for realizing his promises to Abraham, but that does not mean it is permanent or perfect. There is no contradiction in saying, thankfully, that denominationalism has been good for a time and then also saying that its time has come.

What Is Denominationalism?

Christians have long defined themselves by forms of church government. Presbyterian churches are governed by presbyters or elders, representatives of God to the congregation and, in some respects, representatives of the congregation. Local Presbyterian churches are governed by boards of elders, typically elected by the people, and collections of local Presbyterian congregations are organized into regional presbyteries that deliberate and make decisions affecting all the individual congregations. In most Presbyterian churches, the presbyteries are themselves part of a larger organization that meets in "general assembly." Other churches are organized with an episcopal form of government, with a regional or municipal church governed by *episkopoi*, "overseers" or bishops. Local churches are under the direction of a priest or rector, sometimes assisted by a group of lay vestry members. Other churches are organized congregationally. Within each congregation, deacons or elders may have authority alongside the pastor but do not have the same stature as a Presbyterian elder. Congregational churches may be part of district, national, or even international organizations, but they stress what the Assemblies of God calls the "sovereignty of local assemblies," each of which enjoys "full autonomy."[3]

In practice, churches combine features of these ideal types. Every presbytery has its "bishop," a seasoned pastor whose input in presbytery debate carries more weight than anyone's and who takes younger individuals under his wing. Episcopal churches have presbyterial elements, and even in the most rigidly hierarchical system, individual congregations retain some autonomy.

The more fundamental problem with these traditional ways of discussing church organization is that they trade in abstractions. They treat the church as a self-standing entity, without any significant connection to the other institutions and social structures that surround it. In reality, every church—Presbyterian, episcopal, or congregational—is part of an ecclesial meta-structure linked to a complex net of political, legal, economic, media, and other institutions. That network of nonchurch institutions affects the way that churches relate to one another and the way churches are internally organized. We cannot do justice to questions about denominationalism and Reformational Catholicism without paying attention to meta-governmental structures.

William Swatos has developed a helpful typology of meta-structural possibilities, beginning with a distinction between "monopolistic" and "pluralistic" societies:

> In a monopolistic society all facets of life are pervaded and controlled by a single system of ultimate meanings and values. In monopolistic society, there is but one religion, and it is inseparable from the socio-political power structure. Religion thus has a controlling interest over the social structure as a whole and hence a compulsive character. In a situation of religio-cultural pluralism, voluntarism is the key principle for religious organization. In pluralistic society there are both competing religious groups, and competition between "religion" and other discrete institutions for the time, money, and affection of individuals and groups.[4]

Monopolistic societies produce two sorts of religious institutions: churches and sects. A church exists where a single religious institution provides "a life-encompassing organizational structure" in a monopolistic society. A church accepts the world system as it is—and no wonder, because the church enjoys the privileges of monopoly. Sects, too, can exist in a monopolistic setting. An "entrenched sect" is the archetypal dissenting religion, "the 'village atheist' of yesteryear." Entrenched sects may be persecuted or excluded from the mainstream of political life, but the entrenched sect is not bothered by the prospect: it does not want equality with the established church. It stands "against the world," and that includes standing "against the church" that is so intertwined with the world.[5] An entrenched sect exists in a monopolistic society but in world-rejecting opposition. It regards the established church as a sellout and opposes the very idea of a church.

Pluralistic societies produce what Swatos calls "dynamic sects," which are the "churches" of pluralism. A dynamic sect has "high standards," and "its claims sound churchly"—exclusive and dogmatic. It claims to have the truth and only the truth. Yet it is not a church, and it defines itself against the "dominant culture in a way that is explicitly defined and articulated." It engages the culture "only in an emissary way" and rejects "worldly politics in itself." A dynamic sect is often a transitional form that eventually collapses into a different type of organization, the "denomination which exists in a pluralistic situation but accepts rather than rejects the world." It is the "norm of religious organization" in a pluralistic system. It is a voluntary organization: "One may belong to any denomination—*or none!*" It accepts the pluralistic premise that religion is a voluntary activity. It is tolerant and easygoing; each denomination shows forbearance and respect for others. While holding to its distinctive doctrines and practices, a denomination does not treat those distinctives as binding on everyone and can acknowledge a brother or sister who holds different positions on secondary issues so long as they agree on fundamentals. Denominations see themselves as being in a "free market" of religious options, competing with other denominations for market share.[6]

The heart of Swatos's typology is the paradoxically named "established sect." An established sect maintains a close relationship with the political and cultural establishment, but other groups threaten its status. It stands in opposition to a world in which it is forced to compete. Things should not be as they are; the sect should be the church for the whole society. Established sects are transitional and eventually collapse into denominations.[7]

Denominationalism is the meta-structure that has organized the churches of America, and the character profile of the denominational church fits Swatos's description. Denominationalism was *not* the meta-structure of the church in the immediate aftermath of the Reformation. The Reformation split into a Reformed-Swiss branch and a Lutheran-German branch by the mid-1520s, and national Reformed churches appeared outside Switzerland, in Hungary, France (for a time), Scotland, and England. This variety did not turn European Christianity into a "denominational" system. Under the arrangement of the Peace of Westphalia, each prince determined which branch of the church would be the monopoly church of that territory. Other sects sometimes enjoyed limited toleration,[8] but in each territory an established church was supported by tax funds, interconnected with the aristocracy, given access to political authorities.[9] Even when other Protestant groups emerged and even when they were granted a degree of religious freedom, most European countries did not develop denominational meta-systems.

A denomination is not identical to what sociologists call a "church." It is not established by law and has no coercive power to control religious behavior. It does not *want* coercive power, nor does it want anyone else to have it. A denomination is not a sect either. A denomination accepts the world as it is—in all its pluralistic profusion of religious options. A denomination only wants a level playing field where it can compete against other denominations: and may the best person win. It is a courteous way of being church. Denominationalism fits contentedly, cozily into a pluralistic system. Denominationalism is a meta-ecclesial system for a religiously pluralistic society. A denomination is not a *dis*established church. Denominationalism is the *established* church of pluralism.

Original Pluralism

In Europe, pluralism was a late development after a long medieval age of monopoly Catholicism. That was not the case in the United States. From the beginning, America has been a cornucopia of religious possibilities.

America's earliest European settlers had to build a world more or less from scratch.[10] They may have thought of themselves as a new Israel, but the old Israel had at least the advantage of conquering a land of strong cities, vineyards, orchards, fields, and roads. Many American colonists left behind kin networks. In the New World, they did not have family or kin networks any more than they had homes they could move into. Religious life had to be built from the ground up. The ships that brought settlers over were "Noah's arks" containing all varieties of faith (the description is from Mennonite Francis Daniel Pastorius), some radical and divisive. Some groups were like-minded friends, but once in America people kept moving along, seduced by the promise of abundant virgin land. In the transit, "the religious congregation . . . like the family, suffered profound shock from the fragmentation and uprooting which migration to the New World involved." At the same time, the churches bore even more responsibility than ever for their members. It was a gargantuan challenge: fewer hands to handle bigger responsibilities.[11]

This is the setting in which American denominational Christianity took form: "A sense of spiritual and moral kinship, rooted in voluntary adherence to a congregation, was to remain throughout the eighteenth century and long beyond the key to neighborhood stability, ordered family life, and the education of children. Legislation having proven inadequate, pastors and lay leaders of each persuasion united to form an inter-colonial association to counter the weaknesses stemming from the diversity and mobility of the membership of congregations. These associations, later called denominations, became in the eighteenth century the mainstay of beleaguered local brotherhoods."[12] Local churches made up what was lacking in the settlers' social network; denominations provided a faux-clan network beyond the local. Denominational Christianity was the colonial replacement for the traditional networks of the Old World.

Some colonies tried to reproduce European-style establishments in the New World, but it never worked for long. Roger Williams and Anne Hutchinson rapidly challenged the Puritan establishment in Massachusetts, and when they were driven from the colony, they settled down the coast and started their own experiment in religious freedom. Open horizons made an establishment practically unenforceable. In the eighteenth century, the schisms that took place after the Awakenings further undermined any monopolistic pretensions the colonies might have had, and during the French and Indian Wars their religious differences were subordinated to a common national identity.[13] Religious differences were still evident during the Revolutionary era, but the sons of John Winthrop and Roger Williams were largely reconciled in a common political experiment. Battles among denominations could be fierce, as most American churches threw themselves zealously into the competition of the religious marketplace.

Denominational Catholicity

It is not all cutthroat competition. Both in theory and in practice, denominationalism provides ample opportunities for cross-denominational connections. From the very beginning, denominationalism was explained and defended by "catholic Protestants." Contrary to the common perception, the denominational system was not the creation of Enlightenment rationalists who wanted to neutralize the violent public effects of religious difference. At least it was not *only* the creation of such rationalists: "The real architects of the denominational theory of the church were the seventeenth century Independent divines within the Church of England, whose most prominent representatives were the Dissenting Brethren in the Westminster Assembly."[14] Convinced believers provided much of the rationale for the system and provided theological reasons for denominating Christianity into distinct groups, separating Christians by conviction, preference, and name.

In *An Apologetical Narration*, written in opposition to the Westminster Assembly's effort to establish an English church, Independent Congregationalists articulated two principles. First, they found no support in the New Testament for a single model of church government. Second was an anti-traditional principle, a commitment "not to make our present judgment and practice a binding law unto ourselves for the future." This was not relativism but a humble recognition of human limits and frailty: "We had too great an instance for our own frailty in the former way of our conformity, and therefore . . . we kept this reserve . . . to alter and retract (though not lightly) whatever should be discovered to be taken up out of a misunderstanding of the rule."[15] With similar modesty, the New England churches stated in 1639 that they were ready "with great reverence to accept and receive what further light God may be pleased to impart unto us. . . . If anything appear to be unsound and dissonant from the Word, which we for our parts cannot discern, we shall willingly attend to what

further light God may send unto us."[16] Commitment to the authority of
the Word of God over all human traditions, no matter how revered, kept
the New England churches open to further correction from the Spirit
speaking in the Word.

Jeremiah Burroughs, a leading dissenting spokesman, emphasized that
divisions had always existed in the church and argued that they would
continue to exist, even among the most godly of people. This is in part
because Christ has made his people free in conscience: "Godly men are
free men. Christ made them so, and requires them not to suffer themselves to be brought under bondage. They must not, cannot submit their
consciences to the opinions, determinations, decrees of any men living.
They cannot submit to any as lords over their faith." Submitting to the
wise would indeed make "quick work of divisions." Everyone could cede
his conscience to experts. But "this those who fear God cannot do. They
must see everything they own as a truth with their own light . . . received
from Jesus Christ." While honoring those with greater knowledge and
wisdom, "they have the charge of Christ upon them not to acknowledge
it as truth till they understand it to be so." Further, since "the things of
religion are hidden mysteries" that are difficult to discern, free people will
naturally differ at many points.[17] Given the limits of human knowledge,
and the freedom of the Christian conscience, differences of conviction
were inescapable.

Division is inevitable and not altogether a bad thing. Even within a
divided church, Burroughs stated, "God is working out ends above our
reach for his glory and the good of his saints." Divisions give everyone a
chance to test their mettle and grow in grace.

> A little skill in a mariner is enough to guide his ship in fair weather; but
> when storms arise, where the seas swell and grow troublesome, then his
> skill is put to it. In these stormy troublesome times, there had need be much
> wisdom, faith, love, humility, patience, self-denial and meekness. All graces
> are put to it now! They had need put forth all their strength; act with all their
> vigor. Our graces had need be stirring, full of life and quickness, now! God
> prizeth exercise of the graces of his Saints at a very high rate. He thinks it
> worth their suffering much trouble.[18]

Division is one of the methods God uses to "bring forth further light":
"Sparks are beaten out by the flints striking together."[19]

Guided by these principles, denominationalism leaves Christians free in conscience while cultivating the blessings of communion. A dissenter's conscience would be mauled if the Presbyterians established a state church. If dissenters are free to establish their own church, they can form it according to their conscience and insight into Scripture. They do not have to demonize the Presbyterians. They can state their disagreement honestly, openly, and still accept those who differ as brothers and sisters. Denominations enable Christians to live together in peace despite their differences. As Burroughs put it, even though "godly people are divided in their opinions and ways . . . they are united in Christ."[20] Or, as David Martin put it in a widely quoted formulation, "The Jehovah's witnesses claim that they alone have the key; the Roman Catholics claim that they alone have the keys. The denomination merely claims that while there are doubtless many keys to many mansions it is at least in possession of one of them, and that anyone who thinks he has the sole means to open the heavenly door is plainly mistaken."[21] Theoretically, denominationalism permits, perhaps even encourages, fellowship across Christian traditions. If forced into unity, dissenters would fight with Presbyterians, and it could get ugly. Division would happen eventually anyway. Why not separate peaceably, each letting all the others be, and share what fellowship we can?

In many places and ways, denominational catholicity has worked in practice. Interdenominational mission work has been a staple of American denominationalism. On a local scale, churches have often cooperated in mission and ministry. In nineteenth-century Kansas,

> churches often joined forces in sponsoring [revival meetings]. Baptists, Disciples of Christ, Mennonites, Quakers, and Presbyterians all held revivals. . . . One of the largest revivals occurred in Kansas City in 1888 under the leadership of evangelist Samuel Porter Jones. . . . At the conclusion of each lengthy service, Jones appealed to the masses to join their respective churches. "I want every man or woman who'll say, 'I'll join the Christian church, or the Baptist church, or the Methodist church,' to come forward and give me his hands. We'll have the Presbyterians first." . . .
>
> In quieter ways, Protestants worked across denominational lines to provide space for new congregations, hold community meetings, and organize social programs. These activities were well illustrated in southeastern Kansas among the Methodists, Baptists, Congregationalists, and Presbyterians of Winfield, a town of 472 residents in 1870 that grew to more than 5,000 by

1890. . . . The Presbyterian minister occasionally preached at the Baptist Church, and the Baptist minister returned the favor. Dedication services of new buildings typically included brief addresses by all the community's clergy. Each year the churches cooperated in holding a union service on Thanksgiving. During the Christmas holidays, Presbyterians and Methodists each held festivals to which the entire community was invited. The Presbyterian festival, at least one time, was held at the Methodist Church. . . .

In other locations, cooperative Sunday school efforts ranged from small congregations holding joint classes or hosting programs at schools when church buildings were lacking, to enlisting children for larger purposes.[22]

Nor is interdenominational cooperation a thing of the past. The vast majority of American congregations form partnerships with interdenominational ministries:

The average congregation supports about five organizations that provide services to their community and beyond. . . . This is over and above whatever they may do through a regional or national denominational body or on their own initiative. . . . Many congregations (especially Catholics) also channel service money through regular offerings that are administered by regional and national denominational agencies, but they almost all work with other organizations as well. Across traditions, nearly everyone (82%) is connected to at least one outside service organization. Only among the Sectarian groups and the newest groups (Hindus and Muslims, for instance) was it common for us to find congregations that have no connections outside their own religious world. Partnerships between congregations and other community organizations have been institutionalized as an expected pattern in most of American religion.[23]

These partnerships are not permanent or intimate. They are not marriages. They are "strategic alliances. They are connections that allow community organizations to mobilize needed resources and allow congregations to extend their reach."[24] Still, denominationalism need not be an obstacle to the catholic spirit or catholic action.

Denominational Vibrancy

Denominational Christianity has been fertile, creative, and vibrant, as well as catholic. Again, this has partly to do with the unique origins of

American Christianity. American denominationalism was not the end point of a long process of de-monopolization, as it has been in Europe. It is the original condition of American Christianity. This is one of the reasons that some of the "secularization" theories developed in Europe do not transport well to America. According to one version of the theory, secularization is a product of pluralism. In monopolistic societies, only one brand is on sale: any color as long as it is black. In a pluralist situation, religion becomes a shopping mall, and when religious consumers realize they are making choices, they also realize that their choices might have been different. Religion becomes relative rather than absolute, subjective rather than objectively given. Religion weakens. Tolerance increases. Zeal cools.[25]

In Europe, secularization has usually involved either a deliberate disestablishment of a monopoly church or toleration. This typically produces pluralization of a different sort. Religion's influence on public life is diminished as various institutions wriggle free of religious oversight or domination. Society becomes secularized, free to operate without accountability to meddling priests. Sectors of society that were once offshoots of the monopoly religion become autonomous social spheres.

Modernization was supposed to bring secularization everywhere. In the United States it never happened:

> The United States (as a whole) is a religious nation. In general, Americans have high rates of religious *belonging*, *behaving*, and *believing*—what social scientists call the three Bs of religiosity. Eighty-three percent of Americans report belonging to a religion; 40 percent report attending religious services nearly every week or more; 59 percent pray at least weekly; a third report reading scripture with this same frequency. Many Americans also have firm religious beliefs. Eighty percent are absolutely sure that there is a God. Sixty percent are absolutely sure that there is a heaven, although fewer (52 percent) have this level of certainty about life after death. Slightly fewer, 49 percent, are certain that there is a hell.[26]

Not only does America rate high on all three Bs, but belief, behavior, and belonging are at high levels among "conservative" or evangelical Christians. A third of Americans say that Scripture is the Word of God, and Europeans are shocked to discover the high percentage of Americans who have doubts about the theory of evolution and who say that they believe Genesis 1–2 gives a truthful account of the world's origins.[27]

Rational choice theorists have argued that this vibrancy is the fruit of an unregulated religious marketplace. Religious producers aim to serve and meet the needs of religious consumers, and since the market is unregulated, the producers can innovate and adjust their products to meet shifting consumer desires and needs. When religion is unregulated, it is necessarily pluralist, since no single religious institution can meet everyone's wants. As Roger Finke and Rodney Stark put it, "Pluralism arises because of 'normal' variations in the human condition such as social class, age, gender, health, life experiences, and socialization."[28] Even when backed by state power, no religious organization can become a true monopoly; people's needs will demand other sorts of religious offerings. Diverse needs breed specialization and competition to attract free religious consumers. Pluralism thus does not undermine religion but is one of the reasons it stays vibrant. Unregulated pluralism keeps everyone on their toes.[29]

It is a fact, Finke and Stark point out, that religious participation is far lower in countries with a Catholic monopoly than in the United States. They argue that one reason for this is that "monopoly firms tend to be lazy," and clergy who have a secure sinecure for life do not have to work hard to fulfill their modest responsibilities. A Presbyterian who realizes he is locked in competition with the Methodist and Baptist pastor around the corner will be more energetic, more likely to take risks and to try out "innovations in music, communication, religious education, preaching, revival, and organizational strategies."[30] Because the American religious market is unregulated, it is easier to enter the market than it is in monopoly systems. The cost of creating a new religion is low, and the rewards, including the financial rewards, may be great. American pastors do not receive any support from taxation. They are paid only if they attract a large enough number of dues-paying customers. Literal economic motives join together with the forces of religious economy to give a unique energy to American Christianity.[31]

America has never *not* been pluralist; religion has never *not* been voluntary. Since the Bill of Rights passed, Christianity has never *not* been privatized, at least to the extent that it cannot be nationally established. Original pluralism means that the effects of modernization have been quite different in the United States than in Europe.[32] Denominationalism—the established church system of pluralism—has kept American churches from replicating the grand, echoing emptiness of Europe's cathedrals.

From Doctrine to Flow Chart

America is famous, or notorious, for its religious entrepreneurs and innovators. Some of them are religious con men. Some have displayed the sanctified flexibility that new situations demand. This flexibility is evident not only in individual churches and leaders. It is evident also in the macro-structure of denominationalism itself. What makes a denomination a denomination has shifted and changed over the centuries.

Initially, denominations were defined by doctrine and government. Congregationalist dissenters settled in Plymouth colony, Congregationalist Puritans from within the Church of England founded Massachusetts Bay, Anglicans dominated Virginia, Scottish Presbyterians settled in what became the Carolinas, and tolerant Maryland had a large Catholic population. Though each colony had a dominant church, the system as a whole was pluralistic and doctrinally based. This sort of denominational distinctiveness is what denominational officials, pastors, and leaders still focus on when they describe denominational identity: "Those who occupy pulpits, teach in the seminaries, and write adult education materials for churches are likely to look toward beliefs and practices as the core of their denominational identity."[33]

Nondoctrinal factors always had a role in forging denominational identity. Immigrants brought their European forms of Christianity with them. Ethnicity thus became a deep "social source" of denominationalism, often playing a more critical role than doctrine. Much to the dismay of H. Richard Niebuhr, Swedish Lutherans remained separate from German Lutherans who remained separate from Danish Lutherans, despite their identical confessions. Initially, language divided them, but even after everyone learned English the churches went their separate ways for a long time and found plenty of reasons to continue to do so. The timing of immigration was sometimes a factor. After Dutch immigrants had settled in the States, churches in the Netherlands split. When adherents of the newly formed church arrived stateside, they kept to themselves. The recent and older churches had no significant doctrinal differences but diverged over the issue of hymnody versus psalmody. Niebuhr argues that the underlying issue was "the whole subject of adaptation or resistance to the native culture" of the New World.[34] The older church had accommodated more fully to the revivalist ethos of American Christianity.

As noted above, interdenominational cooperation was widespread. Early nineteenth-century America was awash with voluntary societies, some of which had strong denominational affiliations, but almost all of which were interdenominational efforts. Zeal to Christianize America broke churches out of old ethnic enclaves and swept them together into cooperative missionary ventures. Bible societies, mission societies, temperance societies, tract societies, Sunday school societies—all involved interchurch cooperation. The freedom to innovate and experiment inherent in the denominational system enabled churches to meet growing needs in expanding urban areas, fund foreign missions, initiate moral crusades. A modern invention, denominationalism proved a useful framework for churches seeking to address modernity's pathologies.

Doctrine, practice, and ethnicity are no longer as definitive of American denominations.[35] During the past century, denominations, inspired by business models emphasizing efficiency and rationalized procedure, became "modern organizations definable by their bylaws, budgets, and headquarters buildings."[36] The effect of this managerial revolution on interdenominational relations was dramatic. In the late nineteenth century, most tasks of mission and ministry were taken over by individual denominations. Instead of joining with Congregationalists and others, Presbyterians sent out their own Presbyterian missionaries and created their own Presbyterian teaching material.[37]

Denominations have cultural identities quite apart from membership. To the general public, the word "Presbyterian" will hardly conjure memories of Calvin, the Westminster Confession, predestination, or psalm singing. It will more likely conjure a character type—stern, humorless, hardworking, the "frozen chosen." Survey evidence can be misconstrued if this is forgotten. Someone who ticks off "Presbyterian" may not be a member of any church but may have some identification with something about the cultural ethos of Presbyterianism: "There is out there in American culture something defined as Presbyterianism that is not simply a theological tradition or an organizational membership. After a few hundred years of existence, denominational identities have taken on a cultural life of their own. The more established the denomination is, the more pervasive its cultural identity; the more sectarian and separate the group, the more its cultural identity may be at odds with its actual practices and the less likely it is that someone not actually a participant will claim a preference for that group."[38]

Conclusion

In more recent years, fresh cultural trends have changed the shape of American denominationalism yet again, and various lines of evidence suggest that denominational affiliations and allegiances are weakening (see chap. 7 below). Denominationalism may be dying. Or, given the tumultuous history of American denominationalism, what looks like death could be nothing more than preparation for yet another reincarnation.

Denominationalism is imperfect. It can be ugly. Denominational competition can undermine catholicity. In essence, as we shall see, it institutionalizes division and inhibits the fulfillment of Jesus's prayer. But it accommodates difference without sacrificing freedom of conscience, and by virtually every measure it has left the American church far stronger than the monopolistic establishments of Europe. Denominational Christianity has been nothing if not resilient and has carried a living faith into the early twenty-first century. That is no mean achievement.

6

The Case against Denominationalism

One can utter a cheer for denominationalism. One might even add another half a cheer. Denominationalism does not necessarily foster religious hatreds. More often it fosters a live-and-let-live, leave-us-alone toleration. In America it has served the church well. Denominations have cooperated with each other in grand projects of home and foreign missions, in education and welfare, in urban ministry and evangelism. Denominationalism has kept American Christianity lively while the churches of the old Christendom have slowly decayed. Denominationalism has made America a big tolerant tent, a sanctuary where people of every faith can live side by side more or less in peace.

It is not perfect, but what is? Why fix it if it ain't broke?

Even when we acknowledge all this, even when denominations are playing nice as you please, denominationalism is an *alternative* to the one church that the Father promised, the one church that Jesus died to save, the one church being gathered by the Spirit, the one church Jesus asked for. In its *essence*, denominationalism falsifies central Christian truths about the church and her members. Christians are named by the one name conferred on them in baptism, by the one faith they confess, by the one table they share, by the one Good Shepherd who leads his church through his ordained undershepherds. If our name is "Father, Son, and Spirit," then our name *cannot* be Lutheran, Reformed, or Orthodox. If we are named with the name of Jesus, we cannot refuse to acknowledge each other as brothers and sisters, cannot refuse to welcome brothers and sisters to the Lord's table, cannot refuse to take familial responsibility for one another. If we are members of one another, we *cannot* name ourselves as *not*-him or *not*-them. Denominationalism *institutionalizes* division. So long as we are denominational Christians, we will not be one as the Father and Son are one.

We can strive to be what we will be under a denominational system, and many Christians have functioned as denominational catholics. In doing so, though, they are pushing *against* the inertia of the denominational system. At many points denominationalism stymies and frustrates our efforts to be one, and so grieves the Spirit.

In this and the following chapter, my focus is again narrowed to the American church. Denominationalism in the abstract presents theological problems, but my objections are to the concrete form of denominationalism that exists in that most denominational of societies, the United States of America.

Established Division

Denominations are not sects that believe they alone possess the keys of the kingdom. Denominations are tolerant of other denominations, provided all agree on certain fundamental doctrines and maintain certain fundamental practices. American churches have worshiped together, fed the hungry together, cared for orphans together, distributed Bibles and tracts together. They have dedicated each other's sanctuaries and participated in each other's ordination services. They have done God's work, and they will have their reward. Denominationalism does not seem to be an obstacle to expressions of Christian unity.

Yet as Sidney Mead pointed out long ago, denominational churches have an inherent "sectarian" bias as they try "to justify peculiar interpretations and practices as more closely conforming to those of the early Church as pictured in the New Testament than the views and politics of [their] rivals."[1] Since each Protestant denomination claims to derive its practices from Scripture more consistently and thoroughly than others, each sanctifies its own practices "indiscriminately" so that "all the various elements of doctrine and practice that it for whatever reason adopted" are treated as if they came from "a blueprint revealed in the Word of God."[2] This intensifies conflicts between denominations and within denominations. Everyone believes that the whole truth of God is always at stake. This sectarian habit also makes each denomination's claim to be "more biblical than thou" implausible to a watching, often bewildered world. The inability of Reformation-era churches to agree on basic Christian teaching and practice opened the door to secular philosophies that claimed to be capable of discovering a base for consensus concerning truth and goodness. Insofar as denominationalism perpetuates this inconclusiveness, it aids and abets the secularism that many denominations officially oppose.

Sectarianism is not a bug in the system but a design feature of denominational Christianity. Michael Emerson and Christian Smith observe that "in the context of a pluralistic society, social groups construct and maintain collective identities by forming symbolic boundaries." These boundaries are *essential* to the group. Without them, the group does not exist at all. Without strong, clear boundaries, the group will be confused about why it exists: "Groups that stress tolerance, openness to diversity, and inclusiveness typically lack the ability to have strong comparison groups to define their boundaries." In a pluralistic system, churches support the status quo: "As churches constitute themselves agents to promote social change, they are likely to lose, rather than gain, social strength."[3] Every group defines itself negatively, by distinguishing itself from other groups: "Groups must symbolize and utilize symbolic boundaries to both create and give substance to shared values and identities. An ingroup always has at least one outgroup by which it creates identity. Blacks are not whites, Lutherans are not Presbyterians, evangelicals are not mainline Christians, Carolina Tar Heels are not Duke Blue Devils."[4]

Denominational boundary-marking has two damaging effects on the church. On the one hand, denominational churches are homogenous and uniflavored and therefore immature. They are not bodies but collections of eyes, hands, brains, and other disembodied parts. On the other hand, they are set off from each other by a host of symbolic barriers. Symbolically divided, they have few obstacles to further division.

Church Like Me

In a competitive religious situation, the process of defining group boundaries produces homogenous groups. Religious consumers look for religious groups that give without asking much: "Most people want to satisfy their needs with minimal cost."[5] The cost of living in a racially, economically, or socially mixed congregation is comparatively high. It can be difficult to learn how to relate to people who are very different from ourselves. It requires investment of time and emotional energy, which can be unsettling. So "internally homogenous congregations more often provide what draws people to religious groups for a lower cost than do internally diverse congregations."[6] As a result, "congregations become and remain highly racially homogenous. . . . The need for symbolic boundaries and social solidarity, the similarity and homophily principles, the status quo bias . . . all push congregations, and volunteer organizations in general, continually toward internal similarity."[7]

American denominational churches have been ethnic enclaves, and, despite a shifting landscape, some still are.[8] Among the newest immigrants, ethnically homogenous churches are a natural result of cultural and especially linguistic differences. Chinese- or Korean-speaking immigrants worship with other Chinese- or Korean-speaking immigrants. Even after linguistic barriers disappear, churches can retain an ethnic character. In certain parts of the United States, Dutch Reformed churches are full of van-thises and vander-thats. "If you ain't Dutch, you ain't much"—it's a joke but, like all jokes, contains a grain of truth. Lutheran churches still often have a membership that is largely of German or Scandinavian ancestry.[9] Not being part of the ethnic group means being excluded from some of the long-standing networks of power and privilege within a denomination. Not being a Southerner makes you an object of suspicion in some Southern churches. The missions of ethnically homogenous churches "all too easily enter into complex collusions with divisions of class, culture, ethnicity, or status already present there. . . . Rather than reconciling the divided, the gathering of men and women into churches tends to reinforce their divisions." Churches "become artifacts of specific cultures, and their mission becomes the reinforcing of folkways."[10]

Economic and social divisions are even more pronounced. The Reformation division between the "church of the disinherited" and the "bourgeois church" flourishes in America. Many churches draw in a small slice of the American socioeconomic pie. Many of the churches I have attended as an adult are full of professionals—doctors and lawyers and PhDs. It is a comfortable place for me because I share so many unstated assumptions about the world with my friends. It is a church of brains, but we may be missing some other important body parts that are gathered en masse at the Baptist church down the street. In some cases, this homogeneity is the product of a deliberate marketing strategy. Church-growth experts counsel churches to appeal to niche markets. It may be a good way to grow a large church; it is not a good way to grow a church consisting of all sorts and conditions of people. Even when it is not a deliberate strategy, it is implicit in many denominational tics and habits. Black Pentecostals are not going to thrill to the richness of a liturgical service. Many find the theologically weighty preaching in a Presbyterian pulpit off-putting, even if the church members are as friendly as can be. Every variety of church has invisible gatekeepers at the door, habits of expression, liturgy, and church life that hint that some are welcome and others are outsiders. Church shoppers seek out and find something to fit their taste and mood. We worship and live our Christian lives with people like us, and the homogeneity of our brand—the distinctives of doctrine, practice, and "tone"—pre-exclude many, ensuring that our churches remain homogenous and become more so.[11]

If one steps back to look at the "American church" in the aggregate, it is the most diverse community of churches in the world, perhaps the most ethnically diverse collection of churches in church history. But that wide-angle view does not tell the whole story. Individual denominations or churches are full of "people like me."

This is not what the church should be. The church is called to be a community where the weak and the strong, the poor and the wealthy, the enslaved and the free can find a common home and eat at a common table and serve a common Master. Congregations too often reflect the divided condition of the world outside, often becoming a reflection of the Babel of division that exists. The problem is not that the church fails to meet some external standard of diversity. It is that the church mimics and mirrors the world's own divisions. Whatever it might be in theory, denominationalism as it is actually practiced in the United States is an accommodation to the world. As Richard Niebuhr put it, "The evils of denominationalism do not lie . . . in this differentiation of churches and sects. . . . The evil of denominationalism lies in the conditions which make the rise of sects desirable and necessary: in the failure of the churches to transcend the social conditions which fashion them into caste-organizations, to sublimate their loyalties to standards and institutions only remotely relevant if not contrary to the Christian ideal, to resist the temptation of making their own self-preservation and extension the primary object of their endeavor."[12] From the looks of a denominational church, one might conclude that the Spirit never arrived to overcome the divisions of Babel.

Churches become outposts of uniform belief as well as uniform social and economic status. The church is called, of course, to be of one mind and to confess one faith together. *In fact*, though, modern Christians disagree about many things, and denominationalism makes it nearly impossible to resolve long-standing theological disputes. Baptists can remain complacent in their beliefs about baptism in part because they do not have to deal with paedobaptists in their midst. Even if they are on friendly terms with Presbyterians or Anglicans or Lutherans, even if they are engaged in certain forms of common ministry, they know that they can ultimately retreat back to their Baptist enclave where everyone agrees with them. Reformed and Lutheran views of the real presence have divided the church for half a millennium. Apart from the tiny minority engaged in ecumenical dialogues, the dispute is rarely dealt with in any depth. Arminians and Calvinists have their own home bases and can go about life happily avoiding one another. They may not be hostile to one another. They may well regard one another as Christian brothers and sisters and form warm friendships. But Christians of different persuasions live peaceably together primarily because they can do so *without* resolving their differences. It is an easy way. I am sure I would have fewer tensions in my marriage if I never saw my wife, but that would be a legal separation rather than a marriage. Jesus did not say, "They will know you are my disciples by your mutual indifference."

Denominationalism makes us ambivalent about *our own* theological commitments. On the one hand, our theological and practical differences *must* be serious enough to keep us from giving up our identities and uniting as a single church. Sometimes we consider our differences serious enough to keep us from sharing the Lord's Supper together or acknowledging each other's baptism. Ultimate and necessary truths *must* be at stake. Inevitably, this means that we are adding to the gospel. It is not enough that someone profess that Jesus is Lord and live the life of a disciple; if she was not baptized by immersion, or if she does not affirm a Lutheran view of the real presence, or if she does not acknowledge the bishop of Rome as the head of the church, she is not in full fellowship. What makes us a community is not what we hold in common with other believers but what we hold together *against* other believers.[13]

And yet, on the other hand, we willingly acknowledge that Christians in other denominations are fellow believers. We end up double-minded about the importance of our distinctive doctrines and ecclesial habits.[14] Sectarian exclusivism may rule within the church; an easy toleration governs our external relations with other churches, which sometimes shades into indifference. Our differences are important enough to keep us from joining with other Christians, perhaps important enough to keep us from intercommunion; yet they are not so important as to keep us from lower forms of fellowship and cobelligerency. *Which is it?* Are they important enough to separate us or not? Denominationalism liberates us from having to answer that question.

A Reformational Catholic church would also include people of different views and persuasions, but these differences could not be simply ignored. Suppose a Lutheran church wanted to unite with a Reformed church. They could do so with integrity only if they worked through the doctrinal questions that have divided them for five hundred years. They might determine that the divisions are not of the kind that prevent reunion; they might decide that the reunited church can tolerate diversity of opinion on these disputed questions; they might find that they can now discover a common formula that satisfies both sides. They could *not*, however, regard the differences with indifference.

Ecumenists are often accused, falsely, of being indifferent to doctrine. The contrary is true. Ecumenical churches have engaged in deep explorations not only of their own doctrines but also of the doctrinal systems of other churches. It is *denominationalism*, not ecumenism, that minimizes the importance of doctrine. Despite the doctrinal interests of many American Christians, denominationalism makes doctrinal discipline a virtual impossibility. During the Middle Ages, the Catholic Church was the acceptable church, and deviations were judged to be deviations from Christianity itself. Within the church-state system after the Reformation, moral and doctrinal purity was identified with the doctrine and the moral stance of

the established church. John Cuddihy writes, "When the religious organization becomes a purely voluntary association, when the last vestiges of
ascription disappear, we can no longer 'ascribe' moral upstandingness to
any given organization." Denominational churches have difficulty ascribing
moral or doctrinal apostasy to those who deviate. That would violate the
tolerant spirit of denominationalism. When a new church breaks away, it
may be denounced for a time, but it shortly enters the market as another
brand on the shelf. When the churches are divided, it becomes practically
impossible to identify anything *as* heresy and to make it stick.[15]

Liberalism is the great heresy of modernity. As J. Gresham Machen
pointed out near the beginning of the twentieth century, liberalism is less
a variant of Christianity than a rival type of religion. Christianity is rooted
in historical events, in affirmation of certain facts: the Son of God assumed
flesh, lived and died, rose again, and ascended into heaven. If that is no
more than religious symbolism, we are still in our sins.[16] Fundamentalists
vigorously and rightly protested this theological paradigm and often split
to form new, orthodox churches.[17] They had to split because there was
no higher court of appeal that could resolve the theological issues. There
was no place where the buck stopped. Once they split, the churches went
their separate ways. Fundamentalist Presbyterians defined themselves as
not being like the liberal Presbyterians, whom they criticized and attacked.
Thinking of themselves as a separate church, however, the fundamentalists
were relieved of the responsibility of correcting the heresy.

Denominationalism encourages irresponsibility among the churches.
Baptists and Methodists do not consider false teaching in an Anglican
or Presbyterian church as their responsibility. If a Lutheran pastor gets
involved in scandalous sin, the church next door does not take steps to
correct him. It is left to denominational authorities, who are often at
some distance from the situation. Some Presbyterians believe that Baptists make a serious theological error by refusing to baptize infants; some
Baptists think the same of Presbyterians because they do baptize infants.
Occasionally we lob polemics across the divide, but Presbyterians do not
really think they are responsible for correcting Baptists, nor Baptists for
correcting Presbyterians. Denominationalism causes us to forget that we
are part of the same church where some venerate Mary and believe in
transubstantiation, some are debating the legitimacy of same-sex marriage, and some approve abortion. We forget that the pedophilia scandal

is a scandal in the church of Jesus Christ, of which we are members. We push it to the side: "Not my problem."

When we take a step back, we can see that the marketplace analogy is itself an accommodation to worldly patterns of sociality. Recent studies of American religion have emphasized its consumerist character: Americans shop for churches. Again, that is not a flaw but a design feature of American Christianity. It dissolves the norms of doctrine and practice, transforming them from norms into consumer options. Our divisions come to seem "normal," the "natural expression of a Christian marketplace with churches representing different options for a variety of spiritual tastes." A marketplace ideology thus "can anesthetize us to the wound of division."[18] And it seduces us into thinking of the church, or our particular brand of church, as a consumer choice. It is a wonderful thing that Christians have not recently been killing one another over doctrine, but we do not have to be killing one another to hollow out our faith. In our very tolerant niceness, we reduce faith to a preference: to each his own; everyone has their own tastes; that's why they make vanilla ice cream.[19]

Denominationalism infantilizes the church. It forms monstrous churches whose members are all the same body part. It raises Paul's question: If all are eyes, where is the hearing? Denominationalism keeps us safe among people of our own kind, ensconced comfortably in our tribe. It guards us against the vertiginous disorientation of serious debate and upsetting differences of opinion. It justifies our failures of responsibility for our brothers and sisters by helping us forget that they are our siblings. We acknowledge that we are brothers and sisters. Then, in the next breath, we are Cain: Am I my brother's keeper?

Perpetuating Schism

By the same boundary-forming process that makes churches internally homogenized, they are differentiated from other churches. These are two steps of the same dance. Reasons have to be given to justify the group's existence and solidarity, and those reasons inevitably involve reasons to *not* be something else. Presbyterian reasons for maintaining a distinct Presbyterian denominational identity include arguments about why Presbyterians are not-Lutheran, not-Baptist, not-Catholic. The stated reasons are invariably high-minded. They are reasons of deep theology. The gospel is invoked, for the very truth of God is at stake. Everyone knows that many churches are founded for much more sordid reasons—because of unresolved conflict, bitterness, ambition, greed, a desire to be in control. Everyone also knows that we cannot be entirely honest about the real reasons that churches are founded. The high-minded evangelical reasons become a cloak to occlude the actual reasons for division.[20]

The causes of church division are complex, and the effects can be paradoxical. In a study of American Protestant schisms between 1890 and 1990, John Sutton and Mark Chaves conclude that churches do not divide for purely doctrinal reasons but rather "in response to attempts by denominational elites to achieve organizational consolidation."[21] The 1848 schism within the Plymouth Brethren was about open Communion, but "this issue was inextricably linked with the question of whether there would be more centralized control over this religious matter. . . . Schism occurred as a result of an effort to enforce a uniform communion policy on all congregations."[22] Ironically, "mergers and foundings sharply raise the likelihood of schism."[23] Efforts to reunite the church can go wrong and sow further and deeper divisions. Ironically again, schism can reduce the chance of schism, though only briefly: "one year after a founding or merger, rates of schism are five times higher than they are one year after a schism."[24] Pursuing unity or enforcing uniformity may be the quickest way to destroy whatever unity already exists. In some cases, consolidation and centralization can lessen the possibility of schism.[25] At times, it is the very effort to prevent schism that causes it.

A church's membership in an interdenominational federation lowered the likelihood of schism, though the effect seems to be greater if the federation is theologically liberal.[26] Churches that make monopolizing claims are less likely to experience schism. Not surprisingly, churches that say they alone have the truth, or that their tradition is uniquely authoritative, or that only their church has a legitimate claim to apostolic succession, experience fewer schisms. Leaving the church is too costly. As one study puts it, an "organization holds a competitive advantage because it provides an inimitable good or service. From the perspective of potential sect movements, the option for schism is reduced because leaving the denomination would result in the loss of both legitimacy and a host of unique resources."[27]

Denominationalism undermines these schism inhibitors. The first commandment of denominationalism is that denominations are not subordinate to any supra-denominational order. And the second commandment is like unto it: all denominations have *a* key, but none can claim to have *the* key. Denominationalism thus puts few or no obstacles to schism, and denominational Christianity keeps schismating along. New sects and denominations and movements proliferate. The United States has more than two thousand religious groups, one thousand of them distinct Christian denominations.[28] The numbers are much lower when we recognize that these one thousand denominations reduce to a handful of denominational *families* (Lutheran, Presbyterian, Baptist, etc.). That hardly answers the criticism, though, because the obvious question is, If three hundred denominations are all Baptists, why are they not one church?

Schisms not only create fresh divisions but also exaggerate existing differences. Through a process of "schismogenesis," small differences are exaggerated as

> rivalrous groups develop their own identities and objectives through a dialectical process of polarizing opposition and separation. As points of in-group tension become manifest, the emergent factions move increasingly toward disequilibrium, each side defining and valorizing their own respective positions through an intensifying deprecation and negation of the practices and principles espoused by the other. . . . A schismogenic dynamic, in short, is one that progressively transforms the engaged parties into "structural antitypes," as each side organizes itself as "the inverse of the other" [Marshall Sahlins]. Having started from a shared or common orientation, the contending factions are inexorably driven into providing principled rationales or justifications for their disagreements; in the course of placing excessive and pointed emphasis on those differences that form the grounds of disputation, contrapositional identity-markers come to the fore. Failing mediation or compromise, the escalating hostilities will issue in fissiparous rupture and the formation of autonomous or independent communities.[29]

Schismogenesis hardens into a denominational identity. Baptists and Presbyterians rarely meet on a terrain where they can discuss baptism in depth. Worse, Baptists and Presbyterians formulate their theologies and teaching in order to provide continuing justification of their separate existence. Baptists have to minimize or neutralize the force of texts that might lend support to paedobaptism; paedobaptists have to skim past passages that seem to support Baptist views. Calvinists have their favorite texts and avoid others; ditto for Arminians. These tricks of teaching and doctrinal formulation not only betray a cavalier attitude toward Scripture but also help reinforce doctrinal and ecclesial divisions. Honest Baptists and Presbyterians, honest Calvinists and Arminians, who acknowledge the strength of the opponents' arguments, run the risk of being expelled from their own ranks. Anyone who fails to defend the denominational barricades must be a traitor, a heretic at best and a liar at worst.

Established Unity

Institutionalized division is not the only problem of American denomi-nationalism. Equally problematic is the kind of *unity* that exists among the churches of America.

As noted above, the United States has not gone through a process of secularization as Europe did. That is due in part to its unique religious situation, its original pluralism. It did not *become* pluralistic but was from the outset a Noah's ark and a sanctuary, filled with every variety of religious expression. One might call that a free market of religion. One might also say that America has not been secularized because it started out *pre*-secularized.

This secularization is not a defection from denominationalism but its essence. "Denominational pluralism, on the American plan," wrote Will Herberg, "means thoroughgoing secularization."[30] By "secularization," Herberg means a gap between *conventional* and *operational* religion. Conventional religion is what is practiced by religious adherents—the beliefs, rituals, and ways of life of Protestants, Catholics, Jews, Muslims, Buddhists. Operational religion is the set of beliefs, rituals, and values that shape public life. Societies cannot do without some form of operational religion that binds members of the society together and provides a set of reasonably accurate expectations about how my neighbor will behave. In traditional societies, the operational religion is a conventional one. Under Christendom, Christian communities functioned as "churches" in the Troeltschian sense—the national community at prayer—and so the operational religion was one of the forms of conventional Christianity. National rituals were Christian rituals; national symbols included Christian elements; the head of the national church was a public person, integrated into the ruling class.

In a denominational society, *no* conventional religion is the operational religion. None is *permitted* to be. It is unconstitutional in the United States for the operational religion to coincide with any conventional one. Since society cannot be held together with a conventional religion, the governing religious symbols, rites, beliefs must be drawn from somewhere else. By definition, then, denominational societies are secular. As Herberg puts it:

> This country has not had a church since colonial times. The church, in this sense, is essentially the national community on its religious side, the national community religiously organized. Even where the transplanted religious bodies set up in the English colonies on the Atlantic Coast were churches to begin with, widespread religious dissidence, coupled with the diversity of population, soon broke the formal religious unity and induced an incipient denominationalism. Denominationalism became the established religious pattern in the wake of the great revival movements; and in denomination-alism we have a further and very advanced stage of secularization. For denominationalism, in its very nature, requires a thoroughgoing separation between conventional religion and operative religion, and this is the mark of secularization.[31]

What is the *operational* religion of America? Writing in 1962, Herberg could say that the common faith is a trifaith of Protestant-Catholic-Jew,[32] which had recently taken the place of the earlier unofficial Protestant establishment as "the nation on its religious side."[33] Half a century later, this is no longer tenable. After changes in immigration laws in the mid-1960s, large numbers of immigrants from the Middle East and Asia came to America. There are now more than one hundred Hindu "denomina-tions" and seventy-five different forms of Buddhism in the United States. Every town of any size has a Muslim population large enough to sponsor a mosque.[34] Though these groups do not have the prominence of the older American religions, the "trifaith" has become a "multifaith."

Even in 1962, the trifaith was *not* the operational religion of American society. Herberg's own description of the "denominationalization" of the Jehovah's Witnesses points to the real operational faith. He cites an article in a Witness publication instructing the faithful about dressing well and observes that leaders want "Witnesses [to] learn to fit into lower-middle-class suburbia and be accepted by it."[35] The common faith into which they want to be integrated is colored by Protestant-Catholic-Jew, but more fundamentally it is the American way of life. The "nation on its religious side" is no more than simply "the nation."

Markets are never perfectly free. This is the truth obscured in the celebration of competitive American denominationalism. America is the fertile ground from which many new forms of Christianity have grown— Nazarenes, Church of Christ, Disciples of Christ, and Pentecostals, not to mention Jehovah's Witnesses and Mormons. It looks like a land of teeming variety, but this is only partly true. For much of American history the various denominations have operated under the umbrella of a generic Protestantism, what historian David Sehat has called a "moral establishment."[36] States retained established churches until the 1830s, and, more importantly, a general moral perspective was shared by nearly all American churches until the early twentieth century.

By posing alternatives between "monopolistic" and "free market" religious situations, economic theories of denominationalism obscure the degree of monopolization that has characterized and still characterizes American religion. The churches transplanted to and planted in America took on an *American* form and flavor. The United States inherited all of the great churches of Europe and remade them into its American image, remade them into denominations within a denominational structure. Churches that had been established back in the home country dutifully accepted their denominational status when they became American.[37] Herberg knows this. He observes that conventional religions are "integrated into the 'common religion' of the American Way and made to serve a nonreligious function." The result has been "increasingly vacuous" religious life. Though religion is highly valued (in 1962), it is valued because it facilitates participation in the American way, "a religion thoroughly secularized and homogenized, a religion-in-general that is little more than a civic religion of democracy, the religionization of the American Way."[38]

The notion that American churches are "disestablished" is superficial. No single denomination is established and no generic Christian creed is established, but there *is* an established religion in America, one to which American churches have willingly offered their allegiance. It is allegiance to the project of America. During the nineteenth century, denominations devoted enormous amounts of energy and money to carrying out various forms of mission and ministry in the United States. It was an age of denominational cooperation, and much good was done. But the churches cooperated above all in the project of Christianizing the United States. The base of unity was their common Americanness; the goal of their efforts was to advance the moral character of the United States. It was catholicity of a sort, but as much a catholicity of the American way as a catholicity of Christian faith.

Allegiance to the American way means allegiance to the denominational system. American churches accept the American settlement of religious freedom, and that implies, as Sidney Mead puts it, that "only what all the religious 'sects' held and taught in common . . . was really relevant for the well being of the society and the state." Americans need to be religious, and it does not matter what religion it is, so long as it maintains certain publicly useful tenets—including acceptance of the denominational form of American Christianity. Conversely, "the churches implicitly accepted the view that whatever any religious group held peculiarly as a tenet of its faith, must be irrelevant for public welfare." Churches teach their distinctive doctrines and views and so divide themselves from each other, but those things that justify the existence of the denomination are "either irrelevant for the general welfare or at most [possess] only a kind of instrumental value for it."[39]

The price of entering the marketplace of American religion is a commitment to subordinate one's religion to the generic faith of American civil religion, which, as John Cuddihy noted, reduces to a religion of civility. All religions are tolerated, so long as they speak in measured, tolerant terms about other religions.[40] An uncivil religion loses its ticket or is shunned until it learns some respect. We privatize the incivilities of our religion, no matter how critical they may be to our faith, so that we can maintain the civilities of our civil religion.[41] Cuddihy cites Reinhold Niebuhr's call to abandon missionary efforts to Jews as a prime illustration of how American civil religion evacuates central claims of "conventional" religions: "Civil religion exercises an unremitting pressure on traditional religions; it forces traditional theologians into a defensive, apologetic posture. Before he realizes it, the apologist is enticed . . . into representing theological ideas in their public rather than in their private relations."[42] Niebuhr wrote for the "cultured despisers" of Christianity, and in appealing to this public he traded in "scandal . . . for scandal: so as not to scandalize the Jews, the Pauline 'scandal to the Jews' is abandoned as a scandal to the Jews. Civil religion with its discipline of appearances has brought Christianity full circle." Niebuhr did not abandon the mission to the Jews because Christ or Paul forbade it, or because it was contrary to Christianity. It was abandoned "because of appearances: *it was in bad taste.*"[43] He abandoned it because it violated American civil religion's first commandment: Thou shalt be civil.

For the same reasons, American denominationalism softens prophetic voices that might be raised against America. "A key function in most religions," write Michael Emerson and Christian Smith, "is to proclaim what ought to be, what is universally true, what is right and just. We call this the prophetic voice. . . . American religion fragments this prophetic voice, even within the same religion, into thousands of different voices."[44] The result, as W. E. B. DuBois said, is a "pathetically timid and human" church, one that will "stand on the side of wealth and power" and will "espouse any cause which is sufficiently popular, with eagerness."[45] Competitive pluralism in American religion "encourages religious groups to cater to people's existing preferences, rather than their ideal callings." Religious consumers look to congregations not "as an external force that places radical demands on their lives" but to "fulfill their needs." Since pastors are financially dependent on, and beholden to, congregations that tend to support the status quo, pastors have incentives to restrain their prophetic pronouncements.[46] Prophetic voices can take hold, but typically only when they are translated into the terms of the American way. Thus doth denominationalism make cowards of us all.

American responses to war provide one of the clearest examples of the politics of denominationalism. On the one hand, many churches give enthusiastic support to virtually every American war, becoming cheerleaders for American power. On the other hand, some churches *oppose* virtually every American war, some for reasons of principled pacifism and some out of hostility to America's global hegemony. Each side speaks mainly to its own, and differences of opinion about the war widen the gap between the denominations. Because the denominations operate separately from one another, there are few locations for cross-fertilization that might lead to a deepened common witness. From outside, it appears that churches parrot partisan talking points. To the general public, the two sides seem equally vehement in their moral furor and simply cancel each other out. A befuddled onlooker will not be able to discern what insight, if any, Christianity offers into the problem of war. There are always a few individual voices, and a few churches, that can distance themselves from partisanship because they are more deeply rooted in the Christian tradition and more intimately connected with the global church. In a pluralistic setting, though, such voices cannot plausibly claim to speak "for the church," and their contributions are treated as nothing more than one opinion among others. Typically, their nuance gets drowned in the crudely Manichaean world of cable TV and talk radio.

Conclusion

In theory, denominationalism can coexist with catholicity and unity. Various denominations could maintain their own budgets and administrative structures, their own doctrinal statements and standards for leadership, their own models of mission and ministry, all while providing space for interaction, for mutual correction, for "receptive ecumenism."[47] They could acknowledge each other's baptisms, share the Lord's table, cooperate in pastoral care, and issue common statements to address important public questions.

In such a world, denominations would be genuinely companionable, offering mutual support as well as timely rebuke. In such a world, a Baptist pastor could take his Methodist neighbor to task for erroneous teaching, and the Methodist pastor would listen in humility. In such a world, the denominations would acknowledge each other's discipline, cooperate rather than compete in ministry, strive to resolve theological differences, and come to one mind. In such a world, the various denominations would find unity in their mutual share in the body of Christ and their communion in his Spirit. They would be united above all at the Lord's table and in their common baptism. Every denomination would see itself not merely as an American church but as part of a global network of churches. A world of denominational cooperation would be ideal, but we do not live in a perfect world, and the forms of unity that we can achieve will *always* be wanting in many ways. Denominationalism might be a way of being the church that we will be.

At its best, American denominationalism has approximated this ideal. Even then, denominationalism sets up intractable barriers to catholicity. The catholicity of American Christianity has been inhibited by both the divisiveness inherent in denominational Christianity and the peculiar ways Americanist unity has shaped denominational plurality. In combination, the unity and disunity of American denominationalism have made it impossible for the church to manifest the unity of the Father and Son. And, as the next chapter explains in more detail, there are structural barriers to catholicity that prevent American Christians from overcoming some of our longest-standing social rifts.

7

Denominationalism's Dividing Walls

Denominationalism institutionalizes division, and because America is a denominational society, the institutionalized divisions of the church have massive social and political consequences. Whatever its accomplishments, denominationalism is an obstacle to the fulfillment of Jesus's prayer for unity.

American denominationalism infantilizes the church and makes the church impotent to challenge the world. It is impotent to challenge the world because it is too much *of* the world. It cannot overcome Babel because the denominational church is a Christianized Babel. American denominationalism makes the church weak not so much because of its denominationalism but because of its Americanism.

As Newman Smyth wrote many years ago, the cultural impotence is one of the main points of criticism of modern Protestantism.[1] This may seem an unfair criticism, but Smyth argues convincingly that since the gospel promises to transform the lives of human beings, any faith that fails to deliver on that promise must be in need of deep reform.

The cultural and social powerlessness of American denominationalism is evident in many areas, but here I focus on two: race and Catholicism.

Racial divisions have long characterized American Christianity, and they continue to do so. Hostility to Catholicism has happily waned during the past century, but in earlier times it was harsh and sometimes violent. In each case, we see the social and political consequences of the interaction of denominational Christianity and American civil religion.

Black Church, White Church

It was not uncommon in the early nineteenth century for blacks and whites to worship together. As H. Richard Niebuhr observes, they "did not enjoy complete fellowship" and there was certainly not equality between them, yet "they participated in the same services and were members of the same denominations. . . . Domestic servants, if not plantation slaves, often shared with their masters and mistresses the ministrations of the same pastors and communed at the same Lord's table. The Anglican Church was the leading denomination among the Southern masters and this church was officially very mindful of its duty toward the slaves, however inadequately its members may have practiced the ideals set forth."[2] Georgia bishop Stephen Elliott commented that common participation in church services "would tend very much to strengthen the relations of masters and slaves . . . bringing into action the highest and holiest feelings of our common natures. There should be much less danger of inhumanity on the one side, and of insubordination on the other, between parties who knelt upon the Lord's Day around the same table, and were partakers of the same communion."[3]

That quotation hints at the mixed motives that produced the mix of races. We should not imagine idyllic racial harmony: "The white man's fear of Negro independence was as important a factor in the matter as the white man's concern for the Negro's soul." Lest blacks got the wrong idea, theologians and churches made it clear that the freedom the gospel promised was a spiritual rather than a social freedom. Still, there were large numbers of black members in Methodist and Baptist denominations, and majority-white churches had black pastors. When the majority-black First Baptist of Richmond had a revival in 1831, 217 of the 500 people who joined the church were white.[4]

All that changed around and after the Civil War. Already in 1816, after Richard Allen and his friends were forcibly removed from praying in a certain part of St. George Methodist Episcopal Church in Philadelphia, they left to form an African Methodist Episcopal Church. The number of black denominations increased in the middle decades of the century. A mixed church in Mobile dissolved and reorganized without black members, so the black members organized the African Baptist Church. Whites and blacks separated from one another in stages: "The series of steps from fellowship to schism includes complete fellowship of white and Negro Christians in the local church, segregation into distinctly racial local churches with denominational fellowship, segregation into racially distinct dioceses of conferences with fellowship in the highest judicatories of the denomination, and, finally, separation of the races into distinct denominations."[5] The formation of separate black denominations was "largely a movement of self-assertion on the part of the oppressed."[6]

The result was a precipitous decline in black membership in mainline churches: "Of the 208,000 colored members in the Southern Methodist Church in 1860 only 49,000 remained in 1866." At the time Niebuhr wrote in 1929, 88 percent of blacks were in black denominations and most of the blacks in mainline denominations were segregated into African American conferences. Instead of healing, racial divisions within the church were starker than ever: "The color line has been drawn so incisively by the church itself that its proclamation of the gospel of the brotherhood of Jew and Greek, of bond and free, of white and black has sometimes the sad sound of irony, and sometimes falls upon the ear as unconscious hypocrisy." More hopefully, "sometimes there is in it the bitter cry of repentance."[7]

Americanism and Racial Division

The racial division within American churches persists to this day, as nearly 90 percent of Americans attend racially homogenized churches.[8] In some parts of the country, the persistence of Confederate civil religion contributes to ecclesial segregation.[9] But the problem is not confined to Southern Partisan churches. From surveys of evangelicals concerning race, Michael Emerson and Christian Smith found that white evangelicals attribute American race problems to three causes: "prejudiced individuals," "other groups—usually African Americans—trying to make race problems a group issue when there is nothing more than individual problems," and "a fabrication of the self-interested—again often African Americans, but also the media, the government, or liberals."[10]

These simplistic explanations do not reveal latent racism. Rather, these assessments arise from the racial isolation of white evangelicals and the limitations of their cultural "tool kit," the set of "ideas, habits, skills, and styles" by which people engage and evaluate the world.[11] Evangelicals engage the world with the tools of accountable freewill individualism, relationalism, and antistructuralism. Evangelicals are individualists, not because they think they can do anything they please, but because "for them individuals exist independent of structures and institutions." They are "accountable" individualists because they believe that people are accountable, ultimately to God, for their actions. Evangelical "relationalism" arises from "the view that human nature is fallen and that salvation and Christian maturity can only come through a 'personal relationship with Christ.'"[12] Evangelicals transpose this theology of salvation to other spheres, placing "strong emphasis on family relationships, friendships, church relationships."[13]

Using these tools, evangelicals reduce social evils to individual sin. Thus, "if race problems—poor relationships—result from sin, then race problems must largely be individually based. . . . The concept of individual sin lies behind many white evangelicals' accounts of the race problem." What is absent is any acknowledgment that "poor relationships might be shaped by social structures, such as laws, the ways institutions operate, or forms of segregation." Evangelicals find "structural explanations irrelevant or even wrongheaded." When structural explanations for racial tensions are introduced, evangelicals often detect a form of blame-shifting, from the individual to the system.[14] Evangelical theology forces this on them: "It is a necessity for evangelicals to interpret the problem at the individual level. To do otherwise would challenge the very basis of their world, both their faith and the American way of life. They accept and support individualism, relationalism, and antistructuralism. Suggesting social causes of the race problem challenges the cultural elements with which they construct their lives. . . . This is why anyone, any group, or any program that challenges their accountable freewill individualist perspective comes to be seen as a cause of the race problem." The authors believe that evangelicals honestly want a color-blind society. Evangelicals want people to get along, but "white evangelicals' cultural tools and racial isolation curtail their ability to fully assess why people of different races do not get along, the lack of equal opportunity, and the extent to which race matters in America." In spite of being "honest and well-intentioned," the evangelical outlook is "a powerful means to reproduce contemporary racialism" because "a highly effective way to ensure the perpetuation of a racialized system is simply to deny its existence."[15]

As the authors hint, the evangelical tool kit is a thoroughly *American* tool kit. Evangelicals fail to address racial issues insofar as they conform to American presumptions. A long-standing division in the church and society, which typically takes the form of denominational division, becomes intractable because of evangelical adherence to the individualistic assumptions of the American way. The divisiveness and the unity of American denominationalism conspire together to make this sector of the church incapable of having a culturally transformative effect. To address the racial divisions in the churches more effectively, evangelicals have to repent, not (or not only) of our racism, but of our *Americanism*.

Foreign Agents

Protestantism did not originally define itself simply as anti-Catholicism. The Reformers energetically opposed the abuses of the Roman Catholic Church, abuses they considered damnable. Yet the Reformers saw themselves as part of the catholic church and drew on earlier strains of Catholic teaching and practice in mounting their opposition to the Roman church. The Reformers wrote liturgies, stressed the importance of sacraments, affirmed the authority of ordained ministers. To many modern Christians, Luther and Calvin sound like Catholics.

That has not been true of American Protestantism. American Protestantism *has* defined itself over against Catholicism and has often taken direct action to subdue or expel Catholicism's power in the United States. And American Protestantism has typically opposed Catholicism less for Protestant theological reasons than for American civil religious reasons. Catholic churchiness was perceived as a threat to the American religious settlement. With their internationalism and their base in a foreign country, Catholics were suspected of being anti-American or, at best, of having a dubious double allegiance. This American Protestants could not tolerate. So easily had they blended their denominational Protestantism with America that allegiance to the one was virtually equivalent to allegiance to the other.

At the very least, this meant that Catholics were left out of the inter-denominational activities that united Protestants at national, state, and local levels. In nineteenth-century Kansas, "the formal cooperation and interchange that was so frequently evident among Protestant denominations," writes Robert Wuthnow, "seldom extended to Catholics."[16] Despite its reputation for religious radicalism, Kansas Christianity was largely "centrist," except when it came to relations between Catholics and Protestants: "The two had been taught to be suspicious of each other for so long that it was sometimes hard to find common ground. Catholics were still regarded by some Protestants as worshippers of the pope, and some Catholics feared Protestants were trying to convert them, or shut down their churches and schools."[17] By the middle of the twentieth century, Catholics had become more fully integrated into the social life of Kansas, but the 1960 presidential election brought old suspicions back to the forefront:

> Members of the Church of Christ, such as the ones in Courtland and Kiowa, heard sermons about the dangers of Catholicism and were invited to consider arguments against having a Catholic president printed in the denomination's *Gospel Advocate*. Members of Southern Baptist churches received similar advice from the Baptist press. The American Council of Churches, an organization of fundamentalist denominations, met in Kansas City that spring and unanimously passed a resolution disapproving of a Roman Catholic for president. At a meeting in Hutchinson in March 1960, Kennedy received a standing ovation, but afterward, when asked if religion would be a source of opposition, a member of the crowd confided, "It's hidden, it's ugly, but it's there."[18]

Anti-Catholic sentiment was not always so peaceable or hidden. Through-out the middle decades of the nineteenth century, tensions between the Protestant majority and Catholics simmered, as nearly two million Irish, mostly Catholic, immigrated. Will Herberg writes,

> The Irish, precisely because in language, manners, and culture, they were so like and yet so different from the native Americans, seemed to the latter a far greater peril than the more obvious foreigners from the Continent; moreover, they settled in great urban centers, such as New York, Boston,

and Philadelphia, concentrating in ghetto-like quarters, and so were particularly "visible" to the unsympathetic eyes of the natives. Feeling grew
tense; friction developed in many areas, and anti-Catholic passion was fed
by rabble-rousers and agitators, who were responsible for a flood of incendi-
ary books, pamphlets, and newspapers. Catholics were embittered by the
fact that the schools and public institutions to which they were compelled
to resort were avowedly Protestant and were often employed to break down
the Catholic faith.[19]

Violence broke out in the 1830s. St. Mary's Church in New York was
burned down in 1831, and a few years later a mob attacked and demolished a convent near Boston. For three days during 1844, Philadelphia
was in chaos: "Thirteen persons were killed, scores injured; the Catholic
seminary, two churches, and whole blocks of Catholic dwellings went up
in flames." That was nothing compared to Bloody Monday in Louisville
in 1855: "Nearly a hundred Catholics were slain and scores of houses
burned to the ground."[20]

Anti-Catholic animus was not theological but national: "Catholicism
. . . is un-American, undemocratic, alien to American ways, and prone
to place loyalty to church above loyalty to state and nation. Particularly
shocking to many Protestants is the Catholic insistence on by-passing the
public schools and educating their children in their own religious institutions." An editorial in *The Christian Century* (!) charged that the Catholic Church was embarked on a "conscious and well-planned large-scale
attempt . . . to separate Catholics from other Americans in almost every
area of social life." Catholics, it was said, wanted "to create a separate
social order which [would] exist side by side with the rest of American
society."[21] Catholic separatism was not merely a religious concern but a
political threat, and had to be arrested.

The irony is that Irish Catholics were being rapidly Americanized—so
thoroughly Americanized that the Irish nearly fused religion with national
loyalty: "Despite the hatred and persecution he encountered, or perhaps for
that very reason, the Irish Catholic newcomer . . . adopted this country as
his own and transferred his deeply emotional nationalism to his adopted
land. His Americanism took on the same religious fervor and soon came
to be identified with his Catholicism. . . . Irish, Catholic, and American
became almost identical to the Irish-Catholic mind, and the Americanism

of the Irish Catholic developed into something much more than merely the sense of national 'belonging.'"[22] Catholics came to be accepted when it became clear that they were willing to play the American denominational game. Denominational division resolved into unity, an American catholicity that secured the allegiance of Protestant and Catholic.[23]

War on Catholic Canaan

The Mexican-American War was likewise powered by anti-Catholic sentiments that linked American Protestantism with Anglo-Saxonism and Manifest Destiny. Near the heart of the religious justification of the war was anti-Catholicism. The United States could fulfill its world-historical role only by fending off the internal threat of Irish Catholic immigration and the external threat of Catholic Mexico: "If Roman Catholicism was inimical to republican government, and if the foundation of republicanism lay in Protestant Christianity and its hermeneutics, then Americans had a duty to oppose the former and strengthen the latter in order to keep their country free."[24] Protestants had to suppress Catholicism to preserve the particular form of religious liberty for which America was famed. Suppressing Catholicism

> might be the chief of those obligations on the other side of the coin from liberty. This real, felt sense of duty might seem far-fetched, easily getting lost amid the strident religious bigotry, conspiratorial nonsense, and incendiary language of the anti-Catholic movement. Yet to oppose the one particular religion that promised to squelch all others and weaken Americans' hardwon civil liberties seemed perfectly consistent with the principle of religious freedom and not at all hypocritical to a growing number of Americans by the mid-1830s. That is, limiting the freedom of Catholics, especially those recently arrived from a European monarchy with no experience of selfgovernment, actually *ensured* religious freedom, and in doing so it preserved civil liberties as well. The truth of this paradox seemed as sensible and as uncontroversial as confining criminals to jail in order to protect the community from further crime.[25]

Because "Catholics paid homage to a foreign potentate whom Protestants identified with the anti-Christ, were controlled like so many marionettes by their bishops, and slavishly obeyed orders given by priests in the dark of confessionals," they threatened to "enervate the one nation where the true gospel went hand-in-hand with civil and religious liberty and where all humanity looked for help to usher in the millennial reign of Jesus Christ." For American Protestants, "the stakes could not be higher."[26] The war thus took on the character of a religious crusade, an effort to convert inferior Mexican Catholics to superior Anglo-Saxon Protestantism. And the war reinforced anti-Catholic sentiment, as soldiers wrote back accounts of their firsthand encounters with Mexican Catholics, sometimes comparing them "to Canaanites who had to be removed to make way for God's favored people."[27]

Here a violent division between one church and another is fueled not only by divisive factors but also by the American civil religion that guided Protestant politics. American Protestants defined themselves over against Catholics less for theological reasons than for political reasons. The Mexicans had to be suppressed *not* because they taught transubstantiation or venerated Mary but because their commitment to a foreign church made them seem un-American.

Protestant Management, Catholic Labor

Anti-Catholicism was often intertwined with the struggles of the labor movement. David Sehat writes, "By the last quarter of the nineteenth century the corporation had joined the family, the church, and the school as an institution perpetuating Christian moral authority." This created problems because industrialists were not always exemplars of Christian morals: "Their rapaciousness and their seemingly casual disregard for Christian decency in their treatment of workers required some kind of justification." To defend the corporate leaders, "many moral establishmentarians shifted the blame from the owners to the workers, claiming that industrialists were forced to address the degraded moral condition of the workers who, like slaves, required stricter forms of control." Moralists thus supported management in disputes with labor and demanded that the "state ought to support owners over workers . . . because God created the state, just as he had created wealth, to enforce his moral norms."[28] Support of the owners over workers thus typically meant supporting Protestants over Catholics: "Quite a larger percentage of workers were Catholic or

Jewish. . . . Faced with a body of Protestant owners and a larger body of Catholic and Jewish workingmen, the allegiance of the moral establishment seemed clear. Workers needed Protestant owners to guide them. The tendency of Christian writers . . . to bathe industrial mendacity in the cleansing waters of Christian morality combined with anti-Catholicism of writers . . . to support owners against workers through the formidable regime of the moral establishment."[29]

Conclusion

American Protestants may find it easy to work for unity with other Protestants. White churches may also find it easy to reunite with other white churches. Crossing the boundary between Protestant and Catholic is edgier; negotiating the minefield of American race relations is more difficult still. But if American churches are going to make headway in achieving a semblance of catholicity, these are the places where reconciliation must take place. We will not undo the tribalism of American denominationalism by making the Protestant tribe bigger. The racial divisions of the church will not be overcome if white Christians reconcile with other whites while keeping a safe distance from black denominations. Denominationalism will cease to be an obstacle to unity only when we attack the thicker, more impenetrable barriers.

Black-white, Protestant-Catholic: these are the boundaries that must be transgressed, the dividing walls that must be broken through. So long as these walls remain, American denominationalism will go on its comfortable, childlike way, bowing low before the American way of life. So long as these walls remain, we will live with the institutionalized division of denominationalism, and the American church's cultural potency will continue to dwindle. So long as these walls remain, we will not fulfill the prayer of Jesus. In order for American churches to reach greater levels of unity, we must repent of our attachment to the American way of life. We must break the national idols that we have worshiped, strip the flags from our sanctuaries, find our prophetic voice. Only then will we be able to meet the challenges that lie ahead.

In the providence of God, there are signs that this is already happening. It is a cloud no bigger than a person's hand, but small clouds may indicate a coming storm that will flood the world and wipe it clean.

INTERMEZZO

8

From Glory to Glory

The Pattern of History

Before the beginning, there was nothing but God.[1] At the end of the creation week, there was God and the world. God did not form existing material into the world. He made something entirely new. Creation is *absolute* novelty.

Because God is Creator, he does new things *within* the creation, for his mercies are new each morning. From the opening chapter of the Bible, God moves the world forward from glory to glory by tearing and reuniting. Each time he tears and reunites, he makes the world better than it was before. Time moves forward by periodic deaths and resurrections: worlds take form, decay, and collapse, and new worlds take their place. God makes worlds, dismantles them, and rebuilds. This is the pattern of biblical and church history.

It begins in the creation week. Genesis 1 is not a smooth evolution through stages of creation or life. During the first half of the creation week, God wrenches apart the world again and again to put it back together in a new way. He calls light into being, but as soon as that is done, he is separating light-time and dark-time, calling one day and the other night (Gen. 1:4–5). He produces a formless watery expanse of emptiness (v. 2) but then reaches into the waters with his Word to pull some of it up into the heavens, leaving the rest of the waters below. To keep them separate, he inserts a firmament between (vv. 6–9). He reaches into the waters on the earth to separate them, so that dry land appears, in distinction from the portion of the earth that he calls "sea" (vv. 9–10).

He composes something, then intervenes into the something he has made to tear it into pieces, and then harmonizes the scattered notes into a new, richer melody. Each day improves on the previous one. He speaks light, separates light and darkness, and says it is good. Come the next day, and first-day good is not good enough, so he acts again and calls it good. Each day after is good, but as the next day dawns, God is at work doing something new. His mercies—his creativity and glory—are new *every* morning. Each day was good, but each was followed by darkness and dawn that made good better. When he finished, Yahweh God pronounced it *very* good and rested in what he had made.

Of all God's creatures, only human beings were made in this labyrinthine way. Birds and sea creatures were created male and female to "be fruitful and multiply" (Gen. 1:20–22). Land animals rose from the ground male and female. Adam, though, was molded from the dust of the ground, Yahweh shaping him as a potter shapes a vessel to carry his glory. As the Spirit hovered over the waters to form it (v. 2), so God breathed into Adam's nostrils to make him a living soul (2:7). Adam did not arise from the ground sexually differentiated, as the animals did. God put him into a sleep like death and tore a rib from his side to build a woman. Like the creation itself, Adam had to be built, unbuilt, and rebuilt in order to reach his glory. Adam, unlike other creatures, was a creation-in-miniature, a microcosm. And his history will likewise resemble the history of the creation week, a series of deaths and resurrections.

The same rhythm continues after the fall, with God's judgment a critical addition. After the scattering at Babel, God tears Abram from among the nations and sends him as a wanderer through a land not his own, offering sacrifices at oaks and oases under an open sky. The Lord midwives his son Israel through the travail of Egypt and carries him to Sinai, where he teaches him to worship in his tent and live in the land of promise. Solomon reorganizes tribes into districts and builds a temple, a well-watered Eden on Mount Moriah, with the king's palace hard by Yahweh's. Divided, the people of God take a new name, Israel-and-Judah, until Yahweh tears them from the land and melds them back together in the furnace of exile, forming one new man, now all Jews, now all "Judahites," incorporated into the royal tribe. Through the cross and resurrection, we are all separated from our native tribes and nations and grafted into the people of God, taking the name "Christian."

God creates Israel as tribes, then as a kingdom, then scatters them among the nations. Each is good, each is followed by the darkness of the tomb, each brings good brighter than the good that preceded it. At each juncture, God calls his people to shed old ways and old names, to die to old routines and ways of life, including ways of life God himself has previously established.

We do not like this. We do not want our world shattered, even if we know God will rebuild from the rubble. We want to keep our old, familiar names. We do not want to die. Only Jesus makes this bearable. As Eugen Rosenstock-Huessy put it, "Christianity and future are synonymous" because Christians confess that the world ends and begins again and again. Christianity and future are synonymous because resurrection faith alone enables us to meet the world's end and "to die to our old habits and ideals, get out of our old ruts, leave our dead selves behind and take the first step into a genuine future."[2]

The World That Then Was

Two worlds appear and disappear in the course of Genesis. God formed an earth divided among a garden, Eden, and the larger world, but that original order of creation is undone by a series of falls. Adam sinned against God in the garden by eating the fruit of the tree of knowledge. Cain sinned against his brother in the field (land) when he killed Abel. The sons of God intermarried with the daughters of men out in the world. Each sinner was expelled—Adam from the garden and Cain from the land. With the sons of God, things got so bad that the whole world had to be expelled in the flood, which wiped the earth clean and made way for Noah, a new Adam.

The "sons of God" in Genesis 6 were not angels or demons who took human form and reproduced with human beings. As the image of God, Adam was a "son of God" (cf. Gen. 1:26; 5:1–3). In context, the sons of God were the faithful descendants of Adam who carried on the line of

Adam's third son, Seth. When the Sethites intermarried with the descendants of Cain (the "daughters of men"), they produced a world so corrupt that God could only give it new life by killing it and raising it again.

Prediluvian humanity was "flesh," opposed to God's Spirit, and the Spirit became weary of striving (*dyn*)[3] with flesh. Yahweh was pained in his heart over the state of the world. Prior to this, only Eve had been the subject of pain. Here it was Yahweh's own pain, as he began the travail of birthing a new world. Before human beings began to grieve, God grieved and regretted making the earth in the first place (Gen. 6:6). His Spirit, the living Passion of God, had been snubbed, and Yahweh mourned his rejection by his own creatures, his own sons and daughters. The world was full of violence (v. 13) because human beings were living according to flesh.[4] No doubt the violence was perpetrated by the Nephilim who are on the earth prior to the flood, mighty men (*gibborim*) and men of name (*'anshe hashem*). Men had called on the name of Yahweh (4:26), but when the Sethites diluted their witness by intermarriage, each man pursued only the glory of his own name. The Nephilim were ancient heroes, dedicated to war, honor, reputation. A world full of Nephilim could only be a world at war.

The violence of the Nephilim "corrupted" (*shachat*) the earth in the sight of God. The verb is used seven times in the flood narrative (Gen. 6:11, 12 [2x], 13, 17; 9:11, 15). It describes what human beings did to the world with their violence—they *destroyed* it; and it describes Yahweh's eye-for-eye response to the corruption of the world—he would destroy it. Human beings uncreated God's good creation, so he completed the job, uncreating the world in a sevenfold "corruption." God judged, as he often did, by giving human beings over to their sin, by loosening the restraints and letting us have our way.

A *new* world emerged after the flood. Creation was an *absolute* novelty; the world after the flood was not absolute novelty, but it *was* a novelty. Noah was not merely Adam redux; he was Adam advanced. And his world was not a restoration of pre-flood conditions but a world restructured.

Like Adam, Noah was told to be fruitful, multiply, and fill the earth (Gen. 9:1). Noah offered the Bible's first ascension offering (*'olah*) on Mount Ararat outside the ark.[5] Yahweh was pleased with the aroma of the offering and made new promises, sealed by covenant (8:20–22). A new form of worship took shape. Like Adam, Noah had dominion over the creatures, but now Yahweh promised to put the fear and terror of man into the animals to make human dominion more effective. For the first time, God offered flesh to human beings as food, though he prohibited the consumption of animal blood (9:4). Noah was given authority to kill, not only in sacrifice but as a king, avenging bloodshed (vv. 5–6). A right once reserved for God—the right to punish murderers—was now given to man.[6] And like God, Noah planted a garden-vineyard. Adam was allowed to eat from the tree of life, but he never drank wine. Noah, the rest-giver (5:29), entered rest by drinking Sabbath.

Peter thought of the prediluvian world as a different world, the "world that then was" (2 Pet. 3:6 KJV). The world Adam knew became so corrupt that Yahweh dismantled it. Adam's world was truly ended by the flood, and Noah emerged from the ark a new man in a new world. Noah's world had been transformed liturgically (sacrifice) and politically (the power of avenging blood). The human race had been rearranged internally, no longer divided between "sons of God" and "sons of men," between Sethites and Cainites, but organized into families by descent from Noah's sons, Shem, Ham, and Japheth (Gen. 10). In a number of respects, this new world was an advance on the world of Adam—with Noah elevated to have more authority to rule, to eat, to drink. Adam was created a priest in a sanctuary-garden. After the flood, Noah was elevated to kingship. This is his *theosis*, his elevation to a divine royalty that Adam sought but did not reach.

After Babel

The postdiluvian world lasted only ten generations, from Noah to Abraham. The history is recounted rapidly in Genesis, the bulk summarized in the "table of nations" (Gen. 10) and the genealogies of Shem (11:10–32). The only event recorded from this period is yet another fall story, the rebellion at Babel. Like the corruption of the world before the flood, the tower of Babel was the product of "intermarriage," as the descendants of Shem joined with the Hamites who founded Babel and Assyria (10:8–12) to build the tower and city. Yahweh judged Babel not because of violence and destruction but because the human race huddled together rather than spreading over the face of the earth. He acted to limit the ways a united humanity could use its tremendous capacity for evil. Like the Nephilim, the men of Babel sought a "name" (11:4), and they got one. They wanted to be Babel, the "gate of God," but they received instead the mocking name "babble," confusion.

Though far more compressed than the flood narrative, the same dynamics were at work. Yahweh dismantled the Noahic world because of human sin. He brought an end to the construction of the city and tower and scattered the builders over the face of the earth. He disassembled Babel. More generally, he disassembled the human race that had taken form after the flood. In place of a single human race with a capacity to join together in one great project of rebellion, God's judgment at Babel left behind a human race fractured into little pieces, divided both in speech and in lip. The former refers to language, the latter to religious confession. The scattering at Babel was not only geographic and linguistic but also religious.

And from this linguistically and religiously divided world, God called Abram to father a people who would bring blessing to all the nations, the people who would eventually reunite all the nations into one new humanity. The call of Abram was part of the reconfiguration of the world after the fall at Babel. Abram's world was as different from Noah's as Noah's was from Adam's. Liturgically, Abram continued to offer "ascensions" (*'olah*), as Noah did, but he offered them repeatedly, in many places. So far as we know, Noah built only one communion site (*mizbeach*), only one altar (Gen. 8:20), but Abram built one at the oak of Moreh (12:7–8; 13:4), another at Hebron (13:18), and another at Moriah, where he planned to offer Isaac (22:9). Isaac and Jacob also built altars (26:25; 33:20; 35:3). Abram's worship resembled Noah's, but with Abram, Noah's covenant-forming sacrifice became a regular liturgy of covenant renewal. God's people had new names: not "sons of God" or "sons of Noah," but "sons of Abraham" and "sons of Israel."

Politically, the world of Abram was starkly different from the world of Noah. After the flood, humanity was divided into many nations, descending from Noah's sons. At the tower of Babel, they united to build a city in opposition to God and were scattered. With Abram, the world got simplified again. There were still many nations, speaking different languages and occupying different lands and worshiping different gods. But God had reached into that world and reassembled it into a binary system: Abram's household on the one side, all the rest of humanity on the other, with the firmament of circumcision between, the cut in the flesh that symbolizes the cut in the flesh of humanity.[7]

Out of Egypt

Psalm 77:16–20 recounts the exodus in poetic form:

> The waters saw You, O God;
> The waters saw You, they were in anguish;
> The deeps also trembled.
> The clouds poured out water;
> The skies gave forth a sound;
> Your arrows flashed here and there.
> The sound of Your thunder was in the whirlwind;
> The lightnings lit up the world;
> The earth trembled and shook.
> Your way was in the sea
> And Your paths in the mighty waters,
> And Your footprints may not be known.
> You led Your people like a flock
> By the hand of Moses and Aaron.

The psalm is clearly based on the account of the exodus in Exodus 14, but details were added. Not only the deeps but the skies roiled. The waters fled from Yahweh as he came in his cloud, thundering and flashing lightning. When Yahweh came, the earth trembled and the sea split to make a pathway for Israel to follow in Yahweh's footsteps. Heaven, earth, and sea were all shaken at the Red Sea. The threefold world shattered and fell down. God repeated the creative act of day three, separating the waters so that dry land appeared. And he did all this because in the exodus he was forming a new world yet again.

In a narrow, focused sense, the new world that emerged from the exodus involved only Egypt and Israel. Jacob's family was initially welcomed into Goshen, but as their numbers grew, Pharaoh and the leaders of Egypt became alarmed and tried to suppress them—first imposing more intense labor burdens, then carrying out an intensifying program of genocide (Exod. 1). When Pharaoh began to slaughter the boy infants of Israel, Yahweh avenged the blood of his children. In the plagues, he systematically demolished the world of Egypt. Many of the plagues targeted Egyptian gods—the Nile, frogs, Pharaoh and his son. Yahweh made war on the gods of Egypt as he made war on Egypt itself (Exod. 12:12). The plagues separated Israel from Egypt. The first plagues were indiscriminate, falling on both Egyptian and Israelite, but eventually Yahweh targeted his wrath on Egypt. Israel had become indistinguishable from Egypt (Josh. 24), and Yahweh had to forcefully remove her from her Egyptian ways. The decisive separation comes with the exodus itself, as Israel becomes physically distinct and geographically distant.

Though focused on Israel and Egypt, the exodus had wider implications. For the first time, the people of Abram were formed as a political unit rather than a clan network under the headship of a patriarch. Israel became a people and a nation through the experience of Egyptian sojourn and exodus. Now, in the midst of the post-Babel world, God had planted a political entity of his own. Abram fought ad hoc battles in Canaan with his 318 fighting men (Exod. 13–14), but he did not conquer Canaan. After the exodus, Israel had a vast army, leaving Egypt in battle array, ready to fight wilderness marauders and to conquer the land of promise.

At the same time, Israel was reordered and reorganized internally. Advised by his father-in-law Jethro to delegate judicial authority, Moses formalized the clan and family system of leadership that governed the twelve tribes.[8] Heads of tens, fifties, hundreds, and thousands were not selected for their prestige or seniority but were "able men who fear God, men of truth, those who hate dishonest gain" (Exod. 18:21). They were not to rely on their native cunning or common sense but were to follow God's statutes and laws (v. 20). They formed a system of appeals, with major disputes being brought before Moses (v. 22). Israel was still organized by tribes, but the tribal system had been rationalized and routinized.

The most obvious novelty of the Mosaic system was liturgical. Every aspect of worship was transformed, nearly beyond recognition. Abram had built altars wherever he pleased, but Moses strictly forbade Israel to continue the practice. Only at the single sanctuary were they to offer sacrifices (Deut. 12). For the first time since Eden, Yahweh came to dwell in the midst of a people, in a gorgeous royal tent, placed first at the center of Israel's wilderness camp and then at Shiloh. Priestly privilege was narrowed to the Levitical tribe and, more specifically, to the descendants of Aaron. For the first time since Adam, a human being was permitted to enter directly into the presence of God, though only under highly restricted conditions (Lev. 16). New sacrifices were introduced—the purification offering (*hattat*) to cleanse the sanctuary and its worshipers, the trespass offering (*'asham*) for sins of sacrilege, and the peace offering (*shelamim*) as a meal with Yahweh, an unprecedented privilege.

Israelites recognized that all this was novel. Korah and his allies protested the restriction of priesthood to Aaron and his sons (Num. 16–17) and were swallowed alive into Sheol as a result. Nadab and Abihu attempted to offer foreign fire before Yahweh and were destroyed by God's fire (Lev. 10). During the monarchy, Israelites built altars around the land and were castigated by the prophets for their high places.

Though having its own unique variations, the exodus follows the general pattern we have been examining: God forms a world; the world becomes corrupted, and God intervenes to tear it into pieces; then he forms a new world. Building on the Abrahamic world, God gives Israel new forms of worship, a new internal order, a new relation to the nations of the world. The novelty is captured in a name: Israel went into Egypt as "Hebrews," and when they come out, they are "sons of Israel."

Revolution in Israel

The Mosaic order remained intact for several centuries, through the period of the judges. By the end of that period, it was falling apart. Hannah, pregnant with the prophet Samuel, sang of a coming revolution in Israel when the hungry would receive food, the barren would give birth, and the lowly would be raised up from ashes and dust to sit with nobles (1 Sam. 2:1–10). Samuel would be for the rising and falling of many in Israel.

During the lives of Samson and Samuel (whose lives coincide almost completely), the Philistines posed a continuous danger for Israel. At times Israel was under Philistine overlords, and even when they pushed the Philistines back to the coast, the Philistines held large portions of the land, a condition that continued into the reign of David. Internally, Israel was led by Eli the high priest and his sons Hophni and Phinehas. For the writer of 1–2 Samuel, the sins of the priests constituted a more serious threat than the Philistines. Hophni and Phinehas "despised" the sacrifice of the Lord by serving themselves before offering Yahweh's portion on the altar and by stealing nonpriestly portions of sacrificial meat. They fornicated with the women who served at the tabernacle, defiling the sacred precincts (1 Sam. 2:12–25). Because of their sins, Yahweh threatened to break the house of Eli and make him see the "distress of My dwelling" (1 Sam. 2:31–32). They had committed abominations, and the Lord was going to devastate his own house.

When the end came, it came suddenly. The Philistines defeated Israel at Aphek, killing Hophni and Phinehas. Superstitious, the priests had taken the ark of the covenant into the field, and during the battle the Philistines captured it and then moved on to devastate the sanctuary. When Eli heard about his sons and the capture of the ark, he fell off his chair and broke his neck. One battle, and the whole Mosaic order had been dismantled: the priests were dead, the ark captured, the sanctuary in ruins, and Philistines controlled the land.

The devastation was not followed by a return to the *status quo ante*. Creation is absolute novelty. The Creator does not again make absolute novelties, but he *always* does something *novel*. And he does not always form a new world immediately. After Aphek, the evening of Israel is a long one. There is a full century between the dismantling of the tabernacle and the construction of the temple.[9]

By the end of that transition, Israel had been reconfigured once again. Politically, the old tribal organization was replaced by a monarchy (1 Sam. 8), first by the solo king Saul, then by the Davidic dynasty. Monarchy brought centralization. David conquered Jerusalem and made it his capital. Solomon not only reigned from Jerusalem but also organized the land into twelve administrative districts that resembled the tribal areas in number only. Jerusalem became the central city of a system of rural tribute, as each district supplied the palace one month out of the year. Local and regional authorities continued to exist. After Solomon died, Jeroboam and the assembly of Israel appealed to Rehoboam (1 Kings 12:6–11), but the political center of gravity shifted to the palace and court. Korah and others had protested Mosaic innovations at the beginning of the Mosaic era, and tribal allegiances persisted into the early years of the monarchy, dividing Israel even before the kingdom divided.

Israel's relationship to other nations also shifted. David pushed back the Philistines once and for all and extended Israel's territory into the Transjordan. For the first time, Israel received tribute from conquered peoples, and Israel's king became a king of kings (cf. 2 Sam. 12:26–31). Solomon established diplomatic contacts and alliances with gentiles. Hiram of Tyre contributed materials and skilled craftsmen to the temple project, and the queen of Sheba was only one among many royals who came to hear Solomon's wisdom and to observe his kingdom.

The Mosaic tabernacle was never rebuilt. Instead, Yahweh revealed a fresh architectural pattern to David, which David passed on to Solomon. The temple was triple the size of the tabernacle, made of stone and wood, set in one place atop Mount Moriah. New furnishings were placed in the temple courts—a massive bronze sea on the backs of twelve bulls, water chariots that formed a gauntlet of water leading toward the temple, a new and larger altar. Inside there were multiple *menorot*, replacing the single *menorah* of the tabernacle. Previously open to all descendants of Aaron, the priesthood was narrowed to the family of Zadok, which replaced the family of Eli. In addition to the sacrifices on the altar, Levites and priests offered worship in song and musical instruments, a sacrifice of praise that rose like the smoke of the animal sacrifice.

During the course of the monarchy, things were torn and reassembled once again. Israel and Judah divided, a reconfiguration of the internal pattern of the life of the people of God. Jeroboam set up alternative shrines, an alternative liturgical calendar, a non-Levitical priesthood in the northern kingdom. Ahab acted like a son of God from Genesis 6, marrying a "daughter of men," Jezebel of Sidon, and advancing her idolatrous agenda (1 Kings 16:29–34). Instead of participating in the idolatrous worship of golden calves, the faithful in northern Israel assembled with the sons of the prophets, a "free church" movement led by the charismatic prophets Elijah and Elisha. Without temple, official priesthood, or royal support, they kept alive the worship of Yahweh through Israel's darkest hours. Elijah and Elisha expanded prophetic international diplomatic relationships, as Elisha became the first to anoint a gentile king, Hazael of Aram (2 Kings 8).

In the monarchy, we see the same general pattern we have observed in earlier parts of the Bible. A system is established, sanctioned by God. Human beings sin and corrupt the world, and so the Lord comes to dismantle it and erect something new. The new order resembles the old, but it is never a simple restoration. It always involves new liturgical patterns, a new political order and internal organization of Israel, and new forms of relationship between Israel and the nations. As noted above, while the external threat of gentile conquerors is part of the story, the main cause of the collapse of the Mosaic system is the failure of the priests. They are the ones who commit abominations that lead to desolation.

Exile and After

The exile was the most radical reshuffling of Israel since the time of Moses. When Nebuchadnezzar conquered Jerusalem, Judah's political, liturgical, and international life changed dramatically and permanently. Judah lost her land, her temple, her king, her independence. It was in every respect a national death.

In place of a temple, Israel worshiped without sacrifice in synagogues throughout the gentile world. Instead of a king, Jews had to learn the complicated dance of serving and resisting gentile emperors. Israel was no longer organized by tribe or by administrative district, no longer had a central capital city. Instead, Israel was organized, as far as we can tell, under the leadership of a new class of rabbis, perhaps descended from the priests, perhaps not. Prophets took on great prominence, giving instructions to Israel as they entered exile (Jeremiah), envisioning the glories of the return (Jeremiah and Ezekiel), and offering a God's-eye view of the next several centuries of ancient history (Daniel). Plopped down into an exilic community, a Jew from the time of Solomon might have had trouble recognizing the Jewish exiles as his own people.

Even after many returned to the land, Israel did not return to her old patterns and structures. The second temple did not possess the awesome visual glory of the first. Israel gained some political independence, but she continued to be overseen by gentile emperors, who took on some of the responsibilities that had been assigned to the Davidic kings.[10] According to Ezekiel, the priesthood was to be restricted to the sons of Zadok. Once again, Israel was given a new name that signified a new identity in the world—Jew.

The church came into being as another, final revolution in Israel's history. According to the New Testament, the priesthood of Aaron had given way to the priesthood according to the order of Melchizedek, in which all the baptized participate. The temple of stone gave way to a temple of living stones, the holy ones who constitute the holy space where the Spirit dwells. The church retained offices of leadership, but the internal configuration of the church was more diverse than the hierarchically structured configuration of the old covenant. Every believer has access to the sanctuary, and so the structure of priesthood is radically different. Each member contributes to the edification of the whole body, since each member is himself or herself a temple of the Spirit, equipped by the Spirit for the work of building. The division between Jew and gentile is erased within the church, and the church's relationship with the nations around it is a somewhat precarious one. On the one hand, Christians are repeatedly exhorted to submit to the powers that be. On the other hand, Christians must obey God rather than humans.

Christian History and the Future

History is not a seamless garment. It has gaps and tears, some quite rough. There are evenings and there are mornings, deaths and revivals. God tears garments and then sews them back together in new ways. That is the story of the Bible, and it is the continuing story of the church's history. Though we have come to the final covenant order, the pattern of death and resurrection that characterized the history of Israel continues within the history of the church.

For the first three hundred years, the church was an illegal, occasionally persecuted sect. Then came Constantine, and the church's relation to Roman society, and its internal structures and practices, changed dramatically. For the next three hundred years, the Middle East and North Africa were predominantly Christian. Then came Islam, and the church contracted to Europe and Byzantium. Between Constantine in the fourth century and the eleventh century, the Eastern and Western churches, despite tensions and divergences, remained recognizably one church. Then came the schism of 1054, and East and West both were redefined by their separation. For the next five hundred years, the Roman Catholic Church was dominant in the West, though periodically challenged by various reforming movements. Then came the Reformation, and European Christianity, along with the global Christianity that grew out of it, has been divided ever since between Protestant and Catholic, and among Protestants.

At each of these transition points, the church was transformed in its liturgy, in its internal structures, and in its relation to political power. The degree of change is more or less evident in these areas at different times. Constantine's conversion transformed the church's relation to the Roman world, but the church also introduced new patterns of internal government and new liturgical forms. The division between East and West created two churches where there had been one. Orthodoxy and Roman Catholicism were *both* created by the schism, just as Catholicism was formed by the split of the Western church at the Reformation. Protestants adopted new forms of worship—vernacular liturgy, emphasis on preaching, access to the Lord's table—and some groups in the Reformation advocated an anti-liturgy. Protestantism brought a new form of church-state relation. Instead of the centuries-long struggle between pope and emperor, church and state reached an uneasy Westphalian peace, the state arguably the bigger winner and the church the loser, as national churches tended to lose a sense of universal catholicity. The Reformers reached deep into the Scriptures and the catholic tradition, but they were revolutionary innovators for all that. A world came to an end five hundred years ago, and the Western church was reborn in an unprecedented form—as Catholic and Protestant. New kinds of Christians began to appear for the first time, with new names like Lutheran and Reformed and Anglican.

Protestants often act as if the Reformation were the end of history, the moment when the church reached its final condition. For such Protestants, the future of Protestantism can only be more of the same. The only possible future is a future of continued division, denominationalism all the way to the world's end. Catholics think of the future as a Catholic one, and for Orthodox the future is more Orthodoxy.

If God is alive, why would we think that the church reached its final form in 1517 or 1640 or 1965? Why would we Protestants think that the Reformation marks the end of history? Why do we think we can keep *these* names forever?

We cannot. Division *cannot* be the final state of Christ's church. The names we now bear *cannot* be our final names. Luther's protest against Rome was necessary, and we should reverently say that the division of the church, like the division of Judah and Israel, like the division of heaven and earth at the beginning, was in some mysterious sense "from the Lord." Yet if the gospel is true, this division is at best provisional. Jesus prayed that we would be "perfected in unity," and this unity must be visible enough for the world to notice and conclude that the Father sent Jesus (John 17:23). Paul told Peter that refusing to eat with gentiles was an offense to the gospel and an assault on justification by faith. Jesus is our Peace, who died to make the two into one new humanity, in which there is neither Jew nor Greek, slave nor free, male nor female. The promise of unity is internal to the good news. Unity is evangelical because it is the evangel.

God is the living Creator, still at work in his world, and that means that the church of the future will be something *new* and, given the pattern of God's creativity, something *better*. Creation is absolute novelty, and the God who creates is the God who *continues* to do new things.

DIVIDED
CHURCH
DISSOLVING

9

The Restructuring
of Global Christianity

Even before the conflagration of World War I, there was a widespread perception in Europe that the world's solid ground was shifting beneath humanity's feet. "Mass societies, consumerism, mass media, urbanization, big industry and big finance, feminism, psychoanalysis, the theory of relativity, abstract art, and atonal music" all were inducing cultural vertigo before the assassination of Archduke Franz Ferdinand on June 28, 1914, began the engulfing process that led to the killing fields of the Somme and the trenches and the other unspeakable horrors of the war. In the burgeoning cities, people moved on public transportation, bought factory-produced goods, ate food from the other side of the world, worked in factories and offices. Rubber condoms had been invented, handy for the many who were eager to rewrite the rules of sex.[1]

Prior to the war, the cultural inheritance of the West kept the socially volatile effects of new technology, new ideas, and new social forms in check. People could still make sense of the world through traditional ideas of progress, hierarchy, patriotism, heroic sacrifice, and honor. The old tracks still worked. But the war destroyed the rails and released the surging energies of prewar developments, without restraint. Anarchy was loosed on the world. The war was a catalyst that made the world, already whizzing at dizzying speed, go even faster. With the war, the machine age turned on human beings, transforming those who had been cogs in industrial factories into cogs in a war machine.[2] It was an early experience of what in the latter part of the century became known as postmodernism, stunningly captured in Hugo Ball's essay on Kandinsky:

> God is dead. A world has collapsed. I am dynamite. World history has broken into two halves. There is a time before me. And a time after me. Religion, science, morality—phenomena originating in the fear of primitive peoples. An era collapses. A thousand-year culture collapses. . . . The world reveals itself to be a blind battle of forces unbound. Man lost his celestial face, became matter, conglomerate, animal, an insane product of thoughts twitching abruptly and insufficiently. . . . And another element collided destructively and menacingly with the desperate search for a new order in the ruins of the past world: mass culture in the modern metropolis. . . . Machines were created, and took the place of individuals. . . . A world of abstract demons swallowed individual expression, swallowed individual faces into towering masks, engulfed private expression, robbed individual things of their names, destroyed the ego and agitated the oceans of collapsed feelings.[3]

This was written in 1917. It could have been written in the early 2000s by any of a dozen prophets of postmodernism.

A world was ending, said thoughtful intellectuals at the beginning of the twentieth century, and yet here we are at the beginning of the twenty-first. The world is still here; technology has advanced further and faster than anyone a century ago could have imagined; many people live at a level of affluence that was only dimly approximated by the wealthiest of nobility in previous ages. Even many of the poorest billion have opportunity to gain higher levels of wealth than ever before. Yet today some are warning of economic, social, and political disarray on a global scale. The prophets of doom are with us still.

Were the pessimists of the early twentieth century delusional? Or are the pessimists of today delusional? Or are they both delusional? In my view, neither is.

The world does not exist in a permanent steady state, nor is history a smooth progression from one thing to the next. History moves backward in death, then forward in resurrection. Worlds come to an end, and a world undeniably came to an end in the early twentieth century. If it is something of an exaggeration to say that it was a civilization of a thousand years' standing, it was a civilization of at least a hundred years' duration. The post-Napoleonic balance of European power went up in flames, as did the confident predictions of human progress that had dazzled the nineteenth century.

Why then are we still reeling? Why are we still feeling the vertigo of a century-old catastrophe? Scripture provides some insight. The Mosaic order came to an end overnight, with the Philistine victory over Israel at Aphek, the capture of the ark, and the deaths of the priests in the family of Eli. The tabernacle was never put back together, and a new clan of priests had to take over the care of the fragments of the sanctuary. Israel's tribal political structure, with its ad hoc system of judges, remained in place, but there was clearly growing discontent and a desire for something more reliably stable (cf. 1 Sam. 8, which was not a sudden decision). Still, it took a century for the effects of Aphek to completely unfold. The battle of Aphek occurred during Samuel's youth, and his ministry was followed by the forty-year reign of Saul and the forty-year reign of David. It was not until the eleventh year of Solomon that the sanctuary was put back together, now in a new form, the temple.

Would a sociologist writing after Aphek have been justified in saying that the world was ending? Would a sociologist writing in the time of David also be justified in saying that the old days of tabernacle and judge were over forever?

All this is put too negatively, because the history recorded in 1–2 Samuel is not merely a history of decline and fall but also a history of rebirth and renewal.[4] It is a history of evening *and* morning. The Mosaic world collapsed, but over the following decades, Samuel taught and judged Israel and prepared for the new order of the monarchy. As a world was falling apart, a new world was germinating, getting ready to burst through the soil. God was erasing one map and beginning to remap the world.

That same dynamic has been at work over the past century of global history. While the nineteenth-century world was falling apart, a convergence of unexpected developments was preparing for a new Christian world. In 1906 the Azusa Street revival broke out, often seen as the beginning of the Pentecostal movement. Almost simultaneously, world missionary conferences were turning into ecumenical conferences and eventually into an ecumenical movement. Virtually no one in the West knew it, but in Africa, Asia, and Latin America, exotic new Christian churches were being planted and were growing. By the time of the decolonization of Africa and Asia after World War II, these continents were poised for the fastest and most unexpected growth in the history of the church. By the end of the twentieth century, while Europe was languishing in various stages of apostasy and the churches of the United States were involved in what appears to be a losing culture war, Africa, Latin America, and parts of Asia had become filled with Christians. Over the past century, God has remapped and rearranged and redistributed his church. This has chipped away at the institutionalized division of denominationalism and has opened up new opportunities to fulfill Jesus's prayer for unity. It is time for us to adopt a way of being church that fits the new realities we face. The restructuring of the global church offers an occasion to overcome the painful divisions of centuries. It opens an opportunity for Reformational Catholicism.

New Movements

When the World Missionary Conference met in Edinburgh in 1910, *no* representatives from Africa, Latin America, or the Pacific island churches were invited.[5] Today, no international Christian conference would fail to include many leaders from these continents, but our mental routines too often run along rails that were already flecked with rust in 1910. It has been a long time since Will Herberg could accurately summarize the religious life of the United States as Protestant-Catholic-Jew.[6] It has been a long time since we could accurately summarize the church as Protestant-Catholic-Orthodox. Our maps are badly out of date, and it is time to notice and to ask what it might mean.

African Independent Churches

The Swedish Mission Covenant Church entered the Belgian Congo in 1909.[7] Despite early successes in the first decades of the twentieth century, the missionaries were dissatisfied with the results. They were making converts, but conversion was making little difference in the lives of new believers. Leaders of the mission gathered for a retreat in January 1947 for prayer and soul searching.

During the retreat, the mission's head, John Magnusson, preached a sermon on John 3:16 and afterward invited others to pray. A student at the seminary in Ngouedi, Raymond Buana Kibongi (also spelled Kibongui), rose to pray for the seminary, which was, he claimed, "rotting from within." Shaking, Kibongi cried, "Jesus, make me your servant. Jesus, calm me down, calm me down," until he became too exhausted to stand.

The meeting sparked a revival. As Ogbu Kalu recounts, "People confessed their '*kintantu*,' envy or hatred, and poor relationships across racial lines, and they changed dramatically. Others realized their Christian dullness and the low level of church attendance and poor prayer lives in the school and improved."[8] Others were caught up in "the ecstasy of the cross," feeling pain in their palms, and fell to the ground, stiff as corpses. Prophets, *ngunza*, visited the retreat, drank the Spirit, and spread the revival's zeal throughout the Congo. Villages touched by the revival were transformed. Kibongi reflected, "Just as hard iron can only melt in fire, so the black man's stone heart can only be melted in the all consuming fire of the ecstasy."[9]

Kibongi lived until 1998, and in the decades after 1947 he was instrumental in forming the Evangelical Church of Congo, a catholic effort that included white and black churches. In 1950 he became the first head of the Conseil des Églises Chrétiennes au Congo. Brazzaville Pentecostals still think of themselves as "revival churches," tracing their history back to Kibongi's ecstasy and his remarkable lifelong ministry.[10]

The Evangelical Church of Congo is today a member of the World Communion of Reformed Churches. It is organized into presbyteries. With roots in Scandinavian pietism, it has a recognizable Protestant pedigree, but it is not classically Protestant. It has no official confessional statement, and its charismatic and mystical inclinations resemble those of other global Pentecostal movements. As with most charismatics and Pentecostals, the Congolese church recontextualizes distinctly Protestant doctrines like justification by faith alone within a holistic theology of healing and restoration. It is classified as "Protestant" mainly because it is not Catholic or Orthodox, but that classification depends on the assumption that *every* church *must* fit into one of the three categories. That is the assumption we must question. It is as much a new form of Christianity as the Lutheran or Swiss Reformed churches were novelties in the sixteenth century.[11]

Aladura

Since 1937 thousands have gathered in August every year at a location in Nigeria dubbed "Mount Tabieorar" (also "Tabborrah" or "Taborah") to celebrate a thirteen-day festival of prayer and fasting. The Aladura (Yoruba for "praying people") who celebrate the festival consider it analogous to the biblical festivals at Shiloh, Carmel, or Bashan.[12] Six hundred thousand attendees from around the world came to the festival in 1991.

Leaders dress in bright-red cassocks and caps. Lay men and women are robed in stunning white or sky blue, and the women wear headdresses that resemble habits. In vibrant processions, each carries a candle. Choirs sway and clap to the music of brass instruments and drums, singing the Tabieorar anthem:

> The Mount Tabieorar's Festival has come
> Mount Tabieorar is gleeful
> The spiritual anniversary has come
> Mysterious year has come
> All hail the King of Glory
> Praise to the Lord of Mercy.

Judged by its costumes, the Tabieorar might be mistaken for a rambunctious African Catholic or Anglican festival, and the impression is strengthened by "high church" aspects of Aladura theology and liturgical practice. Belief in the efficacy of ritual acts is one of the leading features of the church's belief and practice. The Aladura use holy water, prepare liturgical space with incense and candles, perform rites that amount to exorcisms of new automobiles, and believe that their prayers, fasting, and other ritual acts are efficacious when performed in the right place in the right way. Even these "Catholic" features of Aladura, however, are less a product of influence from Western high-church traditions than remnants of Yoruba traditional religion.[13]

Besides, Aladura has distinctly Protestant features. Beliefs are "based on the principles laid down in the Bible." Aladura Christianity is "biblical in pattern, biblical in the sense that in all matters of faith and conduct, our supreme court of appeal is the Holy Bible."[14] They confess total depravity and justification.

More specifically, Aladura has affinities with African charismatic and Pentecostal movements that are often transplanted from North America, especially in its emphasis on the role of good and evil spirits in every-day life. One summary of Aladura belief reads in part like the Apostles' Creed (belief in the Trinity of Godhead, Father, Son, and Holy Ghost; the second coming; the final judgment; and an endless new creation) and in part like a charismatic manifesto (belief in divine healing and present-day miracles, baptism of the Spirit, and the gifts of the Spirit).[15] Each year the primate of the Aladura prophesies during the Tabieorar festival.[16] In his 1999 sermon at Tabieorar, Primate Rufus Ositelu expressed the wish that the "God of our forefathers, the God of Tabieorar touch every part of your body, your soul, and every part of your life in Jesus' Name." Citing Daniel's encounter with Gabriel and other Scripture passages, he taught that God's touch makes enemies flee; it "can give you success in all your undertakings"; it "can give you great ability and skills which you never had"; it can "make you fearlessly stand for God" and "cleanse you of all your iniquities and remove all your impediments." It can, in sum, "renew your life entirely."[17]

Aladura does not fit easily into a Protestant-Catholic-Orthodox scheme. It is somewhat Catholic, somewhat Protestant, mostly something else entirely—Pentecostalism with an African flavor. Like the Evangelical Church of Congo, it has roots in a Western missionary church. Its founder, Josiah Olunowo Ositelu, was an Anglican catechist and teacher when he began to have visions of a great "eye" of God and began denouncing the nominal Christianity that surrounded him. The Anglican mission super-visor told him to desist, and when he refused, he was removed from his position. After several years of retreat and training, he began to preach in villages, calling people to repentance and promising healing through holy water. The original movement split into four groups—the Christ Apos-tolic Church, the Cherubim and Seraphim, the Church of the Lord, and the Celestial Church of Christ. Over the following decades, the Aladura movement spread throughout West Africa and into the United Kingdom and by the early 1980s had established a church in the Bronx.[18] Aladura groups have formed alliances with American Pentecostal churches, but the attraction of the movement was largely in its promise of Christianity-for-Africans.[19] Aladura is not a continuation of missionary Christianity but was formed in partial opposition to it. Its birth is not unlike the birth of Protestantism.

China Miracle

Most of the explosive growth of the Chinese church took place after missionaries were expelled.[20] Even as missionaries were expelled and missions suppressed, indigenous forms of Christian faith were growing, invisible to the West and to a large extent to the Chinese authorities. The Religious Affairs Bureau was closed down in the 1960s, and when it reopened in the 1980s, the Chinese government discovered that the church had grown rapidly under the pressure of persecution. At the end of World War II, there were 840,000 Christians in China; by 1980 there were more than five million. Estimates today vary wildly between the official figures that put the Catholic-Protestant population around twenty million and estimates that go as high as seventy million.[21]

Scholars divvy up the church that reemerged after the Cultural Revolution into Protestant and Catholic varieties, but, as in Africa, unclassifiable movements have appeared. Some take over Chinese folk traditions, and in several instances leaders have proclaimed themselves to be messianic figures. Others are in the mainstream of Pentecostalism, holding to Christian orthodoxy with an emphasis on the gifts of the Spirit. It was arguably the "radicalism" of Pentecostal Christians that enabled them to endure the horrors of the Communist regime. It certainly kept them at some distance from the missionary establishment even before the missionaries were driven out. Pentecostal experience was intense:

> At one time or another their religious practices involved diverse manifestations of what social scientists call involuntary motor behavior: weeping, trance-inducing, screaming, howling, numbness, glossolalia, weightlessness, shivering, miraculous healings, profuse sweating, rolling on the floor, frothing at the mouth, ecstatic singing and dancing and extended fasting (in one case, for 76 days). It also involved diverse manifestations of demanding disciplinary rituals such as tithing, exorcisms, foot washing, mass public confessions and communal sharing of goods. The theology paralleled the most severe forms of American Protestant fundamentalism. It entailed conversion, biblical literalism, missions to unconverted Chinese, attempts to evangelize other Christian sects (especially Seventh-day Adventists) and fierce denunciation of mainline Christianity and liberal theology. Millenarianism constituted the most conspicuous feature of this radical Protestant theology. Though the details varied from sect to sect, all of them foresaw the imminent end of history in which the Lord would return in glory, smite

his (and, not incidentally, their) enemies and establish a millennial kingdom of peace, justice and prosperity.[22]

Indigenous Chinese churches, while certainly not Orthodox or Catholic, are not entirely Protestant either. Indeed, some of the more extreme groups denounce the mainstream Three-Self churches as anti-Christ, much as the Reformers did with the Roman church.[23] As in Africa, these Chinese movements and churches have roots in Western missions, but the trajectory of their expansion and development has been set not by confessions or a magisterium but by factors that are specifically Chinese.

The Restructuring of Global Christianity

These vignettes are certainly not intended to offer blanket endorsement of African Independent Churches in general or of everything that has adopted the Aladura name. African Christianity is often as riven by rivalry and competition as American denominational Christianity, and this divisiveness can break out in horrific violence.[24] My point is not to endorse but simply to observe.

Observing these brief scenes is enough to indicate that the triad that modern Christians have used to map world Christianity has been completely dismantled. Indigenous churches have stronger or weaker historic ties with European and North American churches. Many of the prophets of Africa started their life working alongside—or *for*—missionary agencies. They bear a family resemblance with Western/Northern churches; despite deviations, many of these movements confess historic Christian beliefs about the Trinity and Christology. But whatever their original relations with the "parent" churches, they have grown up and left home.

Classical Pentecostal churches congealed into denominational structures and are often classified as Protestant. The charismatic movement crossed traditional denominational and national boundaries, but the common dual designations "charismatic Catholic" and "charismatic Episcopal" indicate that the denominational classification was still operative. This was always a distortion. Even in its earliest forms, Pentecostalism was pushing against the borders of the tripartite classification system. Charismatically inflected African Independent Churches and the movements coming out of Asia have pushed the boundaries further, so that the framework itself

is no longer viable.[25] We might group them together as "Spirit churches"
or "indigenous churches," but even that scheme distorts as much as it
clarifies.[26] Better, we should simply acknowledge that our old maps are
as out of date as world maps that show Yugoslavia but not Uzbekistan.
We should keep the old maps in a file out of sheer historical interest. We
would be foolish to use the old maps to navigate the world as it is.

The proliferation of independent churches complicates the pursuit of
catholicity in a number of ways. We cannot assume that every church that
calls itself Christian is in fact Christian. Some movements in Africa, Asia,
and Latin America have abandoned fundamentals of Christian faith—
adherence to Scripture or confession of God as Father, Son, and Spirit—and
are not Christian. Many of these new movements renounce written creeds
in principle, making it difficult to sort out which are purveying truth and
which are preaching a false gospel. Obviously, the effort to come to one
mind and confession, washed by one baptism to eat at one table, is more
difficult when we are dealing with several *hundred* potential table com-
panions rather than three. Yet the proliferation of varieties of Christianity
reconfigures the church and provides an opportunity to approximate more
closely the unity that Jesus prays for. A church like the Church of the Lord
(Aladura) breaks out of the mold of our current groupings and represents
an intersection of Protestant, Catholic, and Pentecostal interests and emphases. Attending to—studying and learning from—these churches may
enable Protestant, Catholic, and Orthodox churches to find some common
ground beyond our historic barricades.

The global restructuring of Christianity breaks down old barriers. New
ones may take their place, as impervious and divisive as the ones that have
been demolished. But while the barricades are down, there is an opportunity to pursue a catholic future.

Restructuring of East and West

Restructuring is taking place at another level too, in Roman Catholicism
and Orthodoxy.

Protestantism began as a conciliar and catholic movement, intent
on reforming the church. The Reformers were eager for an ecumenical
council to resolve the disputes and conflicts that had arisen. In 1560

Calvin wrote, "In order to put an end to the divisions which exist in Christianity, there is need to have a free and universal council."[27] Trent (1545–63) was *not* that council. Because it was convened by the pope, Calvin and the other Reformers were suspicious that it would tilt toward the curia. A few Protestants went to Trent, but none participated in debate. Cardinal Gasparo Contarini, the one high-ranking Catholic who understood Protestant teaching on justification, died before the council began. Dying was probably the safe thing to do. If he had lived, he would have faced censure.

Vatican II (1962–65), though, was a much different affair. Non-Catholic theologians were invited and listened to. The council issued no anathemas. It was indeed a universal council, the largest council *ever*, with "over 2,500 bishops from almost every country in the world. Trent at most was attended by 200 bishops. The largest of the medieval councils never had more than 400 participants."[28]

Many of the results warm a Protestant heart: "The Mass in a local parish has been simplified thanks to the Council's first act, the reform of the Liturgy. . . . The Reformers would now find little to object to and would be delighted that their request for the use of the vernacular has at last been granted. . . . Renewed attention to the Scriptures, encouraged by *Dei Verbum*, has led to the use of a Common Lectionary in many different church traditions." Vatican II "gave a voice to many like Congar, de Lubac, Courtney Murray, and Rahner who had often been silenced. It listened to progressive bishops like Suenens."[29]

Protestants often assume an essentially Catholic account of the Catholic Church—or, better, an *old* Catholic account. According to that view, Catholicism is monolithic and unchanging. It has always taught what it now teaches; it has always been the church it now is. This view of the church is not favored these days by Catholics themselves, but Protestants cling to it. For many, Catholicism—no matter what happens, no matter what changes are made—is the permanent *other* to Protestantism. But the Catholic Church is a very different church from what it was even as recently as the beginning of the twentieth century. From a Protestant perspective, the Catholic Church has gotten worse in some ways. Marian speculations have hardened into dogmas that find little support in Scripture. Though limited with exquisite precision, Vatican II inflated papal authority beyond what Scripture or tradition can bear.

Yet some of the changes of the past century are welcome ones to Reformational Catholics. There was a deliberate, massive shift from a "juridical" understanding of the church to an ecclesiology rooted in the idea of communion. *Lumen Gentium*'s description of the church as "people of God" and body of Christ is a far cry from late nineteenth-century Catholic ecclesiologies.[30] Catholics regard Protestants differently than in the past. We are no longer simply outsiders but brothers, though "separated" ones. In the language of Vatican II, the church "subsists" in the Catholic Church. The council does continue to say that the church exists in fullness only in churches in communion with the Roman church, but Vatican II no longer makes a simple identification between "the church" and the Roman Catholic Church.

These ecclesiological shifts have been accompanied by liturgical reforms. Some Catholic churches have trended in a pop-evangelical direction, but many have retained much of their traditional structure, though much simplified and with much more emphasis on the Word and on the Supper as supper. Communion in both kinds (taking both bread and wine) is normal in many parishes. The Bible plays a much larger role in Catholic life, especially in Catholic theology, than it did before Vatican II. The Catholic Church is home to many of the leading biblical scholars of our time (including Gary Anderson, Harold Attridge, Joseph Fitzmyer, Luke Timothy Johnson, and the late Raymond Brown). Catholic theologians who are not biblical scholars engage the biblical text in some depth (see the works of Hans Urs von Balthasar, Yves Congar, and Henri de Lubac, and of Matthew Levering and R. R. Reno today, among many others).

Admittedly, these changes are more apparent in some parts of the Catholic Church than in others. Polish Catholics do not have the same piety as Americanized Catholics. Catholic theologians have a more nuanced grasp of both Catholic doctrine and of differences with Protestantism than parish priests, much less lay Catholics or converts turned apologists. Admittedly too, Catholics have to do some strange dancing to explain how they still conform to the dogmatic statements of Trent. Catholicism still has some features of sectarianism.

The Catholic Church did not become Protestant in the 1960s. Vatican II was not entirely the universal council that the Reformed hoped for. But it is the closest thing we have, and it should be received as the gift that it is. Catholicism has changed in ways that open new possibilities for engagement with Protestants. Catholics have made generous offers of fellowship. They have issued an invitation to engage in "receptive ecumenism."[31] Protestants would be churlish, even faithless, to refuse.

At the same time that the Catholic Church was generously, humbly closing the gap between Protestant and Catholic, it was at work to renew broken fellowship with the churches of the East. This was partly due to the providential arrival of leading Orthodox theologians in the heartland of Western Catholicism. When Constantinople fell in 1563, Greek-speaking Christians fled to the West, especially to the eastern coast of Italy, where the Byzantine Empire had long had a presence, commercial, political, and cultural.[32] With their Greek manuscripts and knowledge of Greek language and culture, the exiles helped to spark the Italian Renaissance. Exiles have played an analogous role in the renaissance of modern theology, this time exiles from Russia. To list the Orthodox theologians of Russian descent who ended up in Paris in the early part of the twentieth century is to produce a who's who of modern Russian theology: Sergei Bulgakov, Georges Florovsky, Valdimir Lossky, John Meyendorff, Alexander Schmemann.[33] They brought their theology with them, and with that theology they infused fresh life into Western theology.

Proximity has not always made for chumminess. Modern Catholic-Orthodox relations have been testy, and the two churches have not resolved many of their differences. But at the close of Vatican II, parallel ceremonies in Rome and Constantinople removed the anathemas the two bishops had pronounced against each other in 1054.[34] Outside the official channels of ecumenical dialogue, Catholic and Orthodox theologians have been cross-fertilizing one another for a century. Congar was enamored of Orthodoxy, and de Lubac's eucharistic ecclesiology has been fruitfully compared to the theology of Greek Orthodox John Zizioulas.[35] More surprisingly, Protestant theologians have drawn inspiration from Orthodoxy, especially in trinitarian theology.[36] Instead of reading Catholic and Orthodox writers to refute them, Protestant theologians and pastors increasingly read them for wisdom, insight, and edification. No one today, Protestant, Catholic, Orthodox, or otherwise, would presume to discuss theological aesthetics without reference to the magisterial work of Hans Urs von Balthasar. The "trinitarian renaissance," even if exaggerated, was sparked by a triangulation of theological influences: the little book *The Trinity* by Karl Rahner, the expansive trinitarianism woven throughout the *Church Dogmatics* of

Karl Barth, and the discovery or rediscovery of Orthodoxy. Nearly everyone writing on the Trinity since has acknowledged these as touchstones.[37]

Conclusion

The early twentieth-century prophets of doom were right. The world ended. New maps had to be made, with new names and new countries. But we know that when worlds end, the Creator is getting ready to do something new. As war gripped the world, God was quietly beginning a new thing, remapping the church as the world wars remapped global politics. Old denominational maps no longer hold; old denominational barriers are being rearranged. And that opens an opportunity to pursue the union Jesus desires with new vigor.

As we shall see in the next chapter, that global new thing had its direct effect on American denominational Christianity.

10

American Denominationalism and the Global Church

Following the Reformation, Western Europe was broadly split between Roman Catholicism and various forms of Protestantism. National or ethnic Orthodox churches dominated Eastern Europe and Russia, and, though largely forgotten by church historians, various churches continued to exist in the Middle and Far East.[1] Most of the Europeans who settled in early America were Protestants of one variety or another. Catholics settled in Maryland, and many more Catholics immigrated to the United States during the course of the nineteenth century. An Orthodox Divine Liturgy was first celebrated in what became the United States in the mid-eighteenth century, in Alaska, but it was not until 1868 that the first Orthodox church was established in the continental United States, in San Francisco. Orthodoxy was exotic enough that Will Herberg, as we saw earlier, could summarize the religious configuration of mid-twentieth-century America under the triad of Protestant-Catholic-Jew. It is still habitual for many to think of Christianity as divided into three great families of churches, three families with long traditions—Orthodox, Catholic, and Protestant.

The restructuring of global Christianity that I briefly summarized in the previous chapter shows that this triadic categorization is badly out of date. And the global restructuring has local effects on the United States. The most dramatic comes from a homegrown movement, Pentecostalism, that spread from the United States to the four corners of the planet, before returning home speaking in new accents. New immigrant churches bring the latest Christian movements to our doorstep. The old maps of global Christianity are not accurate anymore. Neither are the old maps of American Christianity. The denominational boundaries are changing, and we have an opening to dwell in one another as the Father dwells in the Son and the Son in the Father.

If new movements are restructuring global Christianity and opening opportunities for catholic initiatives, they offer similar challenges and opportunities for American churches.

Pentecostalism

Historians debate the origins of the Pentecostal movement, but on any account it is a late nineteenth- or early twentieth-century phenomenon.[2] We can take the 1906 Azusa Street revival as a convenient "Wittenberg Door" date. In the century since, Pentecostalism has grown rapidly, not only in the United States, but throughout the world, especially in the global South.[3] Total numbers are notoriously difficult to estimate, partly because the boundaries of Pentecostalism are debated. Charismatic movements have sprung up in many Protestant and Catholic churches, and it is not always easy to determine whether to count some of the indigenous churches of Africa as Pentecostal. And should Korean Presbyterians who speak in tongues in private be considered charismatics? What about evangelical churches that borrow their music from the Vineyard or Maranatha?

Some have estimated the total to be nearly half a billion. The cautious David Martin notes that the number of Protestants in Latin America has grown from 1 percent to 10 percent over the course of the twentieth century, with two-thirds of the growth coming from Pentecostals of various stripes. Martin suggests that Pentecostals may constitute the second-largest grouping of Christians on the planet, second only to the billion-strong Roman Catholic Church.[4] Pew Research published in 2006 an estimate that 28 percent of Protestants in the United States are Pentecostals or charismatic. In Brazil the proportion is 78 percent, and in Kenya 73 percent.[5] Philip

Jenkins has called Pentecostalism the most successful social movement of the twentieth century, one that left Marxism well behind in history's dustbin.

A Form of Protestantism?

Martin is typical of scholars who classify Pentecostalism as a variety of Protestantism, but there are many reasons to doubt that classification.[6] The fact that Pentecostals broke from existing churches to form their own denominations does not of itself mean that they constitute a distinct class of Christian churches. Not every break from existing Protestantism is analogous to Luther's break from the Roman Catholic Church. Some are more like Wesley's break from Anglicanism.[7] But the divergence of Pentecostalism from the evangelical Protestantism that gave it birth is more radical than the divergence of Methodism from Anglicanism.

The Reformers maintained continuity with the Roman Catholic Church in many ways: they continued to confess the early trinitarian and christological creeds; most continued to practice formal liturgical worship; they continued to appeal to Scripture and, to a lesser extent, to Christian tradition to justify their theology and practices. Despite these continuities, nearly everything was remixed and recontextualized. The Reformers redefined faith, which took on a prominence it had not had in medieval Catholic theology; they challenged the Augustinian understanding of justification, arguing that it was a forensic declaration rather than a making-just; their worship was conducted in the vernacular, and they placed much greater emphasis on Bible teaching; their Eucharists dispensed with the elevation of the host and every hint of veneration; in place of chants sung by monks and clergy, they composed hymns and metrical psalms to be sung by the congregation. One of the main divergences from Catholicism, of course, was their evaluation of the papacy, an institution the Reformers regarded as anti-Christian because it placed a man rather than the God-man in the position of head of the church.

Pentecostalism diverges from classical Protestantism in the same ways as Protestantism did from Catholicism.[8] The theological divergence from evangelicalism is not absolute, of course; but, as in the case of Protestantism, Pentecostalism rearranges and recontextualizes even the doctrine it shares with evangelical Protestants. The most obvious doctrinal divergence has to do with the work of the Spirit and the continuation of the gifts of the Spirit. For many classic Protestants and evangelicals, the closing of the canon of Scripture is linked with the cessation of the special revelatory gifts of the Spirit. Tongues-speaking, prophecy, and the miraculous healings, exorcisms, and resurrections were part of the founding of the new covenant order but ceased with the apostolic generation. Pentecostalism is *defined* by the conviction that the Spirit continues to work in precisely these same ways, or at least that the Spirit has begun to work again in these ways.

But the difference between Pentecostalism and evangelicalism is more comprehensive. The statement of belief of the non-Pentecostal Willow Creek Community Church follows a very traditional Protestant format. It affirms the authority and inerrancy of the Bible, the Trinity, salvation by grace through faith, the two natures of Christ, the role of the Spirit in remaking sinners, future judgment, the church, and the ordinances of baptism and Communion. The paragraph on the Spirit is critical:

> People in a saving relationship with Jesus Christ are to live in holiness and obedience as they submit to the Holy Spirit, the third person of the Trinity. Sent by the Father and the Son, the Holy Spirit applies Christ's saving work by enlightening the minds of sinners to their need to be saved. He renews and indwells each believer upon salvation, becoming their source of assurance, strength, wisdom, and gifting for building up the church. The Holy Spirit guides believers in understanding and applying the Bible. Appropriated by faith, His power and control empower believers to lead a life of Christ-like character and bear fruit for the Father's glory.[9]

Overall, the statement is a simplification of the Westminster Confession, stripped of its Calvinism.

Many Pentecostals would share most of the beliefs articulated in the Willow Creek statement, but they make additional claims. One of the early classic statements comes from William Seymour, a leader of the Azusa Street revival in 1906. In a seminal article, "Precious Atonement," published in the inaugural issue of *The Apostolic Faith*, Seymour disposed of the normal Protestant emphasis on forgiveness and justification with one line: "Through the atonement we receive forgiveness of sins." The second blessing of the atonement is "sanctification through the blood of Jesus," by which sinners are made children of God and given authority to rebuke humans and demons. Third, Jesus dies for the "healing of our bodies. Sickness and disease are destroyed through the precious atonement of Jesus," Seymour claimed, citing Isaiah 53's promise that "with his stripes we are healed." Atonement is not only for the soul but also "for the sanctification of our bodies from inherited disease." The tainted blood inherited by natural birth is cleansed by the blood of Jesus. Finally, the atonement brings "baptism with the Holy Ghost and fire," so that Christ is "enthroned and crowned in our hearts." Jesus is lifted up "in all His fullness, not only in healing and salvation from all sin, but in His power to speak all the languages of the world." The atonement thus includes "justification, sanctification, healing, the baptism with the Holy Ghost and signs following."[10]

The differences are even more dramatic when we compare the Willow Creek statement with the emphases of the Vineyard movement. Patristic, Reformation, and evangelical elements appear in John Wimber's theological declarations, and to the end of his life, Wimber self-identified as an evangelical. Like evangelicals, Wimber wrote that "the Spirit brings the . . . presence of God to us for spiritual worship, personal sanctification, building up the Church, [and] gifting us for ministry." The sort of ministry he envisioned, however, was quite different: "The Spirit brings the permanent indwelling presence of God to us . . . gifting us for ministry, and driving back the kingdom of Satan by the evangelization of the world through proclaiming the word of Jesus and doing the works of Jesus." The Spirit enabled Christians to do what Wimber called the "stuff," the stuff Jesus did—casting out demons, healing the sick, raising the dead. Following the lead of the biblical theology movement, and especially of George Eldon Ladd, Wimber taught that "God's kingdom has come in the ministry of our Lord Jesus Christ, [and] it continues to come in the ministry of the Spirit through the church."[11]

The issue here is not simply the *addition* of claims about the work of the Spirit or the ministry of the church. Pentecostals place classic Protestant and evangelical doctrines in a new setting and rearrange the emphases to such a degree that they are arguably offering a fresh doctrinal synthesis.

Liturgically, the divergence from classic Protestant and evangelical churches is more obvious. Not all Pentecostal worship is the same, of course, but in the styles of music and the frequent inclusion of tongues and prophecy, it diverges radically from evangelical and classic Protestant worship. The difference is admittedly somewhat obscured by the fact that many evangelical churches, and even some confessional Protestant churches, have adopted this or that element of charisma into their worship services.

Given the Pentecostal understanding of the work of the Spirit, the church also conducts her missions in a very different key. In the early Vineyard movement, for instance, "power evangelism" was done by "signs and wonders"—by miracles of healing especially. Even now, as the Vineyard works its way through to a second generation, most of the churches claim to see at least a few miraculous healings in their communities every year.

Martin summarizes the mash-up that is Pentecostalism: It is a "fusion of a populist Christianity, originally coming out from under the Magisterial Reformation of Luther, Calvin and Cranmer, with a black spirituality, including in that the Afro-Brazilian strain. That has in turn fused with a layer of shamanism from the Andes to Korea and inland China."[12] Martin does not intend that as a criticism, nor do I. It is a description of a Christian movement that does not fit our post-Reformation categories, and therefore forces us to revise those categories.

The Social Profile of Pentecostalism

In its social "sources" and effects, Pentecostalism also does not match the historic profile of American Protestantism. As scholars have remarked before and since Niebuhr, the American church is a racially divided church. The black-white divide is one of the most inflexible social factors that correlates with denominational affiliation. From its beginning, Pentecostalism produced racially mixed churches. In the Azusa Street revival, William Seymour and other leaders sensed that

> God was now assembling a new and racially inclusive people to glorify his name and to save a Jim Crow nation lost in sin.
>
> In retrospect the interracial character of the growing congregation on Azusa Street was indeed a kind of miracle. It was, after all, 1906, a time of growing, not diminishing, racial separation everywhere else. But many visitors reported that in the Azusa Street revival blacks and whites and Asians and Mexicans sang together and prayed together. Seymour [a black] was recognized as the pastor. But there were both black and white deacons, and both black and white women . . . were exhorters and healers. What seemed to impress—or disgust—visitors most, however, was not the interracial

leadership but the fact that blacks and whites, men and women, embraced each other at the tiny altar as they wept and prayed. A southern white preacher later jotted in his diary that he was first offended and startled, then inspired, by the fact that, as he put it, "the color line was washed away by the blood."[13]

Pentecostal churches have remained racially mixed to this day. Between 2004 and 2014, the Assemblies of God increased by a little over 13 percent; white membership increased by only 1.9 percent, while nonwhite membership increased by over 43 percent. As of 2014, 42 percent of members of the Assemblies of God were nonwhite, as compared to 24 percent nonwhite among evangelicals and 14 percent among mainline Protestants. Only the Catholic Church had a comparable mix of races, with 41 percent from ethnic or racial minorities. With its mix of Asian, black, Hispanic, Native American, and white members, the Assemblies of God has a racial makeup similar to that of the United States as a whole.[14]

In the United States and around the world, Pentecostalism began as the faith of the marginal, the down-and-out, the outcasts, the slum dwellers and dump dwellers. Pentecostalism was the latest version of the "church of the disinherited." In some ways, this reinforced the "social sources" of American denominationalism. As the Episcopal Church is the church of the upper class, so Pentecostalism became the church of the poor. Over time, that has not held true. Pentecostalism often facilitates significant upward social mobility. Especially in Latin America, it has become a conduit for bringing the poorest of the poor into something like a middle-class existence. A male convert to Pentecostalism gives up the habits and rites of machismo—drinking, gambling, fighting, wife beating—and becomes a stable and reliable family man and, almost inevitably, a *wealthier* family man. All by itself, giving up drinking can save him a quarter of his income, which can now be put to more productive uses. Like Methodism, North American Pentecostalism has worked among the lower classes and brought them into the middle class. Joining the Assemblies of God no longer bears as much social risk as it once did. Still, the lively piety of Pentecostalism sets it off from the staid piety of mainstream Protestantism. In that sense, it retains features of the "church of the disinherited." By its penetration into mainstream Protestantism, Pentecostalism and the various branches of the charismatic movement may help overcome the long-standing social breach between the disinherited and the bourgeois within the Protestant churches.

Pentecostalism has been as fissiparous as Protestantism. At the same time, it may effect a double move toward catholicity. On the one hand, its sheer existence damages the traditional triad of Christian traditions and is a sign of the restructuring of the church. On the other hand, the fact that charismatic movements exist in various churches perforates the barriers between traditional churches. Charismatic Catholics share the same experiences of the Spirit with charismatic Anglicans, charismatic Baptists, and old-style Pentecostals, and those filled with the Spirit form a connected body across denominations. Waldo Cesar summarizes the catholic potential of the charismatic movement:

> The future of the Christian churches must . . . go along the difficult path of recognizing that a new form of church has emerged on the international scene. It is no longer a matter . . . of an isolated, local parochial movement. It concerns a new dynamism of religious and spiritual life, a challenge to the older churches, their structures, and their relations with social reality. "What Pentecostals are offering to the ecumenical movement is a spirituality of ecumenism—a universal rediscovery of the Spirit for all Christian denominations."[15] . . . If Pentecostalism has not found a space in the historic Protestant churches, it is certainly widening the space of Christian faith in society in our time. Openness to this religious diversity could mean a new era for the ecumenical movement and for the witness of the Christian churches.[16]

The antimodern or postmodern ethos of Pentecostalism fits here as well. David Martin cites a study of Mexican Pentecostal healing that highlights the antimodernity of the Pentecostal movement. Like black culture, and partly because of it, Pentecostalism is characterized by "an emphasis on the spoken as much as the written; the 'telling' of faith and giving of testimony through stories; the extension of participation to all, including women; the inclusion of dreams and visions in personal and public worship; and 'an understanding of the body-mind relationship that is informed by experiences of correspondence between body and mind,' most strikingly through healing in constant prayer."[17] Further, Pentecostalism "attempts to unify individual and community by affirming that healing is a public and communal activity." Martin cites a summary of Pentecostal emphases from Walter Hollenweger that says much the same: "For them . . . the medium of communication is, just as in biblical times, not the definition but the description, not the statement but the story, not the doctrine but the testimony, not the book but the parable, not a systematic theology but a song, not the treatise but the television programme, not the articulation of concepts but the celebration of banquets."[18]

In all this, Pentecostalism is well positioned to catch the cultural shift known as postmodernism. One wonders how much Pentecostalism helped to produce the wave it rides. In any case, Pentecostalism combines rejection of the anti-supernaturalism of modernity with deft use of the latest modern gadgets and technology. It is nicely poised for the emerging culture, whatever we want to call it.

Church of Immigrants

Immigrant churches are having a similar restructuring impact on American Christianity. Today, the missionary opportunity is not "out there" in China or Western Africa or Latin America. For Americans (also Europeans and Australians) the opportunity is down the street and around the corner.[19] One need not don a pith helmet and board a steamer to find these brothers and sisters. They are living in every major city in the world. They are our neighbors. American cars and toys are no longer made in America. Neither is American religion. American Christianity has gone glocal.[20]

Global migration has exploded over the past fifty years. In 1960, 76 million people migrated across a national boundary and stayed in the new country for more than a year. The number for 2005 was 191 million, and by 2007 the figure was at 200 million, fully 3 percent of the world's population.[21] North America has a history of receiving migrants, but this is new. Unlike previous waves, the new migration comes not from Europe but from Asia, Africa, and Latin America.[22] Often spurred by political turmoil and economic deprivation in their home countries, thousands of Africans have migrated to North America and Western Europe. More than ten thousand have settled in Belgium. Over half of the new Pentecostal churches planted in London between 2005 and 2012 were black-majority churches. Between 2009 and 2014, the Redeemed Church of God started nearly three hundred new churches in the United Kingdom.[23]

Between 1900 and 1950, around six hundred Africans came to the United States each year, but African migration has increased dramatically since immigration laws were adjusted in the early 1960s. Jehu Hanciles writes, "By 2003, African immigrants accounted for 7 percent of all immigrants admitted to the United States. . . . In 2002 alone, when the volume of African immigration reached a record high, 60,269 Africans were admitted into the United States."[24] The religious affiliation of these migrants is not always known, but judging by the religious makeup of their countries of origin, many of the migrants to the United States come as Christians. Most of the African immigrants come from Christian rather than Muslim areas of Africa.[25] Many become Christians after arriving in the States.[26] This demographic surge is one of the reasons for thinking that we are living in a period of epochal transition in global history, potentially as far-reaching as the migrations of "barbarians" into the Roman Empire during the early centuries AD.

It is not clear what effect this new migration will have on the shape of American Christianity.[27] The experience of African churches within Africa does not inspire much hope that the African churches will break down denominational boundaries or encourage greater union among American churches. Catholic-Protestant relations vary from country to country in Africa, and many African churches are as full of vicious, petty conflict as your average American denomination. In the mid-1990s, the Baptist Mission of Zambia (related to the Southern Baptist Convention) was locked in a legal wrangle with the Baptist Convention of Zambia over property.[28] Official ecumenical efforts like the United Church of Zambia are rare.[29] African churches are often led by strong and charismatic church planters who, whatever their intentions, can foster personality cults. At times those tendencies get transferred along with the migrants. At the same time, in many local areas, denominational boundaries have become virtually meaningless, as Methodist pastors join Pentecostals and Catholic priests in urban parishes.[30]

When they come to the States, Africans often have little contact with other American churches, including African American churches. Despite their common heritage and similar liturgical and musical instincts, African and African American Christians live in different worlds. Coming from majority-black cultures, Africans do not grasp the effect of racial prejudices on African Americans and so do not share their sensitivities. Africans are the most highly educated immigrant group, more highly educated on average than Americans themselves, and they often migrate because of their professional training and skills. With high levels of education and professional achievement, they are separated socially and economically from many black Americans, whom they sometimes regard as lazy and whiney. Africans are aghast at the breakdown of family life among African Americans, the high rates of illegitimacy, single parenthood, and teen pregnancy. Africans accept many of the stereotypes that white Americans have of African Americans, and they are regarded with some suspicion by black Americans.[31]

At their best, African immigrant churches represent missionary efforts from Africa to the developed world. Africans sometimes migrate with the specific aim of evangelizing and ministering in the increasingly secularized United States. Darlingston Johnson was visiting America in 1990 when his native Liberia fell apart. Making a virtue of necessity, he determined that he had been exiled in order to start a mission. According to Johnson, God told him, "Don't be refugees, be missionaries." The Bethel World Outreach Church that he started in 1990 in Silver Spring, Maryland, now has several thousand members and is the flagship church for a global network of 150 churches. Many African immigrant churches aspire, like Johnson's, to be more than an ethnic enclave for West Africans. Forty-two nations are represented in Bethel's Silver Spring congregation.[32] Not all churches are so successful in attracting non-African members. Despite his best efforts, Oladipo Kalejaiye's International Christian Center in Los Angeles is still a majority-Nigerian congregation.[33]

New immigrant churches may go the way of European immigrant churches—first serving as ethnic outposts, then gradually slipping into the mainstream as yet another eddy in the river of American Christianity. Insofar as American denominationalism is rooted in ethnic identity, the African immigrant churches may simply reinforce American denominationalism and so add to the fragmentation of the American church. In the long run, immigrant churches may provide another piece of evidence for the social sources of American denominationalism and the continuing failure of the church to be the church embracing people of every tongue, people, and nation.[34]

Denominationalism is, however, a mixed curse. While denominations often replicate worldly ethnic, economic, national, and racial distinctions, the very fact of religious diversity creates a certain amount of pressure toward forms of interdenominational recognition and cooperation. In a study of thirteen immigrant religious institutions in Houston, Texas, Fenggang Yang and Helen Rose Ebaugh discovered that various factors pressured the groups simultaneously toward "ecumenism" and "fundamentalism." Buddhism, for instance, is divided into subtraditions that follow the geographic distribution of Buddhism. Mahayana Buddhism dominates China, Japan, and Korea, while Theravada Buddhism is concentrated in Southeast Asia. In Houston, Buddhists of different traditions encounter one another, sometimes for the first time, and they "check out" Buddhist temples from other countries: "Regular attendees at the Chinese Mahayana His Nan Temple include people from Burma, India, Sri Lanka, Thailand, and Vietnam." A Houston Buddhist Council has arisen from these international, "ecumenical" contacts.[35]

This cross-ethnic, cross-tradition contact creates pressure toward what Yang and Ebaugh call "fundamentalism." Despite their differences in thought and practice, Mahayana Buddhists regard Theravada Buddhists as adherents of the same religion; but to determine what they share, both groups reach "back to the original founder and/or some historic, authoritative leaders of the religion, and to the commonly recognized holy scriptures."[36] They discover a basic, common "creed" that unites them despite their differences. Yang and Ebaugh discovered similar catholicizing pressures on Christian immigrant groups. Third-generation "Greek Americans in our Houston study . . . favor a pan-orthodox Christian Church that would unite many ethnic orthodox churches that now exist. . . . By emphasizing common origins, doctrines, and rituals, the pan-orthodox supporters favor the establishment of a united Orthodox church in order to increase the visibility and the religious, economic, and political power of Eastern Orthodoxy in America as well as to emphasize unity among believers."[37] Immigrant churches thus have a built-in bias toward catholicity.

Immigrants, further, do not keep their new religious experiences and insights to themselves. The experiences of American Buddhists do not stay in America. Because many recent migrants are "transnational," maintaining close ties with their home country while living in and even becoming citizens of another country, they export fresh ideas and religious perspectives back to their home country. Buddhist "ecumenism" spreads from the

States back to China and Sri Lanka. Similarly, African immigrant churches might, for instance, encounter varied forms of American Christianity that would lead them to a form of "ecumenical fundamentalism" exportable back to the African context. An ecumenism inspired by Greek Orthodoxy in America could have an impact on Orthodoxy back home in Greece, the Balkans, and Russia.

New ethnic churches have contributed to a "de-Europeanization" of American Christianity. Immigrants often "come from Latin American origins that are predominantly Christian, such as Mexico, Puerto Rico, the Dominican Republic, Cuba, Haiti, El Salvador, and Guatemala. Filipinos (the second largest Asia-origin immigrant group) are predominantly Christian as well. While Christianity is a minority religion in Korea, Vietnam, and India, there has been selective immigration by Christians from those countries."[38] In Europe, large Muslim migrant populations have furthered "de-Christianization" (though even in Europe that is not the whole story), but in the United States immigrants have done more re-Christianizing and de-Christianizing. Latin American immigrants have saved American Catholicism, and Protestant churches have benefited from the influx of committed, vibrant believers from Latin America, Asia, and Africa.[39] Insofar as divisions of the American church are the product of battles fought in Europe, the de-Europeanization of Christianity in the States may ameliorate some of those divisions.

African, Asian, and Latino churches may be smoothed into American denominations, but the nature of their congregants' immigration sets up some obstacles to the process by which they become Americanized. Many current immigrants to the United States do not give up their ties to their home country or their citizenship. They can stay in the United States and connect with family members on the other side of the world by Skype, email, and cell phone. They can hop on a plane and be home in a day. A portion of their paychecks can be electronically transferred back to their family at home. They are residents in the United States, but they live binationally or transnationally. If more churches in America become filled with such strangers, it will become a solvent of the Americanness of the American church. Grateful as the migrants are to their nation of residence, their ties to the home country will protect them from becoming Americanists. And that will prevent them from becoming denominational Christians. Overall, the church in America will look more and more like the global church, and if the churches pursue the agenda that I suggest in this book, local churches will look more and more like the global church, which is to say, the biblical church, the church made from every tribe and tongue and nation and people.

This is the deeper, subtler reason to hope that the new immigrant churches may tilt American Christianity away from denominationalism toward unity. I have argued above that America's denominational churches have implicitly agreed that they will subordinate their public witness to the generic faith of American civil religion. Denominationalism is not *dis*establishment but rather the form that the Protestant *establishment* has taken in the United States.[40] Immigrant churches have the potential to subvert this denominational system in several ways. Though most immigrants come to the States with hopes for economic betterment, they are not participants in the mythologies of American liberal order. In some African countries, the churches are deeply embedded in the life of their nation. For all its ambiguities and failures, the 1991 declaration of Zambia as a Christian nation indicated that African Christians are not necessarily adopting the liberal politics of the modern West.[41] African Christians seem instinctively aware that politics cannot be religiously neutral, that political struggles are always also spiritual struggles. African migrant churches in America have an implicit political theology sharply at odds with Americanism and sharply at odds with the denominationalism that is the ecclesial face of Americanism. They offer something more in continuity with medieval Christendom than with American liberal democracy.

Though some immigrant churches had their origins in the States, those following what Jehu Hanciles calls the "Macedonian model" were deliberately planted by Africa-based churches. The Church of Pentecost, based in Ghana, now has a US branch with seventy local "assemblies" and over ten thousand members. The Nigerian Redeemed Church of God has 175 churches in the United States and also has more than ten thousand members.[42] The Anglican Mission in America is a variation on this theme—a collection of Anglican congregations in the United States ruled by the Anglican bishop of Rwanda. These churches weaken American denominationalism insofar as they are part of networks that extend beyond American borders and are not beholden to the American civil religion. And by weakening American denominationalism they open up the prospect of bursting the denominational system wide open.[43]

Welcome the Stranger

None of these shifts will lead automatically to deeper unity. The slow, partial Americanization of the Catholic Church suggests that migrant churches might well become as American as any other church, adapting over the generations to the American order, American civil religion, and the denominational system. Besides, we might, out of fear, envy, and self-protective pride, blow it. Mark Gornik worries that, faced with unclassifiable new Christian movements, the Western church might "seek to protect or even try to establish its position as normative" or "to acknowledge other viewpoints but ignore any deep engagement."[44] Migrant churches might become another "church of the disinherited," kept at arm's length by the mainstream church of bourgeois respectability.

It has happened before, among missionaries who either ignored or denounced indigenous Christian movements without any real effort to listen, engage, or understand them. Dean Gilliland spent two decades as a missionary with the United Methodist Church in Nigeria. He confessed that for the first decade and a half, he paid no attention to the African Independent Churches, except to denounce them: "I considered it my Christian responsibility to warn all pastors and interested laymen against them," since he considered them "heretical" and even "satanic." Churches transplanted from Europe and North America were ignorant of the goings-on in these exotic communities, and what little they knew scared them.[45] Gilliland's experience was not unique. Some churches enter the mission field in order to advance their own theological tradition, sometimes in competition with other Western churches: Presbyterians who need to win Asia for Presbyterianism, Anglicans who want an Anglican Africa. As a result, Western conflicts are globalized. The gospel is preached, people convert, but it is a great waste of energy and talent. For the point is to win the world for Jesus, not for any denomination. When that point is lost, denominations cease to be denominations and become schismatic sects.

Leave aside questions about the legitimacy of Western missionary "paternalism" in the nineteenth century. It is past time for first-world Christians to acknowledge that in dealing with, for example, Aladura believers or members of the Redeemed Church of God, we are dealing with *brothers and sisters*, from whom we may learn at least as much as we can teach.[46] Emmanuel Katongole has complained that "Africa has not become the

subject of serious theological inquiry in the United States, or generally
in the West." African issues—issues like healing and medicine, miracles
and spirits, prophecy and gifts of the Spirit—"remain peripheral to the
theological project of the West." Katongole thinks that this negligence
could be "disastrous for the future of World Christianity." Without serious
theological engagement, clichés about the growing importance of African
Christianity will be "hollow."[47] We Westerners should get used to being
challenged to revisit our faith when we hear it sung in a new tongue.

Capitalizing on the opportunity will require mortification of old habits
and instincts. It will mean seizing what Andrew Walls called the "Ephesian
moment," a moment in which the encounter between different Christian
traditions involves mutual giving and receiving, mutual listening and learning and teaching, openness among Western believers to the new forms
of faith that are emerging from worlds we barely know and certainly do
not understand. Only in this way can we reach the fullness of Christ, for,
as Walls says, "none of us can reach Christ's completeness on our own.
We need each other's vision to correct, enlarge and focus our own; only
together are we complete in Christ."[48] Only together can we realize Jesus's
prayer that we would be one.

To exploit the catholic potential of the glocalized church, Christians will
need to get out of their denominational ghettos. Pastors and churches that
want to pursue global catholicity can start locally. Large-scale ecumenical
efforts have borne fruit, some nourishing, some rotten, but most pastors
will never have the opportunity to engage other churches at that level.
That does not prevent them from advancing the unity of the church. It is
not rocket science or labor-intensive. A few minutes on Google will locate
the Chinese or Korean or Kenyan or Somali or Colombian or Ecuador-
ean churches in town. Pastors can search out a handful of international
pastors who are willing to pray and study Scripture together every week.
Churches can find ways to serve and share with immigrant churches by
offering language training or by helping to navigate the job or housing markets. European, North American, and Australian churches can experience
Pentecost all over again by worshiping with churches from various tribes,
tongues, nations, and peoples. God is remapping the world, and it is high
time for us to die to our institutionalized divisions and reorient ourselves.

11

American Denominationalism in the Twenty-First Century

During a visit to Florida in the summer of 2015, I enjoyed a Wednesday-evening dinner at one of the largest churches in the small inland community where I was staying. The church hosts two dinners a week, serving meals to about four hundred people each Tuesday evening and another six hundred each Wednesday evening. You have to buy a ticket, but the food is cheap and tasty—a seafood pasta dish prepared by a small army of kitchen volunteers.

The church has several thousand members spread over three campuses. The main campus holds five Sunday morning services. Seven men and one woman are listed on the website as pastors, and another twenty-plus are listed as "ministers" responsible for various aspects of the church's work—group life, hospitality, recreation, children, music. A culinary director is responsible for the meal. One campus has a day-care service and kindergarten. When I visited, the lead pastor had just returned from a mission trip to Africa, where he had a chance to inspect the two dozen church buildings that the congregation had raised money to build. Everywhere a building went up a revival broke out. Jetlagged as he was, and recovering from a malaria scare, the pastor's excitement about Africa kept breaking out.

Over the past few decades, the church has grown from a few hundred to its current size. The congregational care minister has been at the church through most of its growth period. When I asked him how they account for the church's growth, he answered, "We try to be biblical in everything we do. Whenever we're faced with a question, we don't just stick with our traditions or the way we've always done things. We strive to be biblical." The church could be one of the large nondenominational churches that have mushroomed all over the United States in the past fifty years, but buried deep at the bottom of the webpage is a notice that the congregation is part of the United Methodist Church. The church I visited is hardly unique in its size, its range of ministries, or the muting of its denominational identity. It is one of many churches groping toward a way of being church beyond denominationalism.

Global Christianity is being dramatically, confusingly reconfigured, and the aftershocks are unsettling American denominational Christianity. Besides, factors specific to the United States indicate that denominationalism is losing its grip on the American church. Denominationalism's death certificate has been signed many times before, and the reports have proven greatly exaggerated.[1] I might as well say it up front: the following analysis and projection may be mistaken too. Denominations may persist for some time. That large church in Florida where I had dinner may keep its identification with the United Methodist Church indefinitely, albeit tucked away at the bottom of its home page. Denominations may maintain their denominational headquarters, even if they move from Manhattan to more affordable locations in the heartland, towns like Cleveland or Louisville or Springfield, Missouri.

But the persistence of denominations does not necessarily entail the persistence of the central *importance* of denominations. Benedictines, Franciscans, Jesuits all still exist, but they are no longer the bearers of the Catholic Church's future that they were when they first formed. The persistence of denominations also does not imply the continuing importance of the denominational *system* in American Christianity. Churches may retain their denominational affiliations, continue to contribute to denominational causes, continue to gather at denominational meetings, while the real center of the life of a congregation, and the life of the church beyond the congregation, moves from denomination to location. The Methodist, Baptist, Lutheran, Catholic, and Presbyterian pastors of a town might find more to do with one another than with their respective denominations. A local pastors' assembly might take precedence over the distant denominational offices as churches minister to their towns. Plus, it is entirely possible that *some* denominations will disappear. It has happened before. It can happen here. And if it does happen, it would not be surprising if denominational executives were the last to discover it.

I *know* that denominationalism will not last forever. The denominational map of Christianity cannot be permanent. The future of the church cannot be a future of institutionalized division. Jesus, who prayed that we would be one, will not be satisfied with that. Yet I cannot know when denominationalism will finally end or what exactly will replace it. In chapter 3, I speculated about a future Reformational Catholic church, the church I dream of. I do not know if that church is about to emerge or how much the future church will resemble it. What I offer is an argument founded on my best judgment of the evidence I can find, sifted through the biblical framework outlined in chapter 8.

Not knowing what comes next is one of the glories of being human. Confidence in the face of uncertainty is the life of faith, and faith is the source of all genuine catholicity. We follow Jesus and the Spirit where they lead, even when we do not know where they are leading us—which is all the time. The biblical paradigm in chapter 8 implies the same thing: no one could have anticipated that the temple would replace the tabernacle, just as no one living in 1450 could have anticipated the post-Reformation configuration of the church.

At the same time, that same biblical paradigm points us to certain critical indicators of epochal change—major shifts in the church's relation to political powers, internal rearrangement of the church's structures and polity, and, at the heart, new liturgical forms and directions. My aim is to show that American Protestantism is undergoing epochal shifts in each of these areas. Worship styles have changed, and there is a surprising revival of liturgical interest in traditionally anti-liturgical churches. Our denominational boundaries are sagging and becoming increasingly porous. The relationship between America's churches and American legal, political, and cultural institutions has shifted dramatically over the past half century. The time seems ripe for a seismic reconfiguration.

I take some comfort in the fact that the practical agenda I offer in the next chapter will be relevant regardless of whether I am right about the direction of American Protestantism presented in this chapter. Even if denominations remain strong, we are still called to pursue unity in faith, still called to reach the end of Protestantism by achieving the end of Protestantism.

Nondenominationalism

The rise of nondenominational churches is one sign that something is up. Megachurches like Willow Creek near Chicago or the former Mars Hill in Seattle are not affiliated with any long-standing denomination but create networks of their own. They are often recognizably Protestant in certain respects, but they do not line up doctrinally, liturgically, or in ethos with any of the main denominational traditions. Their worship and music are typically soft-charismatic, their doctrine generically evangelical, with a baptistic twist.[2] Like the church in Florida, many of the most successful denominational churches cleverly disguise themselves as nondenominational churches. Saddleback in Southern California is a member church of the Southern Baptist Convention, but I was not able to find any indication of that affiliation on the church's website, nor any statement of the church's doctrinal standards. At a further remove from the mainstream of Protestantism is the Calvary Chapel movement, founded as a Jesus People church in 1965 and now with six hundred churches in the United States and another one hundred overseas.[3]

During the past few decades, many new nondenominational resources for worship, instruction, and ministry have been developed. Liturgical churches often follow a lectionary, so that every member congregation hears a sermon from the same set of texts each Sunday. Worship was standardized by the use of a prayer book or missal. Denominations without lectionaries or liturgies maintained a continuity of teaching and worship by providing standardized teaching materials for Sunday schools, Bible studies, and so on. Today's Protestant churches have a far larger array of choices than they had in the past. Many churches do not use hymnals at all, much less a denominational hymnal. Music is chosen from one of the many "worship music" providers, printed in a bulletin or projected on a screen. Children are taught not from denominational Sunday-school manuals but from guides published by one of dozens of publishers of children's Bible-study material. Denominational authority weakens as each church in the denomination chooses which direction it will go with liturgy, music, teaching. The range of options varies from church to church, of course. Confessional churches place tighter limits on what sorts of songs may be sung and what Sunday-school materials are usable, but every church has a range of options that they did not have before, and that erodes the organizational rigidity and centralization of the denomination.

Missions have followed much the same trajectory. American mission agencies of the early and middle part of the nineteenth century were often interdenominational. As business and managerial models took over denominational headquarters, denominations brought many of these ministries under denominational control. Today that trend is being reversed. Alongside denominational missionaries, many churches support nondenominational ministries and organizations like Wycliffe Bible Translators, World Vision, or Habitat for Humanity.

With this expanded market in religious materials, nondenominational producers compete with denominations for the attention of individual congregations.

Porous Boundaries

Large-scale social changes have played a role in weakening denominational loyalties. Families were once primary transmitters of denominational identity, but the breakdown of the family has made it an ineffective instrument for passing on a religious heritage to the next generation. Among whites, ethnic identification has dissolved in a generic American identity, and this has weakened the traditional links between ethnicity and religious affiliation. As I noted in an earlier chapter, there are still correlations between ethnicity and religious affiliation in some churches, but the religious climate has become more "individualistic." Here "individualism" is not a slogan but a precise sociological descriptor: the individual, rather than family or clan, determines what religion he or she will associate with.[4] There is no ethnicity that has a "natural" fit with nondenominational Christianity.

By the end of the twentieth century, the old "social sources" of denominationalism had become far less intimately linked with denominational identity:

> The ascriptive bases of the religious communities have declined, creating a more fluid and voluntary religious system. Class, ethnicity, region, race—all have lost force in shaping religious and cultural identities. Old class and ethnic patterns especially have diminished in importance while at the same time new aspects of each have emerged. . . . Niebuhr himself anticipated a fluid and changing situation and was struck with the potential for religious mobility in a democratic, achievement-oriented social order. He foresaw old lines of cleavage being erased and new ones emerging as the society experienced change. . . . Since the 1960s the country has undergone something of an "equality revolution," as one movement after another has challenged the limits of ascription and opened up opportunities for individuals to pursue their goals. Weakened ascriptive ties and greater ease of movement for individuals facilitate greater religious choice.[5]

Geographic and social mobility is tied to greater religious mobility. As people move from one side of the country to the other, they go church shopping and often make decisions less on the basis of their denomination of origin than on other factors—ministry offering, liturgical styles, proximity.

As a result, nearly every church has a large number of religious "switchers," members who did not grow up in the denomination but came to it later in life as a result of a conscious decision.[6] Switchers have various effects on their newly adopted church. When an Arminian becomes Reformed, watch out! He goes through what Douglas Wilson has called the "cage stage," ready to tilt at every Arminian windmill with all the Calvinist ferocity he can muster.[7] Protestant converts to Catholicism often become fervent Catholics, eager apologists to their former colleagues and friends among the separated brethren.[8] Eager converts can nudge a church in a fresh direction, giving it new life. It is hard to imagine the Antiochian Orthodox Church having the kind of impact it has had in the past few decades if it had not been for the influx of trained, zealous, biblically knowledgeable evangelicals from Campus Crusade.[9] On the other hand, in many cases the switchers lack deep loyalty to either their former or their new denomination. Both are relativized by the fact that the member has changed. If he thought the Wisconsin Evangelical Lutheran Synod was *the* true church, why would he become a Methodist? Yet most will admit, though perhaps only after the passing of time, that their previous church *also* preached the gospel.

It has been argued that switching has largely gone in one direction, from squishy liberal mainline churches to their hardier conservative competitors. Reality is more complicated. Switching has sometimes been to the benefit of liberal churches, sometimes to the benefit of conservative churches. The reasons for switching are too varied for the phenomenon to be unidirectional. Dean Kelley's argument that "strong" conservative churches grow because they demand more from members than "weak" liberal churches explains *some* of the data.[10] But the weakening of liberal churches has been going on for much longer than is usually believed. In a 1994 study of denominational identity, Dean Hoge and a team of researchers agreed that the mainline was declining in membership and vitality because of "ebbing strength." Presbyterian churches that were once strong had become weak and were leaking members to stronger denominations.

Once upon a time, Presbyterians expected their members "to abstain from using alcoholic beverages, to avoid 'worldly amusements' in general, to dress modestly, to conduct family devotions, not to practice birth control, and not to seek a divorce unless their spouses had deserted them or committed adultery." By the mid-1960s, though, "*all* these disciplines had fallen by the wayside." The church slipped into a "disciplinary silence" on virtually every cause, the dissipation of the older standards never replaced by "the imposition and enforcement of new standards." By the middle of the decade, "it was difficult to give a clear-cut answer to the question, 'What do Presbyterians do that makes them different?'"[11]

So, blame it on the sixties? Not quite. If we start not with the 1960s but with the 1920s, we can see a decades-long "weakening" of Presbyterian moral expectations: "Concern about worldly amusements and family altars had subsided by the middle of the 1920s, but support for Sabbath observance and national prohibition remained strong for several more years. Among Presbyterians, the dissipation process involved *sloughing off* some elements of tradition that seemed burdensome or pointless, while *retaining* other elements, at least for a time." The supposed revival of the 1950s did not change the trend. There is "no evidence of either a slowing or a reversal of the relaxation of old Presbyterian disciplines during the

1950s." During that period "conservative churches increased their share of the Protestant market by the smallest percentage in decades," and "mainline denominations had gained more members from conservative churches than they had lost to them." Conservatives feared that their churches were "slowly draining away."[12]

The growth that swelled the mainline during the 1950s was fueled by people looking for "a more relaxed, less legalistic, less dogmatic version of the faith." Despite numerical growth, however, the mainline churches did not grow "stronger"; growth "concealed an ongoing weakness that a few years later produced an unprecedentedly steep decline in membership."[13] The drift in the mainline resulted from an accommodation to cultural trends: "The American cultural climate has shifted during the twentieth century in the direction of greater relativism and skepticism in matters of religion, and toward greater degrees of individualism. Acceptance of diversity in belief, lifestyle, and ethnic and racial background has broadened markedly." Initially promoted by elites, the shift became popular, and "the leadership of the mainline Protestant churches accommodated the shift within their own ranks." American churches had always followed the American way, and when that way took a new turn, many continued to follow. When the sixties hit, the mainline Protestant churches were already sailing by the same wind that carried the sexual revolution and the challenge to settled authority: "The mainline Protestant churches did not initiate the new shift, but they were unable and unwilling to resist it."[14] Not surprisingly, Presbyterians lost the next generation: "The children have asked over and over what is distinctive about Presbyterianism—or even about Protestantism—and why they should believe it or cherish it. The answers have apparently not been very clear. Today Presbyterians should not bemoan the lack of faith and church commitment exhibited by their youth, since they have no one to blame but themselves. No outside power forcibly pulled their children away from the faith."[15]

The increase in the number of switchers is linked with the widely observed rise of the "Nones," people who tick the box marked "no religious preference" when they take a survey. Nones now outnumber members of the mainline churches.[16] Whatever that trend might mean in other countries, in the United States it is not a sign that the country as a whole has become less religious. Nones come in a variety of shapes and colors:

Nonaffiliates are . . . a diverse constituency, made up of secularists who claim no religion and others whose faith is so privatized that they retain little or no connection with organized religion. They are very liberal on issues of civil liberties, women's liberation, and personal morality. Quests for social and economic justice are important, as is openness in matters of personal moral behavior. Themes of self-fulfillment and sensitivity to interpersonal relationships appeal to a young, educated, middle-class clientele who, exposed to the idealism and expectation of the cultural changes of the 1960s, have had to face the realities of the "adult" world of bureaucratic constraints. An expressive ethic and secular utilitarian values seem to fulfill many of the needs that others meet by more conventional moral and religious commitments. A cosmopolitan outlook, strong commitment to liberal causes, and weak ties to organized religion characterize nonaffiliates and Jews and thus contribute to their labeling by some as secular humanists.[17]

If the Nones are not a-religious, they are a-denominational, and the increase of their tribe is another piece of evidence that denominationalism is weakening.

Behind all these trends is an individualism that corrodes association with and commitment to any larger organization. Again, "individualism" is not a philosophical position but describes a rearrangement of social life that leaves the individual person freer than ever to make his or her own choices. Communications technology makes it possible to be a consumer of a wide variety of religious products, a different religious product for each mood. On the iPod or iPhone, everyone constructs his own culture. Each can also, as Thomas Jefferson already hoped, become "my own sect," patching together a religion suited specifically to my desires and needs. We are not only bowling alone; we also have the technology to worship alone. This is not an entirely new thing in American religious life, of course: "From the beginning, large numbers of Americans have held 'privatized' or 'individualized' understandings of faith that ultimately accept only the conscience as the final arbiter. Given the heritage of voluntarism, such expressions of personal faith are hardly surprising."[18] Denominations continue to exist, and some continue to flourish, in spite of this corrosion, but individualism is corroding them from within: "The threat of religious individualism lies not so much in a militant and anti-institutional sentiment as in growing subjectivism of religious belief and practice." Churches provide a "second language," but the primary religious language is one of "radical individualism."[19]

Radical individualism is radically different from Reformational Catholicity. But systems are always dissolved before they are reconstituted, and the dissolution of denominationalism in the solvent of consumer choice may be the flood that sweeps the world clean and makes way for a renewed church.

Denominations in the Culture War

Over the course of a century, broad cultural changes have shaken denominational Christianity. Social issues, many of them concerned with sexual morals, came to the forefront of American politics during the culture wars of the 1980s.[20] With the rise of the Moral Majority, the Christian Coalition, and other institutions of the religious right, conservative Christianity entered the fray of American politics with a boldness and bluster that took many by surprise. It was hardly unprecedented in American history. Moral majority movements are a recurring feature of American Christianity. For some, especially among the media, academic, and political elites, the evangelical/fundamentalist resurgence was deeply threatening. Here was a religion that refused to stay put in the place where good liberals wanted to keep it—in homes and churches and other private places where it did not have to be seen or heard. Here was a movement that seemed intent on undoing the secular settlement of American society, on making a conservative form of conventional religion the operational religion.

The first volleys were fired before Jerry Falwell emerged on the scene, with the Supreme Court decision outlawing prayer in public schools. For much of American history, the public schools had effectively been training grounds for Protestant children, inculcating a generic and moralistic and Americanist form of Protestantism. It was one of the reasons Catholics built their own educational system: they did not want to subject their children to attacks on the papacy. The Supreme Court took the schools away from the Protestants who had controlled them, apparently turning the schools into officially God-free zones. The introduction of sex education added to the crisis. The reaction to this was not prudery; it was a reaction to the legally enforced secularization of sexual morality. Kids would learn about sex not from their parents or the Bible but in a place where they were not allowed to pray. Some churches responded by creating a still-growing network of alternative schools. Others responded by attempting to reverse the secularization of the schools at the local and national levels.

Roe v. Wade played a major role in galvanizing an evangelical opposition. The Supreme Court decision not only overturned laws restricting abortion—laws rooted in Christian understandings of persons and life—but also explicitly dismissed religious opposition as legally irrelevant. The only opposition to abortion comes from religion. In America, religion cannot be established by law; therefore, no law that is based on religion meets the test of the First Amendment establishment clause. That aspect of the decision confirmed the pattern of the prayer decision and the more localized efforts to bring sex education into the public schools.

More recently, gay rights and related issues have taken a leading role in the continuing battles over sexuality. With the *Obergefell* decision in June 2015, the Supreme Court determined that marriage could not be defined as a union of male and female without discriminating against homosexuals. Traditional laws and constitutional definitions of marriage were overturned at a stroke.

Through these political and cultural struggles, the churches have been divided along moral lines, opening up gaps not between but within denominations. Presbyterians who want to protect the unborn, who uphold traditional beliefs about sexuality, and who believe that education is a religious enterprise take one side; Presbyterians who support abortion rights and gay marriage and who do not care about school prayer take the other side. Similar divisions have emerged throughout American Protestantism: Methodist versus Methodist, Episcopal versus Episcopal, Baptist versus Baptist, Lutheran versus Lutheran.

As fissures open up within denominations, the boundaries *between* denominations have become more permeable. Presbyterians war with Presbyterians over abortion and sodomy, but conservative Presbyterians ally with conservative Methodists and conservative Lutherans in the same battles. A new set of alliances has emerged, and it includes Catholics along with Protestants. Catholics were in the forefront of the pro-life movement when some Protestants were still wringing their hands in indecision. Catholics and Protestants have picketed together at abortion clinics for four decades. During the heyday of Operation Rescue, Protestant activists shared jail cells with their Catholic counterparts. It is the kind of experience that makes it difficult to see the other as a damned pope-worshiper or as a schismatic heretic on the fast track to hell. Perhaps the most effective ecumenism of the past several decades has been what Timothy George has described as the "ecumenism of the trenches," the ecumenism of the street and the picket line.[21]

The fact that these divisions overlap with partisan politics is incidental. It *happens* to be the case that the Republican Party has upheld traditional sexual morality and opposed abortion more consistently than the Democratic Party. It did not need to be so. There is no *necessary* connection between support of liberal policies regarding health care, social security, environmental regulation on the one hand and social libertarianism on the other. One could support the Great Society and think that unborn children should be part of it. As it happens, though, the Democratic Party has hitched itself to social as well as political liberalism, and Christians of conservative morality end up, by default, being associated with the GOP.

This moral and political division is one aspect of what Robert Wuthnow has called the "restructuring" of American religion.[22] Ideological and moral divisions have become more prominent boundaries in American religion, and denominational boundaries have become less prominent. Alliances across denominational lines have replaced alliances within denominations. One can no longer predict where a person stands on some of the great moral issues of our time by knowing that he or she is Methodist or Presbyterian. At the very least, one has to determine which sort of Methodist or Presbyterian the person is.[23] Asking how often someone attends church is an even better predictor of his or her theological and moral inclinations.

Conclusion

Cracks have appeared in the walls separating denominations. Just as importantly, the hold of the American way of life on the churches has weakened. As I argued above, denominationalism works by a combination of religious pluralism and civil religious uniformity. As theologically, liturgically, and missionally diverse as they are, American churches have joined in enthusiastic support of the American way, including the American way of being church.

Denominationalism is weakening from one side because of internal differences within denominations and because of new cross-denominational alliances. Denominationalism is weakening from the other side because the American way itself has come into contention.[24] For some churches, being American means upholding our nation's historic moral and religious traditions, which include a tradition of sexual restraint. For other churches, being American means supporting an infinite expansion of personal freedom. For some, it is un-American to advocate abortion or gay marriage; for others, these freedoms are essential to America. If American civil religion no longer unites the churches of denominational Christianity, what does? What will?

What we are looking at is not only the collapse of the Protestant establishment, not only the erosion of the American civil religion that depended on the Protestant establishment.[25] We are witnessing the hollowing out of the American way of life itself. Some have wondered whether America can hold together in the absence of a consensus about the good, about what it means to be America. That is an issue. But the more fundamental question for the churches is what sort of meta-structure of churches will emerge after the American civil religion shatters. Can denominationalism survive the end of a unifying American way? Here's to hoping it cannot. Might the erosion of the seductive false catholicity of the American civil religion that shattered the institutionalized division of denominationalism open the possibility for Reformational Catholicism, a *Christian* catholicity, to unite America's churches? Dare we hope that we will see Jesus's prayer for unity more fully answered in our time? This entire book is written in the hope that there is a place for Reformational Catholicism on the new map of American Christianity, and the final chapter explores specific ways we may capitalize on the opportunity.

UNITED
CHURCH
REBORN

12

A Way Forward

From Present to Future

Jesus prayed that we would be one, and we are called to join his prayer and to live in the confidence that it will come to pass. We are called to die to our divisions, to the institutionalized division of denominationalism, in order to become what we will be, the one body of the Son of God. God is answering Jesus's prayer and the prayers of countless Christians who have pleaded to the Father to pour out his Spirit to make us one body in Christ. God is remapping the Christian world under our very feet, tearing down the old to make way for the new, and we must prayerfully follow the Spirit on the way toward unity. In the Spirit, in union with the Son, we must die to what we are and have been, so that we may become what we will be.

Pursuing unity, even on a small scale at a local level, can be painfully slow and apparently unfruitful.[1] Reunion cannot be achieved by negotiation or consensus building, because the church is not a political community or social club. It is the body of Christ, animated by the Spirit of God. Reunion, when it comes, will be a gift of God, a work of the Spirit. Yet we must act, and our actions will either preserve current divisions, make them worse, or move toward the unity for which Jesus prays. The way of reunion is the way of prayer. We are called to act in accord with the future

unity that God has promised to his people. We are called to die to what
we are so that we may be what we will be.

Beyond that perennial vocation to preserve the unity of the Spirit in
the bond of peace, the church today has a particular need to seek unity.
The church can face the challenges of this new century only as a *united*
church. Nothing has so weakened our witness as our tragic divisions.
Nothing has made the gospel so implausible, if not preposterous. Division
has deprived us of the weapons we need for the spiritual battles that are
on the horizon. We don't pursue unity for pragmatic reasons, so that we
can win the culture wars. The gospel demands that we live at peace with
our brothers and sisters. The German Reformed theologian John Williamson Nevin said that the "unity of the church . . . is a cardinal truth
in the Christian system," involved in the very "conception of Christian
salvation itself." When we lose sight of the unity of the church, we "make
shipwreck of the gospel."[2] Because we must be passionate for the truth
of the gospel, *for that reason* we must be passionate also for the unity
of the church.

The church needs to pursue unity and, as I have argued in the previous
chapters, we have a unique opportunity to do so. God is redrawing the
maps of world Christianity, and American Christianity is being redesigned
in the process. This may lead to even greater fragmentation, a Babelic
scattering of the church. But it also affords a fresh opportunity to heal old
wounds and break down old misunderstandings and to come, in prayer
by the Spirit, to fresh knowledge of God and his Word.

What is offered here draws on a number of ecumenical models. Much of
what I outline below fits with what has come to be called the "federative"
model of ecumenicity. Federative catholicity focuses on common action
and does not require intercommunion, mutual recognition of ministries
and sacraments, or doctrinal uniformity. Confessional commitments will
limit the cooperation of some churches; cultural, linguistic, and other
factors will also place limits on how far a congregation might cooperate
with others. Churches may not be able to achieve as much as they hope
for, but on the federative view, churches work and worship together as
much as each church is able.[3] Yet I do not believe the federative model
achieves what Jesus prays for in his high priestly prayer. As outlined in
earlier chapters, I believe that the future of the church is a catholic one and
that nothing less than full reunion and fully committed communion will

please our Lord.[4] Only union in faith, sacraments, ministry, and mission will express the full unity to which the Spirit drives us.

Getting from division to federative unity to full communion will be a long, difficult, strife-filled, and frustrating process. We would not even dare to venture into it without confidence that the Lord has promised just this as our future, without believing that we are to strive to be what we will be. Yet we are not completely without direction. Two models of ecumenicity are especially pertinent as we attempt to build the bridge from present schism to future reunion. Walter Kasper rightly emphasizes the central importance of prayer in his outline of "spiritual ecumenism." Jesus prayed for unity, and our first ecumenical task is "a humble but faithful sharing in the prayer of Jesus, who promised that any prayer in His name would be heard by the Father."[5] As we pray together for unity, we become aware of "how much harm has been caused by pride and selfishness, by polemics and condemnations, by disdain and presumption," and we are awakened to the reconciling power of the Spirit and the gospel.[6] All the other practices that Kasper endorses—common Bible reading and study, sharing sacramental celebrations, taking advantage of opportunities for common witness and ministry—are linked to and infused with prayer. In prayer we acknowledge that unity is a gift from God rather than a human achievement, that communion is not a sociological but a spiritual phenomenon, and that we come to full union with one another as we are more deeply united with and rooted in the Father, Son, and Spirit.

Catholic theologian Paul Murray advocates a "receptive ecumenism"[7] of hospitality, welcome, and listening, an ecumenism of gift exchange. It is rooted in our acknowledgment that we do not know or possess everything we need in our own branch of the church. Every Christian church is tempted to think it possesses all the resources to be healthy and faithful. Catholics, Orthodox, Anglicans, Presbyterians, Lutherans, Baptists—we all think that the church will be perfected when everyone else is enlightened enough to become like us. We are deluded. We are all Laodiceans, boasting of our health and wealth when we are poor, blind, wounded, and naked. No tradition has been spared the desolation of division. *Every* Christian tradition is distorted insofar as it lacks, or refuses, the gifts that other traditions have. *Every* Christian tradition must be as ready to receive as to give.

Receptivity does *not* mean loosening doctrinal standards. To modern liberals, dogma appears to be inherently divisive, but that is a prejudice.

In Scripture, truth divides, but it divides in order to unite. The creative Word of God tears the world apart so that it can be knit together in new ways by the same omnipotent Word. Jesus the living Word comes with a sword to divide Israel in two so that he can create one new humanity in the cross, and that same sword of the Spirit still cuts to joints and marrow and discerns the thoughts and intents of the heart. Far from undermining unity, doctrinal discipline is essential to achieving unity. As the Princeton Proposal for Christian Unity puts it,

> Authentic commitment to unity is always commitment to unity in the truth of faith and doctrine. When truth and unity are played against one another, both are misrepresented. In many American churches, doctrinal discipline is collapsing and internal divisions are emerging. In these circumstances, effort is often focused on the maintenance of present denominations' mere institutional unity, without reestablishing unity of apostolic faith and doctrine. In order to defend doctrinal discipline, renewal movements in some churches justifiably threaten bureaucratic forms of unity. . . . Modernist and revisionist distortions within Christianity are best addressed by a united Christian voice under a common doctrinal discipline.[8]

Receptivity does not involve diluting our identity, either. In receiving from others, we are enriched as the particular kinds of Christians we are. Murray suggests that Catholics become more fully Catholic as they become appropriately Anglican, Lutheran, Methodist, Orthodox. We listen to each other to answer the question, "What can we *learn*, or *receive*, with integrity from our various others in order to facilitate our own growth together into deepened communion in Christ and the Spirit?"[9] Pursuing receptive ecumenism, Christians fall in love with the presence of God in the people, practices, and structures of *other* Christian traditions.

If it does not mean abandoning our past, receptive ecumenism also does not leave the various Christian traditions *intact*. More than enrichment, more than clarification or mutual understanding, receptivity aims at *transformation*, at conversion. Pollinated by Baptist theology and practice, Catholicism will become something other than the Catholicism it was; enhanced by exchanges with low-church biblicist evangelicals, Orthodoxy will not remain the same. In the long run, the transformation must be a transformation into the one, holy, catholic church. As Eugen Rosenstock-Huessy put it, "We respond, though we shall be changed."[10] Receptivity is not an easy path to unity. At times, it is not easy to recognize, much less to receive, a gift. Receptivity is as difficult—as impossible—as change; it is as painful as death. Yet we must pursue receptive ecumenism in the hope that through our dying we will all find ourselves raised up in a place where "apparently irreconcilable differences . . . become genuinely navigable,"[11] where impasses of long standing can be overcome. Those impasses are not overcome by relativistic indifference. Receptive ecumenism pursues truth, recognizing that the truth of the gospel may be distorted by hardened confessional formulas. We must be prepared to remove our tribal badges when they inhibit our life together, which is life *in the gospel*.

This may seem a utopian program, encouraging loyalty to a church that does not exist. Admittedly, there is something to the utopian charge. The church we know is not the church we shall know. We cling to the wrinkled, blemished, divided church in the hope of what she will someday be, the spotless Bride without wrinkle or blemish or any such thing. Yet hope is not utopian, and we pursue Reformational Catholicism in the confidence that the head of the church is the one Lord Jesus, who gave his life so that we may be made one.

Too Catholic to Be Catholic

As I have suggested above, the path to reunion for Protestants is *not* to become Catholic or Orthodox. The Reformation recovered central biblical and evangelical truths and practices that Protestants ought not to sacrifice. Even after Vatican II and the ecumenical movement, even after the joint Lutheran-Catholic statement on the doctrine of justification, many of the traditional Protestant criticisms of Catholicism and Orthodoxy (of the papacy, of Marian doctrines, of icon veneration, of the cult of the saints) hold. We can achieve certain forms of unity with Catholics and Orthodox, and we ought to seek those. But full reunion will occur only when *all* the churches are reformed by the Word of God, only when Jesus purges each church in the unique way that each needs to be purged.

We cannot see the future. We cannot know *how* God is going to put back the fragmented pieces of his church. We can trust and hope that he is and will, but all we have access to are the configurations of the past and present. It is tempting to imagine that the future of the church will be an extension of some present tradition—Protestant, Catholic, Orthodox, Anabaptist, whatever. That is tempting because it is so easy to imagine. But if the biblical pattern holds, the church of the future is *not* continuous with the church of the present, any more than the temple was simply a refurbished tabernacle or the church a slight upgrade of Judaism. The future is *never* a simple extension of the past and present. How can the future church be simply more of the same, with the massive surge in Christianity in the global South?

Catholicism and Orthodoxy have, furthermore, their own entrenched forms of tribalism. In important respects, Protestants are free to be more catholic than Catholics. Here is the question for Protestants considering a move into Catholicism or Orthodoxy: What are you saying about your past Christian experience by moving to Rome or Constantinople? Are you willing to start eating at a eucharistic table where your Protestant friends are no longer welcome? How is that different from Peter's withdrawal from table fellowship with gentiles? Are you willing to say that every faithful Protestant or Pentecostal saint you have known is living a sub-Christian existence because they are not in churches that claim apostolic succession, no matter that they live lives fruitful in faith, hope, and love? To become Catholic or Orthodox, I would have to agree that I have never presided over a valid Eucharist. To become Catholic, I would have to begin regarding my Protestant brothers as ambiguously situated "separated" brothers rather than full brothers in the divine Brother, Jesus. Why should I distance myself from other Christians like that?

Reformational Catholics are too catholic for that.

Catholicism and Orthodoxy are impressive for their heritage, the seriousness of their theology and intellectual tradition, the depth of their cultural engagement, the passion of their ministry to the weak and poor. Both are impressive for their sheer size. But when I attend Mass and am denied access to the table of *my* Lord Jesus, I cannot help wondering what really is the difference between Catholics and the Wisconsin Synod Lutherans or the Continental Reformed who practice closed Communion. My Catholic friends take offense at this, but I cannot escape it: Size and history apart, how is Catholicism different from a gigantic sect? Does not Orthodoxy come under the same Pauline condemnation as the fundamentalist Baptist churches that close the table to everyone outside? To become Catholic I would have to *contract* my ecclesial world. The communion I acknowledge would become smaller, less universal. I would have to become *less* catholic—*less catholic than Jesus.*

Given Protestant objections to Roman Catholic and Orthodox theology and practice, why should we consider them Christian brothers at all? Why should Protestants think of these churches as churches at all? The Reformation discussion of the marks of the church is illuminating here. According to one formula, the church is a body of people who profess the gospel, celebrate Christian sacraments, and enforce Christian behavior. Protestants disagree with Catholics on many of these points. We have significant doctrinal differences, different sacraments and different views of how the sacraments work, different methods of discipline. Protestants believe that our views on these subjects are biblical and that Catholic views are erroneous. Yet, in fundamental ways, the Roman Catholic Church self-evidently exhibits these marks. They affirm foundational truths about the Triune nature of God and the God-manhood of Jesus; they confess the gospel, which is the narrative of Israel, incarnation, death, and resurrection. Though they understand the sacraments differently and practice additional sacraments, they do practice baptism and the Eucharist. The Catholic Church today is the world's primary teacher and defender of biblical ethics. To say, as some Protestants do, that the Roman church is not a Christian church is preposterous. If Rome is not a Christian church, what *is* it?

Much the same can be said of Orthodox churches. They too confess fundamental Christian truths, practice the biblical sacraments, uphold Christian morality. Orthodoxy has not defined itself over against Protestantism, as Catholicism has to some degree, and so it is in some ways less repellant to Protestants. For Protestants, its errors are less doctrinal than liturgical.

It may seem strange to charge these churches with serious error and yet treat their members as brothers and sisters, but there is biblical precedent. After the reign of Jeroboam, the northern kingdom of Israel adopted calf worship as its official cult. Jeroboam instituted a new religious calendar, ordained non-Levitical priests, and set up shrines for idolatrous worship. Later, Ahab led Israel into Baal worship. Yet according to 1–2 Kings, Israel and Judah remained "brothers" (1 Kings 12:21–24), and even after a long history of rebellion, Yahweh had compassion on Israel because he regarded them as his covenant people (2 Kings 13:23; 14:25–27). His prophets Elijah and Elisha rebuked Israel's kings but also aided them. When Israel and Judah went into exile, Yahweh did not abandon the northern tribes but promised that in exile Israel and Judah would be tied back together again as one Israel (Ezek. 37:16–20). If our God remains faithful to his people despite idolatry and apostasy, surely he calls his people to remain faithful to one another.

In any case, no Christian has to leave home to become a full member of the one, holy, catholic, apostolic church, despite Catholic (and Orthodox) claims to the contrary. If I were addressing Catholics, near the top of my list would be the wish that Catholics would abandon—repent of—even the moderated exclusivism of Vatican II. Catholic tribalism is no more defensible than Protestant tribalism, no matter that Catholics have a bigger tribe.

So, if the solution to disunion is *not* to squeeze everyone together into one of the existing churches, what *is* the solution? Here, as throughout this book, I do not pretend to address everyone. I speak only to that part of the church with which I am most familiar—the conservative Protestant wing. There is plenty to say to my tribe, and perhaps it will be instructive to others. In general, I am urging my tribe to grow out of its tribalism. It is time to bring Protestantism to its end by turning Protestants into Reformational Catholics.

Reformational Catholicism for Theologians

On many fundamental points of teaching, Protestant churches are united doctrinally with one another and with Catholic and Orthodox churches. Protestants in the great confessional traditions all confess the Trinity, affirm the Christology of the ancient creeds, and agree on the basic outlines of the gospel story—the Son of God comes in the flesh, lives a sinless life, dies on the cross, is raised again in glory, and ascends to heaven to pour out his Spirit upon his disciples.

Virtually every tradition within the Christian church has gone beyond these fundamental affirmations.[12] And in many churches the further elaborations function as identity markers that justify division from other Christians. Doctrinal formulations function as shibboleths to expose and exclude those who mispronounce. This use of doctrine is inherent in American denominationalism, since every denomination has to justify itself by claiming that *its* distinctive doctrines and formulations are important enough to the defense of the gospel and the advance of Jesus's kingdom to keep its people in a separate church. If they flinch and acknowledge that this or that is not essential to the gospel, if they concede that this other church has a good point or that their particular formulation is relative to very particular historical circumstances, then it becomes difficult to explain why a separate church need still exist.

That instinct to protect our distinctive elaborations of the gospel is a significant obstacle to reunion, but it is not overcome by ignoring doctrinal differences, loosening doctrinal commitments, treating doctrine as an optional extra, or pretending that truth does not matter. Doctrines have mattered and do matter; they have mattered enough for people to kill and die for them. Many have believed that the gospel is at stake in their formulations, and it will not do simply to assert the contrary. At the same time, it *cannot* be the case that our doctrinal differences are fixed for all time. If Jesus promised to unite his church, he promised to unite us in one mind with one mouth. We can put it into a syllogism:

1. Jesus prays for unity, and therefore the church will be united.
2. Doctrine is one of the divisive factors in the church.
3. Doctrine is essential to the church.
4. Therefore, in the process of overcoming the divisions of the church, Jesus will overcome divisions of doctrine by his Spirit.

There *must* then be a way of insisting on doctrinal truth while simultaneously striving to overcome doctrinal division. That way will be, in part, the way of humility. Especially in the church, all disputants must acknowledge that we see through a glass darkly, know only in part. We should all be ready to be corrected by brothers and sisters, whatever tradition they inhabit. We should all do theology with a prayer for brighter, more comprehensive light. There is a responsible way of doing theology that strives for doctrinal unity. A successful catholic doctrinal formula has to be biblically grounded, theologically sound, historically plausible. It has to answer to the truth that the churches in their various traditions have affirmed, yet it must at the same time attempt to move beyond the barricades to stake out fresh ground.

Let me illustrate in two areas of historic debate. The first, soteriology, is a struggle between Protestants and Catholics, and the second, sacramental theology, is a struggle between different varieties of Protestant.

Reformational Catholic Soteriology

Soteriology was arguably the central point of struggle during the Reformation era. Protestants claimed that justification is a forensic act, a legal declaration about the standing of a sinner before God, an act of sheer unmerited, unsought grace, and that faith is the unique instrument for the reception of this gracious declaration. Since Augustine at least, Catholics had defined justification as the renovation of human beings in their totality, not merely a matter of their legal standing. To justify was to remake a sinner into a righteous person. Contrary to Protestants, Catholics did not believe that faith is the sole instrument for justification. Faith itself must be formed by love, and faith, hope, and love together form the proper human response to God's gracious work of justification.

The stark differences between these two understandings of justification can be moderated somewhat. Catholics were concerned about the potential for antinomian libertinism they saw in Protestant soteriology, but many Protestants emphasized the grace of sanctification and the necessity of good works. John Calvin saw justification and sanctification as the *duplex gratias*, the double grace, that flows from union with Christ, and the Westminster Confession emphasizes that although faith alone receives justification, the faith that receives God's gracious verdict is never alone in the person justified. Love and hope are Protestant emphases, only they are not viewed as being linked to justification.

That is not to say that the difference is merely terminological. The Reformation was not merely a dispute between Catholics who use the word "justification" to refer to what Protestants call "justification and sanctification" and Protestants who use the word more narrowly. Large and deep systematic differences are at stake, and they have been the subject of heated debate, detailed theological investigation, and intense ecumenical dialogue for the past five centuries. I do not pretend I can resolve the debate here. What I can suggest are a few guidelines that might set the debate on a fresh trajectory.

Catholics and Protestants must stop caricaturing one another's theology. Caricatures can be pedagogically useful. More usually, they are *rhetorically* useful, useful for the purposes of exercising power, rallying the troops, identifying the enemy, and bullying the opposition. Caricatures can also be lies. Avoiding caricatures means listening carefully to one another. This is difficult because over the centuries each tradition speaks a different language and puts puzzle pieces together in different ways. We must try to learn one another's language and not translate what the other says into our own terms in order to dismiss or condemn it. When a Catholic denies that justification is by faith alone, it is essential to ask what the Catholic *means* by "justification" and "faith." If "faith" means mere "assent to truth," then surely every Protestant would agree, and together we could all agree with James: "The devils also believe, and tremble" (James 2:19 KJV). Protestants should gladly concede the Catholic apologist's point that "faith alone" appears only once in the Bible, when James says that "a man is justified by works and not by faith alone" (James 2:24). Trying to skirt that verse—trying to minimize the Letter of James, for that matter—is dishonest and undermines the Protestant boast that our faith is rooted in Scripture alone. Catholics for their part need to acknowledge (as many do these days) that "justify" was indeed a legal term in first-century Greek and that Paul regularly connects justification not with love but with faith.

All this involves making the difficult effort to get behind the slogans to the systematic and sub-systematic issues that determine the slogans. "Faith alone" and "faith and good works" contradict one another. It may be that Protestants are completely right and Catholics completely wrong. It may be the opposite. Logically, though, it may *also* be the case that the apparent contradiction arises from the fact that both Protestants and Catholics are addressing the question from within the same, perhaps misleading, framework. It may be possible that *neither* side has really grasped the depth of the biblical teaching on justification. It may be that Paul was addressing some other set of questions entirely, and that each side has grasped some fragments of a total picture that still eludes both. Instead of Catholics trying to persuade Protestants and vice versa, both may have to admit that we had it partly wrong. Instead of persuasion of one side by the other, perhaps we should change the questions we expect Paul to be answering.[13]

Reformational Catholic Sacramental Theology

Issues of sacramental theology divided and still divide Protestant and Catholic. Since Luther and Zwingli went their separate ways, sacraments have also divided branches of Protestantism from others. The debate between Luther and Zwingli focused on the question of Christ's real presence in the Lord's Supper. Luther insisted on straightforward trust in Jesus's words of institution—"this is my body, this is my blood." Zwingli ran Jesus's statement through a hermeneutical grid that contrasted spirit and matter, spirit and letter. He took Jesus's explicit statement as a metaphor analogous to Jesus's claims to be "the door" and "the way" and stressed that the Supper was a covenant meal for the body of Christ.

In addition to debates over the real presence, Lutheran and Reformed wings of the Reformation diverged in their understandings of baptism. Both continued the Catholic practice of infant baptism, but they gave quite different rationales for it. On the Reformed side, infant baptism was linked to the old covenant sign of circumcision; because circumcision was a covenant sign applied to infants, the new covenant sign of baptism should also be given to infants. Statements about what precisely baptism accomplished for the baptized were surrounded by ambiguity. Baptism was the "solemn admission" into the visible church (Westminster Confession) and a sign and seal of the covenant, of regeneration, and of union with Christ, but the meaning of "sign and seal" remained obscure. Lutherans tended to be much more straightforward: baptism gave the infant the gift of faith and new life.

Once again, systematic and sub-systematic frameworks are deeply implicated in this debate. Luther and Zwingli brought different hermeneutical principles to bear on the words of institution, different understandings of symbols and rituals, different conceptions of the metaphysics of presence. It is difficult to discuss the issue because systematic assumptions define the terms. Because the systems are different, the terms mean different things, and the two sides seem to be speaking different languages. Careful, patient listening is the starting point for working through the impasse.

Here again, I do not have a unifying formula for either the real presence or for baptism, though I can suggest a few parameters for discussion.[14] Without ignoring differences concerning the real presence, it might be the case that there are larger frameworks for understanding

Communion that might encompass the opposed positions of traditional debates. Debates over the real presence have had the unhappy effect of obscuring the obvious: the Supper is a supper, a communal meal of joy and thanksgiving. Were the meal-ness of the Supper made the starting point for theological reflection, we might find that the divisive issues could be fruitfully recast.

On the baptism issue, those who resist notions of "baptismal regeneration" should be willing to admit that there are passages in the New Testament that sound suspiciously like baptismal regeneration. Whether Paul was talking about baptism when he referred to "the washing of regeneration" (Titus 3:5) is disputed, but it is not obvious that the statement is *not* about baptism. That would be obvious only to a reader who has a prior bias against a strong view of baptismal efficacy. The bizarre notion, still advocated by some interpreters, that Romans 6 is *not* about baptism is a flagrant example of special pleading.

In these and other disputed doctrinal areas, Protestants should operate on one overriding principle: Scripture is the final source for and judge of theological controversy. That is a Protestant emphasis, but properly framed and qualified, it can be agreeable to Catholics. The Bible is, after all, *the* ecumenical book of the church. Beyond that, these disputed areas of doctrine in a reunified church can be worked through only if everyone believes that the Scriptures have the capacity to shed fresh light on old debates. This belief is based on the conviction that the Spirit can still speak to his church in the Scriptures. It is based on Jesus's command to take up the cross, because all theologians who strive for truth and unity with their separated brothers and sisters will have to die many times before they see the dawn of resurrection.

Despite my disclaimers, some might take this as an exhortation to abandon the passionate pursuit of truth. It is the opposite: If Roman Catholicism is simply outside the church, we can leave it to its errors. But if we are one body, Catholicism's errors are errors within the church *of which we too are members*. Siblings correct siblings, and certainly the correction is *mutual*. It is easy to criticize from a distance; it is much harder to patiently correct family members.

Practically, consultations should be deliberately interdenominational. No single church should attempt to settle a theological dispute in its midst without input and advice from a wide spectrum of other churches. When a denominational body determines a doctrinal dispute on its own, it reinforces and sharpens doctrinal differences and might feed prejudices against other traditions.[15] And more practically still, all Reformational Catholic theology should be surrounded, infused, founded on, and overarched with prayer and worship. We must pray that we may be of one mind before we get down to the business of hashing through our lack of oneness. Worship together should frame all our debates, so that our debates emerge from communion and mutual indwelling. Denominationalism makes us "nice." But doctrinal unity does not come when we are nice. Unity comes when we are truthful in prayer, prayerful in truth.

Reformational Catholicism for Pastors

Pastors are crucial to Reformational Catholicism. They are more critical than theologians, though theologians are exceedingly important. Pastors are more critical to the future than denominational bureaucrats and leaders, as fruitful as some denominational-level ecumenical efforts have been. Pastors are crucial because the reunion of the churches will take place primarily at the local and metropolitan level. That is where interdenominational relationships are already developing.

Large-scale denominational ecumenism has made significant strides, but it has gone off the rails. It was always dogged by liberal theology, but much of it has collapsed into a parroting of secular liberalism and political correctness. Questions of doctrine, order, and mission have taken a back seat to trendy causes like global warming. The church—which means the *local* church—is the place where the real action happens.

The local church was always the best place to pursue unity and catholicity, and was the central focus of the ecumenical movement. It is the only place where one can engage in real face-to-face debate, dialogue, and worship and common prayer on a regular basis. Denominational loyalties have been weakening for decades, and differences regarding doctrine and social issues have weakened them further. Conservative Protestants have more in common, doctrinally and practically, with Roman Catholics and Orthodox than we do with mainline Presbyterians or Methodists. As more churches accept same-sex marriage wholesale, that divide will grow bigger, with those who accept a biblical view of marriage and sexuality separated from those who accommodate to the world's standards. There is common ground for us to build.

What should we build?

Bible, Liturgy, and Unity

Within each local church, Protestant pastors should pursue the vision of a biblically and liturgically reformed church that I laid out in chapter 3. To say that Protestant churches need to rediscover the Bible may seem as redundant as the proverbial coals taken to Newcastle. Sadly, it is not so. Despite formal commitment to Scripture and its authority, many churches fail to teach the Bible in any breadth or depth, include very little Bible reading in their worship services, and leave members sometimes appallingly ignorant of the Bible's contents. Reinstituting the central place of Scripture in the church will mean that more and longer sections of Scripture are included in worship services; it will mean that pastors will preach from the text rather than offering commentary on the news or showing video clips with a light gloss of Bible-talk; it will mean that the churches provide venues—not necessarily the sermon—where members can be taught the entire Bible and review it on a regular basis; it will mean that lectionary churches will have to expand the repertoire of lectionary texts and bolster Bible *teaching*.

Merely teaching more of the Bible will not be sufficient. A central part of the "catholicizing" program of Reformational Catholicism is renewed appreciation for pre-Reformation modes of reading and interpreting Scripture. Protestant interpreters have always engaged in various forms of typological or figural interpretation, but in many churches and institutions this approach to Scripture has become an object of scorn. Historical and grammatical and moralistic teaching dominates some sections of the Protestant church; amoralistic redemptive-historical preaching is found elsewhere. What is needed is a deep combination of these two: Scripture read and taught as the story of Christ and, precisely *because* it is the story of Christ, as a demand placed on those who are in Christ. Both grace and command; both the indicative of the gospel and the imperative that follows from the gospel. Both acceptance with God in Christ and spiritual fruit are *promises of the gospel*, and evangelical preaching must stress both equally as *evangelical* promise and demand. Reformational Catholicism

thus involves a hermeneutical revival, a revival of christological interpretation of the whole Scripture that is simultaneously practically instructive.
It means the revival of the medieval Quadriga—a method of reading that
combines literal historical meanings with various dimensions of spiritual
significance—or something like it.

In their teaching and preaching, pastors need to stress the New Testament's call to unity among believers. If pastors want their churches to
catch a Reformational Catholic vision, they have to demonstrate that it
is a biblical vision. Without patient, careful, diligent teaching over many
years, any efforts churches make toward reunion are likely to end badly.
Ecumenical efforts have often done more to cause schism than to prevent
it. Though denominational allegiances have relaxed, many Christians still
have deep commitment to being a certain brand of Christian. A pastor is
asking a lot to ask his congregation to share in the cross of Jesus by dying
to their old name and identity to assume a new one. He should not shrink
from calling them to take up the cross, but he has to explain why this is a
cross they should bear. This will be the work of years. In some churches,
it will be the work of a generation or more.

Liturgically, at a minimum, the pastor or pastors should strive to institute a weekly celebration of the Lord's Supper in the church. They need to
convince the members that this is a good and right thing to do, but it is less
important to understand the Supper than to obey Jesus's command to "do
this." In many settings, pastors will have an uphill struggle to achieve this
goal. Many conservative Protestant churches are deeply, un-Protestantly
anti-sacramental and anti-liturgical.[16] It may not be easy to convince such
a church of the importance of the Supper at all, much less of the importance of a frequent celebration of it. When pastors become convinced of
the importance of this practice, they need to be careful to guide their flock
patiently and carefully and generously. Pastors who push through liturgical
reforms without preparing the church are abusing their office; fortunately,
they will not be able to abuse it for long because they will be forced out.[17]

Instituting weekly Communion will not make life easier. It often makes
things quite a bit more difficult. In the Supper, we commune in the body
and blood of Jesus. Those who do so unworthily get sick and some die,
Paul says (1 Cor. 11). When Jesus comes to dinner every week, things
happen. Strange things: Hidden sins get exposed. Smoldering marriages
explode. The church may split. All hell breaks loose, and the pastor and

other leaders have to pick up the pieces and try to reassemble them. This is not a mistake or an accident. It is the effect of Jesus coming near every week to inspect and judge, as well as to feed. When we set the table each week as a memorial of Jesus, we are calling on God to remember his covenant, his covenant jealousy as well as his covenant faithfulness. In the love feast of the Eucharist, we call on God to come near in all his jealous faithfulness, his faithful jealousy, which are but two sides of the passion that is the inner life of the Triune God.

The table at the center of Christian worship is Jesus's table. It belongs to him and must be open to all his disciples. The table is the center of the church's discipline as well as of her worship. Flagrant, impenitent sinners must be rebuked and if necessary cut off from the Lord's table. Pastors must not allow anyone excommunicated from another church to commune at the Lord's table. Otherwise, though, there are no valid grounds for excluding any believer from the Lord's Supper. Christians of different traditions differ in their understanding of what happens at the Lord's table, but those differences of theological formulation should not separate members of the corporate body from a common share in Christ's eucharistic body. In context, Paul's warnings about "discerning the body" (see 1 Cor. 11:29) do not have to do with the theology of the Supper but with factionalism in the church. Those who exclude other believers because of different beliefs about the Supper *fail* to discern the body.[18]

Out on the Town

Outside the confines of their own churches, pastors should make it a priority to foster relationships with pastors from other denominations. When called to a pastorate, pastors should set a goal of having coffee or lunch with at least two other pastors each month. They can begin with the pastors of the churches nearest to them. They should find out if there is a pastoral association in town and start attending. Pastors who are willing can meet together regularly to pray for the unity of the church or to discuss the lectionary or sermon texts that they are working on. The goal should not be to convert other pastors to one's own tradition. The goal should not be simply to get along in spite of differences. The goal should be to begin to work through differences in a context of communion and prayerful friendship. Each pastor should enter the relationship ready to receive as well as to give. A healthy Reformational Catholic relationship will not be easy or smooth. Doctrine is important, and so doctrinal differences are important and need to be hashed out honestly, patiently, carefully. More difficult than this is the problem of doctrinal *in*difference, for the catholic Protestant will definitely encounter pastors who consider doctrine a sideshow to the real work of ministry. Reformational Catholics will devote themselves to convincing their fellow Protestants to take doctrine seriously. Pastors must simultaneously take doctrine seriously and explore possibilities beyond the current boundaries of practice and doctrine.

Pastors can work toward a common confession among local churches. During the Reformation, every city or confederation of cities formulated its own confession of faith. Reformational Catholic pastors can spearhead efforts to formulate a general confession of faith to unite the various orthodox churches in their cities, or work to establish a local "Council of Nicene Churches."

In addition to the problem of doctrinal indifference, the problem of anti-creedalism arises here. Many of the most biblical churches in the United States renounce all humanly written creeds and confessions. At the extreme, this can turn into heretical denial of the Trinity or of the two natures of Christ. Even when the church and its pastor are perfectly orthodox, though, they will be resistant to a creed. An appeal to the use of creeds in church history may have some effect, but most likely it will not. After all, to the Bible church pastor, church history is the fallible record of human approximations of truth. It is the problem, not the solution. The best way around this difficulty is to find some common affirmation of scriptural teaching short of a formal creed. It would be a tragedy if the most Bible-centered churches were excluded from a biblically based catholicity.

Even if a church cannot get cooperation from other churches, it should commit itself unilaterally to honoring the discipline of other churches. No church should accept a member from any other church without investigating, touching base with previous pastors, if necessary sending the member back to work things out. Churches should not be possessive about members who leave. Churches should respect the membership commitments of other believers and not attempt to seduce faithful members from another church into their church.[19] Pastors can develop ad hoc structures for overseeing one another in a local area, constructing a metropolitan disciplinary structure and getting commitments from a group of churches to work within that structure whenever a discipline case involves more than one church.[20]

In all these efforts at unity, it is essential for American pastors to reach out to the pastors and people of the immigrant churches. This is critical not only because welcoming the stranger is a biblical demand. It is critical because only catholic efforts that reach across the class and racial barriers that have traditionally divided the American church can be effective in achieving unity. The division between the church of the disinherited and the bourgeois church of the comfortable opened early in the Reformation, and it has never closed. New churches are thrown off from Protestantism, denounced by the mainstream, and eventually rise to respectability, whereupon they are welcomed in.[21] Then the process begins all over again. This pattern will replicate itself yet again with the immigrant churches unless existing American churches make deliberate efforts to overcome the class and economic divisions. American churches have much to learn, much to receive, from the immigrant churches.[22] And it will only be by fraternal giving and receiving, only in that exchange of the Spirit, that the American churches will be one. American Christians are increasingly strangers in our own country. We should welcome immigrants and learn what it means to be resident aliens.[23]

Reformational Catholicism in Action

This is not a utopian dream. Pastors throughout the United States and the world have been pursuing these sorts of local catholicity for a long time. A young pastor friend in Tokyo was ordained by two Anglican pastors, a Reformed Presbyterian pastor, a Roman Catholic priest, a Baptist pastor, and an evangelical pastor. The Ukrainian Orthodox priest did not participate in the ordination but did greet the young pastor with a kiss of peace immediately following the ordination. Ministers are ordained to serve Christ and his body in his body. That is a universal ministry, and ordination services should be moments to express the catholicity of the church.

Before he died of esophageal cancer in 2014, Pastor Tom Clark celebrated twenty-five years of ministry at Tri-City Covenant Church (TCCC) in Somersworth, New Hampshire. He counted the local Catholic priest and the Congregationalist minister among his closest friends. Father Michael stopped by a few weeks before Pastor Tom's death to perform evening prayers and lay hands on him, and the Congregationalist pastor joined Pastor Tom's family at his deathbed. A veteran, Pastor Tom was the chaplain of the local American Legion post, as well as chaplain to the Somersworth police department and the ambulance service. He was so deeply involved in the life of the town that he was awarded the Somersworth Chamber of Commerce Citizen of the Year award in 2014—this in a New Hampshire town that not long ago elected the state's first openly gay mayor. "As a pastor, you have to fall in love with your community," Tom says.

Nathan Ketcham is a pastor in a small town in Colorado and knows nearly all the pastors in town. The local ministerial alliance has monthly meetings for prayer and fellowship. The churches cosponsor a Vacation Bible School each summer, and they celebrate Easter together with a sunrise service at the high school football stadium. When the local Episcopal priest had a stroke, the other pastors all visited him as he recovered in the hospital. All the pastors have committed to respecting the membership of one another's churches. Nathan writes, "If a family leaves for theological reasons, that is fine, but we don't actively recruit members from other churches. We recently had a family leave our church to go to the Assemblies church, and when it happened I made sure I went to the pastor to prepare him for the family coming." If someone leaves the church because of sin, "we will help one another resolve these matters before allowing a family to change churches."

David Sayler knows all the pastors in Kearney, Nebraska. The evangelical pastors meet in a ministerial association, hold an annual community-wide Good Friday service, and have been involved in service projects together. He knows some Roman Catholics in town and has become a good friend of the Antiochian Orthodox priest, with whom he has serious theological discussions. They are aware of their differences and try to preserve their friendship in the face of those differences.[24]

Demolishing Denominational Identity

Do we dare go further? Is it possible that the churches in a locale, the churches of a particular city, could establish something more than interdenominational cooperation and fellowship? Is it possible that churches could *eliminate* their denominational affiliations and assemble together as the churches of Christ in a particular place, as one church of many congregations in a single city?

We *ought* to dare. This effort is no more utopian than the more modest aim of establishing communion between denominations. The Church of South India united Presbyterians, Methodists, and Anglicans. For the first time in history, episcopally organized churches joined with non-episcopal churches, with each recognizing the validity of the others' ordination and ministry.[25] Every member of one of the uniting churches became a member of the united church, and that meant that the baptism of every member of every church was recognized by all the churches and that every member of every church was welcome at the Lord's table in all the other congregations of the united church. The churches were quite aware that they were leaving theological differences to the side for the sake of reunion, but they did not plan to leave them aside permanently. The whole point of reunion was to "initiate a process of growing together into one life and of advance towards complete spiritual unity." Union left "freedom of opinion on debatable matters, and respect for even large difference of opinion and practice . . . with regard to forms of worship or the conditions regarded as necessary for the valid celebration of Holy Communion."[26] The remaining practical and theological differences would be worked out in the context of the reunited church. Even to arrive at that decision, the churches had to struggle through the process of identifying which truths were essential and nonnegotiable and which could be left for future resolution.

The problem of orders has been one of the most intractable points of division during the past century. It is most intractable among ecumenical Catholics and Orthodox, but it arises in Protestant churches as well. It is essential to distinguish between forms and theologies of episcopacy that may edify the church, not least by contributing to the church's reunion, and forms and theologies of episcopacy that have arisen in the midst of division and have been formulated and practiced in a way that deepens division. The former should be seen as permanent features of the future church; the latter are provisional and should not be obstacles to reunion.[27]

Micro-Christendom

Years ago, members of a Boulder, Colorado, ministers' association determined that they were responsible for Boulder's civic health. Taking a cue from the early chapters of John's Apocalypse, they resolved to serve as the guardian angels of the city. They began to invite civil officials to address the pastoral association. Heads of city bureaus, the district attorney and police chief, and officials at the University of Colorado all visited. Each time, the pastors made the same offer: "Tell us," they would say, "the problems you face for which there are no human solutions. We want to pray for solutions." A pastor friend of mine who has been intimately involved with the group says that no one ever refused. No matter how secular or post-Christian, the leader sat tight as the pastors scrummed round to lay hands and pray.[28]

My friend has countless accounts of answered prayer. Out of the meetings, the pastors developed close personal relationships with Boulder's leaders. When crises hit, as they always do, city officials turned to the pastors for guidance, advice, prayer, encouragement, and friendship. Some of these officials converted or recommitted to their earlier faith. The pastors became, as my friend likes to put it, "advisors to the king," prophet-pastors like Daniel to Nebuchadnezzar—and this in one of the most secular cities in the United States.

Every time I tell my friend's story, someone comes back with a similar story about another part of the country. During the 1990s, the murder rate in Aurora, Illinois, was higher than in Chicago. As recently as 2007, there was a murder every month in Aurora. In 2012 there were *no* murders in the city.[29] Police crackdowns on gangs have played an important role, as have efforts by community groups who work with troubled youth, but churches have also been visible players. Beginning in the mid-1990s, the ecumenical Prayer Coalition for Reconciliation, founded by Dan Haas of the Aurora Community Church and David Engbarth of St. Nicholas Catholic Church, began holding a prayer vigil at each murder site.[30] Vineyard pastor Robby Dawkins was recently recognized by the city for his work with gangs.

Ecumenical, transformational ministry is happening not just in the United States. Another friend has been a missionary in northern Peru since 2000. With the blessing of the Catholic bishop, his missionary team took pastoral responsibility for a sector of his city. They built their first church in a depressed part of town on a piece of ground donated by the city. They run a medical clinic, provide micro-financing for small business startups, and train woodworkers at one of the local churches. They offer seminary training for Peruvian pastors and plan to start Christian schools.

There are two constants in these stories. First, churches from different denominations minister *together*. Second, churches cooperate with political leaders on projects that benefit the entire community. Christendom is being rebuilt on a human scale in town after town across America. It is a model of ministry suited to our historical moment. As the Yoderites and Hauerwasites have been telling us for some time, Christendom is dead. The religious right was its last, long suspiration. Though there are millions of Christians in the United States and Europe, Christian faith no longer provides the moral compass, the sacred symbolism, or the *telos* for Western institutions.

America's Protestant establishment has collapsed. Neither evangelical Protestants nor Catholics nor a coalition of the two is poised to replace it. Christian America was real, but—whatever its great virtues and great flaws—it is gone, and the slightly frantic experiments have failed to revive the corpse. It is past time to issue a death certificate. That's a sobering conclusion, and it is tempting for Christians to slink back to our churches. For innovative, visionary pastors and civic leaders, though, there are hundreds of realistic, locally based, ecumenically charged opportunities to foster experiments in Christian social and political renewal. Christendom is dead! Long live the micro-Christendoms!

Reformational Catholicism for Lay Christians

Reformational Catholicism can look like a clerical plaything. It involves pastors and theologians and denominational officials, but it leaves the lay believer out in the cold, watching as the church reunites. That would be a grievous ecclesiological error, since the laity is the church, the *laos theou*, the people of God. A reunion among the clergy that did not involve renewed relationships among the people would be a farcical union.

Practically, though, how are lay Christians involved in the reunion of the church that is proposed here? Pastors are again critical. If they fill their teaching with half-truths about other Christians, they will stoke ignorant prejudices and fracture the already broken church. Truthful, careful teaching is essential. Pastors should also recognize that the members of their churches are likely to have a more diverse network of Christian friends and associates than the pastor does. Some businesses are owned and operated entirely by Presbyterians or Lutherans, but those are rare. Most businesses of any size will include members from a variety of churches, as well as employees who attend synagogues and mosques or have no religious affiliation at all. While pastors spend much of their time with church members and other pastors on in-church business, lay Christians have daily contact with a wide variety of believers and unbelievers. Evangelicals have always known this and have capitalized on it by unleashing lay Christians as evangelists in the workplace.

Prayer has been central to ecumenical efforts since the early part of the twentieth century, and it must be at the center of any Reformational Catholic effort. Lay Christians can facilitate prayer in many ways. They can include prayers for reunion in their personal prayers, praying for unity among the churches of their city. They can contact churches other than their own to gather prayer requests for prayer meetings and pastoral prayers. They can pray for wisdom to know how best to follow Jesus, where they need to die in order to be what they will be. They can pray for their own pastors to have the vision and courage to pursue reunion.

Lay Christians are involved in the many interdenominational mission and ministry efforts that give much of the energy to American Christianity. Lay Christians go on short- or long-term mission trips to help rebuild New Orleans or Haiti. They volunteer to coach soccer teams in the inner city to keep kids out of gangs. Lay Christians serve at soup kitchens and homeless shelters and homes for women escaping from the sex trade. Lay Christians picket the abortion clinic, teach English to inmates and recently released prisoners, and volunteer at the local thrift store. In each of these contexts, they serve alongside Christians from many other churches. They can engage in these forms of ministry with the deliberate intention of crossing denominational barriers. Lay members might seek opportunities to serve churches in other denominations, churches that may be understaffed or in need of particular gifts.[31] They might decide to attend a Wednesday-evening prayer meeting at a different church or to visit a new congregation once a month. A group of churches could make a "lay free agent" website that would enable pastors throughout the city to contact Christians who have particular gifts. Methodist churches could borrow gifted members from Lutheran and Presbyterian churches, and vice versa.

Lay Christians who have been gripped by a vision of church unity can be "evangelists" for reunion, and their interdenominational contacts in ministry can serve as bridges for reuniting the church. In both the work-place and ministry, cooperation happens more or less naturally. When making widgets, there is no Jew nor Greek, male nor female, Lutheran nor Methodist. They are one in widget-making. And the same is true, though not as effortlessly, when Christians of various denominations cooperate in ministry. It is not as effortless because differences in theology and practice do affect the way they carry out their ministries. Even the simple act of "presenting the gospel" may take on a somewhat different texture and tonality from different mouths.[32] Questions will surface over what to do with someone who wants to become a Christian: Do you pray the sinner's prayer, or do you go to the faucet to get some water? Theological issues will arise in how Christians of different persuasions deal with poverty: How much is due to culpable irresponsibility, and how much is due to inescapable victimization?

The temptation will be to sideline theological questions, but a lay be-liever who is striving for reunion will not be satisfied with that. In some contexts, of course, the theological issues can be put to the side as everyone pitches in. Over time, common ministry may result in modified theology on one or both sides. But on the program offered here, there need to be times when the theological and practical questions are brought into focus and made the subject of direct discussion, debate, and even battle. When dealing with broken families, the difference between infant baptism and believer's baptism makes a difference in how the children are regarded. How we think of the relationship between forgiveness and repentance will be implicit in how we deal with anyone who has sold their body for money, and that must be made explicit. The goal here is not to use ministry as an occasion for theological dispute. The theological dispute is there, whether ignored or engaged. The goal is to make everyone more effective in ministry by achieving deeper unity in ministry. This does not make ministry easier. On the contrary, it may make ministry much more challenging and contentious. It may cause fragmentation and splitting of ministries. But if the differences are profound, they had the potential to split the ministry anyway.

Outside the ministry context, lay Christians might also look for op-portunities to move beyond the "agree to disagree" stage of interdenomi-national relations. They should talk about differences of practice, liturgy, and theology, and they must listen carefully. Laypeople must strive to put the prejudices of historical debates to the side while listening to what another believer actually believes. They should not assume that a Catholic "worships" Mary or believes that every word from the pope is a fresh addition to Scripture. They should be skeptical of the caricatures and lies that have been spoken about other believers. As Luther said, put the best construction on everything. All Christians should treat their brothers and sisters as brothers and sisters.

The political dimensions of Reformational Catholicism are also crucial for lay believers. As I have argued above, the denominational system of American Christianity has long been in a symbiotic relationship with American civil religion. That has made it exceedingly difficult for many churches to disentangle the kingdom of Christ from the American empire. Few equate the two at a theoretical level, but in practice the two are for most purposes identified. Many American Christians believe that protecting America's interests in the Middle East and avenging the deaths of thousands of Americans on 9/11 were legitimate reasons for invading Iraq. And many believe that illegal immigration is a threat to the fabric of American society and must be opposed. I do not make any judgment about the political issues here. I only note that churches err if they regard these public issues as merely political and not preeminently ecclesial issues. Christians pitch in to help refugees; they send aid to displaced people in the Middle East. But few churches oppose American wars, instruct their young men to refuse to fight, or vigorously criticize American foreign policy.

Reformational Catholicism implies that the most basic political base for the Christian is the church. The church, not America or its interests, is the international context for evaluating and responding to global political events. When American authorities instruct Christians to drop bombs on their brothers and sisters in other countries, we should simply refuse and take the consequences. American interests do not override Christian communion.

Conclusion

Someone once asked me how I respond to the charge that Reformational Catholic churches do not exist. My response is, "That's right. They don't." There are pockets; any church may become a Reformational Catholic congregation in spirit and in practice. But as a visible body it is a church of the future, a city yet to come. That may be bewildering, but it is where Protestants *always* are; it is where all Christians ought always to be. One of the great contributions of Protestantism has been our insistence that we walk by faith, not by sight: here we have no lasting city. Being a Reformational Catholic Christian is a circus ride, a high-wire act with no net but the loving arms of our faithful Father. Christian faith is not safe if you suffer from vertigo, if you are not willing to have your world upended.

It is only in this faith that we can embrace the death that God demands of us. I dearly hope that the Protestant tribalism of American denominationalism dies. I will do all in my power to kill it, not least in myself. I long to see churches that neglect the Eucharist blasted from the earth. I hope to see fragmented Protestantism, anti-liturgical and anti-sacramental Protestantism, thinly biblical Protestantism, anti-doctrinal and anti-intellectual Protestantism, anti-traditional Protestantism, rationalist and nationalist Protestantism slip into the grave—and I will not hesitate to turn that grave into a dance floor. Insofar as these are the things that make Protestants Protestant, I am hoping for the death of Protestantism.

But death is never the last word for the church of the living God, the God who is faithful to death, and then yet again faithful. Christianity and future are synonymous. If Protestant churches must die, they die in faith that they will be raised new, more radiant with glory than ever. If they die, they die to become more and more what we will be. The Creator who said in the fifth and ninth and sixteenth and nineteenth centuries, "It is good," will not finish his work until we come to the final Sabbath, where everything will, once and for all, be very, *very* good.

Notes

Chapter 2 Evangelical Unity

1. For discussion of the sons of God and daughters of men, see chap. 8, under the heading "The World That Then Was."

2. For more on Babelic unity, see my *Between Babel and Beast: America and Empires in Biblical Perspective* (Eugene, OR: Cascade, 2012).

3. The ecumenical leader Willem Visser 't Hooft made a similar point in a 1968 speech at a World Council of Churches meeting at Uppsala:

> The vision of the oneness of humanity is an original and essential part of the biblical revelation. Centuries before Alexander the Great's Oikoumene began to give Mediterranean man an idea of a wider human family, Israel had already recorded its insight that all men are made in the image of God, that they share a common task: to have dominion over the earth, that all were together included in the covenant of God's patience, made with Noah; that all are to be blessed in Abraham. And the Second Isaiah had already prophesied in one of his songs concerning the Servant of Jahveh that he would be a "covenant of humanity" and a light to the nations. . . . This prophecy is fulfilled in Jesus Christ. He is the manifestation of God's love for the whole of mankind. He dies for all and inaugurates the new humanity as the second Adam. When it is said that God makes all things new this means above all that through Christ God re-creates humanity as a family united under his reign. Mankind is one, not in itself, not because of its own merits or qualities. Mankind is one as the object of God's love and saving action. ("Mandate of the Ecumenical Movement," in *The Ecumenical Movement: An Anthology of Key Texts and Voices*, ed. Michael Kinnamon and Brian Cope [Geneva: WCC Publications; Grand Rapids: Eerdmans, 1997], 41)

4. For further discussion of Galatians 3, see N. T. Wright, *Climax of the Covenant: Christ and the Law in Pauline Theology* (Minneapolis: Fortress, 1993), 137–74; also my *Delivered from the Elements of the World* (Downers Grove, IL: InterVarsity, 2016).

5. Wright, *Climax of the Covenant*, 171.

6. As Lesslie Newbigin emphasized regularly, unity is not some marginal desideratum but a central thrust of the gospel itself: "The Gospel comes to men not only as a set of ideas; it does not even come only as a set of ideas which includes the idea of historical actuality. It comes in the concrete actuality of an encounter with God's people. The redemption which God has wrought in Christ is for the world. Its purpose is a new humanity, mankind made one in Christ, converted from that egocentricity which cuts man off from God and his neighbor, restored to

that life of communion for which mankind was created. The firstfruits and instrument of that purpose is the Church. . . . There is no reconciliation to God apart from reconciliation with the fellowship of His reconciled people" (*The Reunion of the Church: A Defence of the South India Scheme*, rev. ed. [1960; repr., Eugene, OR: Wipf & Stock, 2011], 28). See also his powerful tract, *Is Christ Divided? A Plea for Christian Unity in a Revolutionary Age* (Grand Rapids: Eerdmans, 1961). See the similar emphasis in the Princeton Proposal for Christian Unity, published as Carl E. Braaten and Robert W. Jenson, eds., *In One Body through the Cross* (Grand Rapids: Eerdmans, 2003), 13.

7. For Paul, the union of believers with Jesus is so intimate that he can call the church itself "Christ": "As the body is one and yet has many members . . . so also is Christ" (1 Cor. 12:12). This is the biblical source of Augustine's idea of the church as the *totus Christus*, the "whole Christ," Jesus with his Spirit-animated body.

8. Eugen Rosenstock-Huessy, *The Christian Future: Or, The Modern Mind Outrun* (1946; repr., New York: Harper Torchbook, 1966), 62–63.

9. Ibid., 114. Rosenstock-Huessy argues that these three unities form the focal points of the first three millennia of Christianity's history. During the first millennium, the one God of the Bible triumphed over the many gods of Greco-Roman paganism. With the age of exploration during the second millennium, humanity discovered a single world. Toward the end of the second millennium, as communications and transportation technologies advanced, the world grew smaller. Now we can go halfway around the world in a day, write or speak halfway around the world in seconds. Under the oversight of the papacy and the nation-state, modern science disclosed universal physical and chemical realities, and modern politics unified the world in a network of states. The wars that rocked the world early in the twentieth century were symptoms of this unified world: for example, without one world, the United States and Japan would not be proximate enough to fight each other. The work of the third millennium, Rosenstock-Huessy argues, is the establishment of "Man, the great singular of humanity, in one household, over the plurality of races, classes, and age groups." Totalitarianism is a false attempt to unify the race, but it is a sign of the obsessions of the coming centuries: "The theme of future history will not be territorial or political but social: it will be the story of man's creation" (115). Rosenstock-Huessy goes on to match these three unities with the articles of the Apostles' Creed—God the Creator, Redeemer, and Revealer. The first three millennia of the Christian era match these three attributes of God, but history does not follow the order of the creed. The first millennium "was wholly concerned with being the Body of Christ" and thus focused all its attention on the second article, "Jesus the true Christ, his father the true God, the spirit of his Church the Holy Spirit." The second millennium reached back to the first article of the creed, because "after the Christian soul had found its dwelling place in God, the external world could be purged of all ungodliness." Magic and demons were banished from the world, as science made nature "a realm of universal law and order," becoming "a process within the story of salvation." The third millennium lies ahead, and it will take up the challenge of the third article, "to wrestle with the task of revealing God in society." That will partly involve "the revivification of all dead branches of the single human race" and "the reinspiration of all mechanized portions of the single human life" (116). It is not entirely clear what Rosenstock-Huessy has in mind here, but he perhaps is referring to the revival of marginal peoples in Africa, Asia, and Latin America. His prediction of the reinspiration of mechanized humanity is doubtless a reference to the overcoming of Fordist organization of labor. Writing as he was in 1946, his foresight is remarkable.

10. I have noted a few passages, but the theme of unity is a constant one in the New Testament. Jesus is the Good Shepherd who gathers the sheep that there may be "one flock with one shepherd" (John 10:16). Jesus says of his cross, "I, if I am lifted up from the earth, will draw all men to Myself" (John 12:32). As Caiaphas inadvertently predicts, Jesus dies for the nation, "and not for the nation only, but in order that He might also gather together into one the children of God who are scattered abroad" (John 11:52). The resurrection of Lazarus is a

proleptic sign of this great gathering. Jesus prays that his disciples would be one "even as You, Father, are in Me and I in You, that they also may be in Us" (John 17:21). After the Spirit falls at Pentecost, the church continues "with one mind in the temple, breaking bread from house to house" (Acts 2:46). Paul castigates the Corinthians for their divisions (1 Cor. 1:12–15). Each member of the body of Christ receives a gift that he or she is to use for the good of the whole body, but these gifts all come from "one and the same Spirit" (1 Cor. 12:11). The body animated by the Spirit, built by those gifted by the Spirit, is "one" even though it has many members (1 Cor. 12:12). "The body is not one member, but many" (1 Cor. 12:14), but even with its many members it is "one body" (1 Cor. 12:20). There ought to be "no division in the body," and the members preserve unity as they "care for one another" (1 Cor. 12:25). The unity of the body of Christ is so profound that "if one member suffers, all the members suffer with it; if one member is honored, all the members rejoice with it" (1 Cor. 12:26). "There is neither Jew nor Greek, there is neither slave nor free man, there is neither male nor female; for you are all one in Christ Jesus" (Gal. 3:28). In Christ, Jew and gentile are made "one new man" (Eph. 2:15). We are called to Christ's peace, "to which indeed you were called in one body" (Col. 3:15). Jesus died to purchase people "from every tribe and tongue and people and nation" (Rev. 5:9). A great multitude from every tribe, tongue, nation, and people unite in the praise of the one God who is enthroned in heaven (Rev. 7:9).

11. Summarized in Harding Meyer, *That All May Be One: Perceptions and Models of Ecumenicity* (Grand Rapids: Eerdmans, 1999), 46.

12. A classic statement of evangelical suspicion is J. Marcellus Kik, *Ecumenism and the Evangelical* (Philadelphia: Presbyterian and Reformed, 1958).

13. See the brief, not altogether flattering review of the ecumenical movement in Braaten and Jenson, *In One Body*, 18–26. See also Richard John Neuhaus, "Christian Unity: Beginning Again, Again," *First Things*, June 2003, http://www.firstthings.com/article/2003/06/christian-unity-beginning-again-again.

14. What Ephraim Radner describes as the "Church as such" never suffers division. *A Brutal Unity: The Spiritual Politics of the Christian Church* (Waco: Baylor University Press, 2010), 121–68.

15. See the searing critique of such ecclesiologies in Radner, *Brutal Unity*.

16. I lay out the case for "evangelical unity" from a biblical perspective, but a similar argument has been made from a trinitarian starting point. Lutheran theologian Robert Jenson starts from "the patristic concept of *theosis*," or deification, which he describes as "the most precise and compendious possible evocation of the end for which God creates us" ("The Church as *Communio*," in *The Catholicity of the Reformation*, ed. Carl Braaten and Robert Jenson [Grand Rapids: Eerdmans, 1996], 3). *Theosis* does not imply that the Creator-creature distinction is somehow erased; that difference is "indeed absolute and eternal." Far from compromising the Creator-creature distinction, *theosis* is premised on the difference between the infinite God and his creatures: "Precisely because God is the infinite Creator there can be no limit to the modes and degrees of creatures' promised participation in his life." If God were finite, we would run out of new depths of knowing love. Because he is without limit, there is no limit to the fresh ways we may love and know him. Jenson emphasizes that "it is of God's life that we here have to think. Our end is not participation in an abstract essence of Godhead, but in the love that the Father, Son, and Spirit have among themselves." We are what we are—every thing is what it is—as "anticipation of its own participation in God's being." We are *nothing* except the form now of what we will be when we see him face-to-face. And there is no *koinonia* now except one "founded and defined in the *koinonia* that, under the traditional label *perichoresis*, is the life of the triune God." Each hypostasis in this fellowship is "real as and only as the poles of that fellowship," but in this way "the triune hypostases subsist genuinely, as identities capable of fellowship." Again, the Creator-creature distinction is the basis for the possibility of our *theopoiesis* (deification): "As the communion that is God, their communion is at once infinitely intimate and infinitely comprehensive; therefore

they can even make room among them for others. And by God's free choice, that room is opened to created persons, and the church is taken to be those persons" (3). Since things now exist as anticipations of what they will be, the church is presently an anticipation of the entire assembly of the saints. And as the *hypostases* exist only as poles of a fellowship, so churches exist only as communions communing with the larger communion of the saints. As Jenson puts it, "Each local fellowship can know itself as the one church of God only in fellowship with all those other fellowships that know themselves in the same way and with which it will at the end be joined" (4). Trinity is the ground for *theosis*; trinitarian *theosis* is in turn the ground for a catholic ecclesiology. The link between trinitarian theology and catholic ecclesiology is a commonplace of ecumenical theology. See for instance the "Report of the Section on Unity" from the 1961 World Council of Churches assembly in New Delhi, in Kinnamon and Cope, *Ecumenical Movement*, 88–92.

Chapter 3 A Reformed Church

1. For a brief review of the ecumenical import of Vatican II, see Paul D. Murray, "Vatican II: On Celebrating Vatican II as Catholic and Ecumenical," in *The Second Vatican Council: Celebrating Its Achievement and the Future*, ed. Gavin D'Costa and Emma Jane Harris (London: Bloomsbury, 2013), 85–103.

2. Scholars working in the framework of the new institutional economics talk about "path dependence." In developing policy reforms, leaders cannot ignore past developments that have brought us to the present circumstance. Past decisions, conflicts, and actions set constraints on present decisions and actions.

3. In what follows, I have attempted to be realistic. But the nature of the exercise lends itself to idealism, and I have not wholly escaped that trap.

4. The future church will operate according to the standard laid out in "The Faith of the Church," a portion of the Basis of Union for the Churches of South India: "The uniting Churches accept the Holy Scriptures of the Old and New Testaments as containing all things necessary to salvation and as the supreme and decisive standard of faith; and acknowledge that the Church must always be ready to correct and reform itself in accordance with the teaching of those Scriptures as the Holy Spirit shall reveal it" (quoted in Lesslie Newbigin, *The Reunion of the Church: A Defence of the South India Scheme*, rev. ed. [1960; repr., Eugene, OR: Wipf & Stock, 2011], 124). See also Newbigin's explanation and defense of this statement on pp. 124–47.

5. One can imagine, of course, that five thousand years from now, when the reunited church has been lumbering along for several centuries, it too will wear thin. Some of the churches will forget their first love. Some churches may take up the banner of a charismatic leader. The churches will need to be recalled to the faith, and there will be some who will insist on persisting in faithless nominalism. Another Luther may arise, and the church may again be splintered. The church is ruled by the Word of God, and that means she is ruled by the living Lord Jesus by his Spirit. As long as that is true, it remains possible that the churches will divide, fray, and die. And from the stump of a decayed church, a new growth will miraculously emerge. That is not only possible, not only probable; it is a virtual certainty.

6. In the church of the future, the word "sacrament," like the word "ordinance" or some equivalent, will cease to function as a tool of division. Churches will have somewhat different understandings of the mechanism and meaning of the sacraments, but that will not prevent them from acknowledging and sharing one another's sacraments. All churches will recognize that the Lord's Supper is "Communion" and "Eucharist" and "Mass."

7. For a biblical defense of this pattern of "covenant renewal" worship, see Jeffrey Meyers, *The Lord's Service: The Grace of Covenant Renewal Worship* (Moscow, ID: Canon, 2003).

8. I can dream in more detail: Churches in the future will use bread, not specially prepared wafers, stressing the continuity between the church's feast and the meals of daily life. They will use wine, not grape juice, not only because Jesus drank wine but because wine symbolizes

the maturation of the goods of the earth and because wine induces Sabbatical contentment and restfulness. Churches will stress that the Supper is a meal by sitting to eat, as the crowds did in the Gospels. Members will be enthroned as kings and priests to receive the bread and wine of Jesus's royal table. Pastors will pray prayers of blessing and of thanksgiving, as Jesus instructed, and they will pray two prayers, one for the bread and one for the wine, as Jesus did.

9. Inevitably, this will have bureaucratic features. When bishops meet for an ecumenical council, *someone* has to make the arrangements and keep things running on schedule.

10. These are not spiritual beings. Why would Jesus tell *John* to *write* to spiritual beings? Why couldn't Jesus just *talk* to them?

11. Though often accused of emphasizing centralized bureaucracy, the vision of the ecumenical movement has always been oriented to local unity. See Eugene Carson Blake, "A Proposal Toward the Reunion of Christ's Church," in *The Challenge to Reunion*, ed. Robert McAfee Brown and David Scott (New York: McGraw Hill, 1963), 272; Newbigin, *Reunion of the Church*, 12.

12. World Council of Churches, "New Delhi Statement on Unity," December 31, 1961, https://www.oikoumene.org/en/resources/documents/assembly/1961-new-delhi/new-delhi -statement-on-unity.

Chapter 4 The End of Protestantism

1. World Council of Churches, "New Delhi Statement on Unity," December 31, 1961, https:// www.oikoumene.org/en/resources/documents/assembly/1961-new-delhi/new-delhi-statement -on-unity.

2. This distinction is made by H. Richard Niebuhr, *The Social Sources of Denominational-ism* (1929; repr., New York: Living Age Books, 1957), chap. 2. According to Niebuhr's account, the earliest followers of Luther followed him because they were attracted to his appeal to the Sermon on the Mount as much as his appeal to Paul. This impulse continued in the Anabaptist movement, a movement of peasants who insisted on voluntary membership in the church, who rejected sacraments and hierarchy, and who brought into social expression Luther's doctrine of the priesthood of believers. The Peasants' War showed them, Niebuhr said, "that the new Protestantism they had espoused so heartily protested less against their masters than against their masters' enemies and that the new faith dealt with their extreme necessities even less ef-fectively than did the old. The priesthood of all believers, they found, meant deliverance neither from the abstruseness of dogma and the formality of sacramentalism nor from the inequality of political and economic ethics." As a result, "the disinherited were ruled out of Protestantism" and a rift developed between the bourgeois respectability of the Magisterial Reformation and the underclass of the sects.

3. For a critique of the characterization of these wars as "religious," see William Cavanaugh, *The Myth of Religious Violence: Secular Ideology and the Roots of Modern Conflict* (Oxford: Oxford University Press, 2009). Cavanaugh places the "religious wars" in the context of early modern state-building, on which see Charles Tilly, *The Formation of National States in West-ern Europe* (Princeton: Princeton University Press, 1975), and Benedict Anderson, *Imagined Communities: Reflections on the Origin and Spread of Nationalism*, rev. ed. (London: Verso, 2006). Ephraim Radner has critiqued Cavanaugh in *A Brutal Unity: The Spiritual Politics of the Christian Church* (Waco: Baylor University Press, 2012). For a monumental history of the Thirty Years' War, see Peter Wilson, *The Thirty Years War: Europe's Tragedy* (Cambridge, MA: Belknap Press of Harvard University Press, 2011).

4. Mark Greengrass, *Christendom Destroyed: Europe 1517–1648* (New York: Viking, 2014).

5. The boldest recent statement of the effects of the Reformation is the much-debated Brad Gregory, *The Unintended Reformation: How a Religious Revolution Secularized Society* (Cam-bridge, MA: Belknap Press of Harvard University Press, 2012). For an accessible introduction to the controversy, see the forum in *Historically Speaking* 13, no. 3 (2012). Thanks to my colleague Chris Schlect for alerting me to this forum.

6. John T. McNeill, *Unitive Protestantism: The Ecumenical Spirit and Its Persistent Expression* (Louisville: John Knox, 1964), 77.

7. Ibid., 69.

8. Ibid., 71–72.

9. Ibid., 56–57.

10. Ibid., 40.

11. Ibid., 47.

12. Charles Clayton Morrison makes a similar point, noting that because the Catholic Church had been reduced to the hierarchy, the actual body of Christ, one body with many members, had been rendered all but invisible (Morrison, *The Unfinished Reformation* [New York: Harper & Brothers, 1953], 69–70). The terminology of "juridical" and "monarchical" is common in recent *Catholic* critiques of Counter-Reformation ecclesiology.

13. McNeill, *Unitive Protestantism*, 65. That this was more than a rhetorical maneuver is evident, albeit in an extreme form, in an exchange between Luther and Eck at the Leipzig Disputation (1519). McNeill summarizes, saying that for Luther,

> Christianity was vastly wider than Romanism. Against Eck he cited the Greek Church as proof that the "rock" passage in Matthew is not applicable to the Pope, whose connection with "My Church" is with a section of it only. This argument Eck tried to dismiss with contempt: the Greeks, in separating from Rome, he said, became exiles from the faith of Christ. Luther insistently returned to the point, expressing the hope that Eck, "with Eccian modesty," will spare so many thousands of saints, since the Greek Church, though separated from Rome, has endured and will endure. Eck in turn, while he avoids condemning the Greek fathers, has little hope for the salvation of any in the modern East except a few who hold the Roman obedience (*qui Romanam obedientiam tenent*). . . . Eck's expressions were calculated to confirm the differentiation that had arisen in Luther's mind between "catholic church" and "Roman obedience." (66)

14. Quoted in ibid., 73.

15. Quoted in ibid., 80.

16. Ibid., 86.

17. Eamon Duffy, *The Stripping of the Altars: Traditional Religion in England, 1400–1580* (New Haven: Yale University Press, 1992), 379–81.

18. Ibid., 377–78, 384.

19. Carlos M. N. Eyre, *War against the Idols: The Reformation of Worship from Erasmus to Calvin* (Cambridge: Cambridge University Press, 1989); Lee Palmer Wandel, *Voracious Idols and Violent Hands: Iconoclasm in Reformation Zurich, Strasbourg, and Basel* (Cambridge: Cambridge University Press, 1994); Joseph Leo Koerner, *The Reformation of the Image* (Chicago: University of Chicago Press, 2004), part 1.

20. Heiko A. Oberman, *The Two Reformations: The Journey from the Last Days to the New World*, ed. Donald Weinstein (New Haven: Yale University Press, 2003), 62–69. This tradition was carried on by Franciscan theologians such as Bonaventure and Duns Scotus, who developed the "two propositions" of Francis himself, namely, that God is a personal Lord and his action is covenantal. In the place of the Thomists' Supreme Being and Unmoved Mover, the Franciscans taught that God was "the highly mobile covenantal God who acts, a God whose words are deeds and who wants to be known by these deeds." Luther attacked what he viewed as the Pelagianism of the nominalists, but "within a larger frame of reference that, without the Franciscan paradigm, would have been inconceivable."

21. David S. Yeago, "The Catholic Luther," in *The Catholicity of the Reformation*, ed. Carl E. Braaten and Robert W. Jenson (Grand Rapids: Eerdmans, 1996), 13–34.

22. Ibid., 17.

23. "Enjoy," for Augustine, means "enjoy for its own sake, as an end in itself." According to Augustine's formulation, therefore, the only "thing" that should be "enjoyed" is God himself,

and all other things should be used as means to achieve this enjoyment. There is thus a twofold potential for idolatry: enjoying anything other than God turns that thing into an idol, and "using" God to enjoy something else is also an idolatrous attempt to master God, thus in effect making a claim to be God (Augustine, *On Christian Teaching*, Oxford World's Classics, trans. R. P. H. Green [Oxford: Oxford University Press, 1997], 9–10).

24. Quoted in Yeago, "Catholic Luther," 19.

25. Quoted in ibid.

26. Quoted in ibid., 20–21.

27. Ibid., 21.

28. Ibid., 29.

29. Quoted in ibid., 27–28.

30. Quoted in ibid., 31.

31. Calvin's assault on the idolatry of relic veneration also hinged on a turn in sacramental theology. Hence, alongside a satiric burlesque of relic veneration, Calvin insists that relics were spiritually destructive because they pointed sinners away from those designated sites where Christ had promised to make himself available—in baptismal water, through his Word, at the Lord's table, in the fellowship of saints. See Calvin, *An Admonition, Showing the Advantage which Christendom Might Derive from an Inventory of Relics*, in *Selected Works of John Calvin: Tracts and Letters*, 7 vols., ed. and trans. Henry Beveridge (Grand Rapids: Baker, 1983), 1:289–341.

32. For a superbly detailed account of Poissy, see Donald Nugent, *Ecumenism in the Age of the Reformation: The Colloquy of Poissy* (Cambridge, MA: Harvard University Press, 1974).

33. Anthony Milton, *Catholic and Reformed: The Roman and Protestant Churches in English Protestant Thought, 1600–1640* (Cambridge: Cambridge University Press, 1995), esp. chap. 4 ("The Errors of the Church of Rome").

34. Quoted in ibid., 170.

35. Ibid.

36. See ibid., esp. chap. 3.

37. Ibid., 132.

38. Ibid., 133.

39. Ibid., 133n18, refers to Robert Some's *Godly Treatise . . . Touching the Ministerie, Sacraments and the Church* (1588), which included "apposite quotations from Calvin."

40. Some of the arguments got twisted in startling ways. Since her baptism was valid, the Roman church "met the crucial requirement for any church—that by baptism she brought forth children unto God." But the church was so utterly corrupt that some Anglicans thought the children born into her by baptism would inevitably be poisoned. For Richard Field, the best hope was that after baptism infants would die before being poisoned by Catholic doctrine. For some, "the only hope for salvation in the Church of Rome was thus to die immediately after baptism" (Milton, *Catholic and Reformed*, 135). Another argument arose from the conviction that the pope was the antichrist: "Robert Some advanced as his first argument to show that 'the Popish Church is a Church, though not a sound Church' the point that 'the pope is Antichrist, therefore the Church of Rome is a Church.' He was able in 1588 to remark complacently that 'no Protestant doubteth of the antecedent.' If there were no marks of God's church in the popish church, so the argument ran, then Daniel and Paul would not have foretold that Antichrist would sit in it. To deny Rome to be a church was to give Romanists a great advantage, since it implied that the pope could not be Antichrist" (ibid., 139). An underhanded compliment, to say the least.

41. For a fine introduction to this controverted concept, see Ute Lotz-Heumann, "Confessionalization," in *Reformation and Early Modern Europe: A Guide to Research*, ed. David M. Whitford (Kirksville, MO: Truman State University Press, 2008). Lotz-Heumann reviews the literature and includes an extensive bibliography.

42. McNeill, *Unitive Protestantism*, 258.

43. Benjamin Kaplan, *Divided by Faith: Religious Conflict and the Practice of Toleration in Early Modern Europe* (Cambridge, MA: Belknap Press of Harvard University Press, 2010), 37.

44. Ibid., 41–42.

45. Lotz-Heumann, "Confessionalization," 140–41, summarizing the arguments of Wolfgang Reinhard.

46. Luther Peterson, "Johann Pfeffinger's Treatises of 1550 in Defense of Adiaphora: 'High Church' Lutheranism and Confessionalization in Albertine Saxony," in *Confessionalization in Europe, 1550–1700: Essays in Honor of Bodo Nischan*, ed. John M. Headley, Hans J. Hillerbrand, and Anthony J. Papalas (Aldershot, UK: Ashgate, 2004). I found the Peterson quotation in Cavanaugh, *Myth of Religious Violence*, 168. Cavanaugh (170) also cites the conclusion of R. Po-chia Hsia: "The process of political centralization, discernible in the fifteenth century—the adoption of Roman Law, the rise of an academic jurist class, the growth of bureaucracies, and the reduction of local, particularist privileges—received a tremendous boost after 1550. Conformity required coercion. Church and state formed an inextricable matrix of power for enforcing discipline and confessionalism. The history of confessionalization in early modern Germany is, in many ways, the history of the territorial state." Confessionalization was largely sponsored by the state, which "usually played a more crucial role than the clergy in determining the course of confessionalization. . . . Having become the head of their territorial churches, princes understood the imposition of confessional conformity both as an extension of their secular authority and as the implementation of God's work." Necessarily, this enforcement of uniform confession meant that "local and particular privileges had to be swept aside; estates, towns, cloisters, and nobility resisted confessionalization behind the bulwark of corporate privileges." The resistance worked for a longer while than we think. Even in 1624, in the region around Osnabruck, most of the clergy could not be easily categorized as Lutheran or Catholic. Hsia, *Social Discipline in the Reformation: Central Europe, 1550–1750* (London: Routledge, 1992).

47. Scott M. Manetsch, *Calvin's Company of Pastors: Pastoral Care and the Emerging Reformed Church, 1536–1609* (Oxford: Oxford University Press, 2012), 96.

48. Ibid.

49. In 1500, Europe had five hundred independent political units. Four centuries later, it had twenty-something. The streamlining of the map of Europe was not accentual but rather the result of deliberate efforts at state building. According to Charles Tilly, "State-makers only imposed their wills on the populace through centuries of ruthless effort. The effort took many forms: creating distinct staffs dependent on the crown and loyal to it; making those staffs (armies and bureaucrats alike) reliable, effective instruments of policy; blending coercion, co-optation, and legitimation as means of guaranteeing the acquiescence of different segments of the population; acquiring sound information about the country, its people and its resources; promoting economic activities which would free or create resources for the use of the state" (*The Formation of National States in Western Europe* [Princeton: Princeton University Press, 1975], 24). It wasn't pretty. Any consolidation of power like that of early modern Europe leaves a lot of losers behind, and victorious state builders frequently consolidated by force: "For all their reputed docility, the ordinary people of Europe fought the claims of central states for centuries. In England, for example, the Tudors put down serious rebellions in 1489 (Yorkshire), 1497 (Cornwall), 1536 (the Pilgrimage of Grace), 1547 (the West), 1549 (Kent's Rebellion), 1553 (Wyatt's Rebellion), all responding in one way or another to the centralizing efforts of the crown." During the seventeenth century, the revolutions "grew most directly from the Stuarts' effort to concentrate power in the crown. The result was an enormous amount of conflict and resistance." By the time of the Glorious Revolution of 1688, "conspiracy and rebellion, treason and plot, were a part of the history and experience of at least three generations of Englishmen. Indeed, for centuries the country had scarcely been free from turbulence for more than a decade at a time" (23).

50. Greengrass, *Christendom Destroyed*, 19.

Chapter 5 The Case for Denominationalism

1. I focus on the configuration of the church in the United States, but not because the churches of Europe or of the non-Western world are less important. I focus on the churches I know best. I do not pretend to know all the churches of America intimately, but I know American Christianity better than I know the Christianity of any other part of the world. It also happens to be the case that I am an American, comfortable in my Yankee skin. I hope that some of what I have to say about American denominationalism will be applicable more widely.

2. The literature on denominationalism is vast. H. Richard Niebuhr's *Social Sources of Denominationalism* (New York: Henry Holt, 1929) deserves its reputation as a classic in the sociology of religion, as does Will Herberg's *Protestant-Catholic-Jew: An Essay in American Religious Sociology* (1960; repr., Chicago: University of Chicago Press, 1983). Russell E. Richey, ed., *Denominationalism* (1977; repr., Eugene, OR: Wipf & Stock, 2010) is a compilation of key essays. Ernest Sandeen, "The Distinctiveness of American Denominationalism: A Case Study of the 1846 Evangelical Alliance," *Church History* 45, no. 2 (1976): 222–34, argues that scholars have overstressed the contrast between English and American systems and that denominational Christianity in the States has arisen as much from evangelical pietism as from church-state separation. See also Sidney Mead, "Denominationalism: The Shape of Protestantism in America," reprinted in Richey, *Denominationalism*, 70–105. Mead argues that a denomination is "not primarily confessional" or "territorial" but rather "purposive." A denomination "has no official connection with a civil power whatsoever" but is a "voluntary association of like-hearted and like-minded individuals, who are united on the basis of common beliefs for the purpose of accomplishing some tangible and defined objectives" (71). This situation has produced a distinctive pattern of churchmanship, which Mead summarizes under six heads: (1) a denominational church has a "sectarian" tendency to "justify its peculiar interpretations and practices as more closely conforming to those of the early Church as pictured in the New Testament than the views and politics of its rivals" (75–76); (2) denominations are based on a voluntary principle and depend on persuasion rather than coercion; (3) denominations are missionary organizations, and this mission-mindedness has accounted too for the "interdenominational or superdenominational consciousness and cooperation which has been such an outstanding aspect of the American religious life" (84); (4) denominations are revivalist; (5) in America, many denominations have defined themselves in opposition to Enlightenment reason while paradoxically accepting the parameters of a church-state settlement rooted in Enlightenment reason; finally, (6) denominational churches are competitive institutions in a religious free market. For more recent treatments, see Robert Bruce Mullin and Russell E. Richey, eds., *Reimagining Denominationalism: Interpretive Essays* (Oxford: Oxford University Press, 1994). Richey, "Denominations and Denominationalism: Past, Present, and Future," *Word & World* 25, no. 1 (2005): 15–22, is a recent update of Richey's arguments. Robert Wuthnow's *Restructuring of American Religion* (Princeton: Princeton University Press, 1990) sets the terms for much of the current discussion of the loosening of denominational loyalties. David Roozen and James Nieman, eds., *Church, Identity and Change: Theology and Denominational Structures in Unsettled Times* (Grand Rapids: Eerdmans, 2005), contests the consensus that denominations are dying; see the editors' introduction (1–14) for a discussion of the meaning of "denomination." William Swatos begins his *Into Denominationalism: The Anglican Metamorphosis* (Storrs, CT: Society for the Scientific Study of Religion, 1979) with a nuanced treatment of the differences between church, sect, and denomination (1–16); see also Swatos, "Beyond Denominationalism?: Community and Culture in American Religion," *Journal for the Scientific Study of Religion* 20, no. 3 (1981): 217–27. David Martin has the virtue of placing the American denominational system in global context; see his *Pentecostalism: The World Their Parish* (Oxford: Blackwell, 2002), 8–9, 28–33. See also Martin's old essay "The Denomination," *British Journal of Sociology* 13 (1962): 1–14. Though my focus here is on American denominationalism, scholars have studied denominationalism on other continents. See, for instance, Erik Berggren, "Pieces in the Puzzle:

A Local Study of Denominationalism and Ethnicity towards Unity in South Africa," *Swedish Missionary Themes* 93, no. 1 (2005): 87–113; Sam Kobia, "Denominationalism in Africa: The Pitfalls of Institutional Ecumenism," *Ecumenical Review* 53, no. 3 (2001): 295–305; Setri Nyomi, "Christian World Communions in Africa: Their Impact in Overcoming Denominationalism," *Ecumenical Review* 53, no. 3 (2001): 333–40.

3. "Our Form of Government," Assemblies of God, March 1, 2010, http://ag.org/top/about /structure.cfm.

4. Swatos, *Into Denominationalism*, 9. See also Swatos, "Beyond Denominationalism?," 217–27.

5. Swatos, *Into Denominationalism*, 12–13.

6. Ibid., 13–14.

7. Ibid., 53–54. The established sect is a key to the history of Anglican denominationalizing that Swatos tells. Following the Glorious Revolution, the Nonjurors broke from the Church of England over Parliament's demand that they swear loyalty to William and Mary. They saw "Parliament's attempt to dictate religion as a . . . serious offence. From their point of view the entire question of the prerogatives of the church with respect to the state re the monarchy was in serious jeopardy of being answered wrongly. Parliament had first been so presumptuous as to remove God's Anointed from the throne and to crown another as the lawful monarch. It was now even further." The Nonjurors saw "pluralism and secularism . . . creeping into the bishops' chairs" (53). Swatos argues that the Nonjurors were sociologically self-aware. They represented what he calls the "exclusivism" and "anti-denominational" tendency of Anglicanism: "It is the sectarian element in Anglicanism that stands over against the much more frequently noted Anglican comprehensiveness. In the church-sect sense, it is a two-edged sword. It militates for churchliness [in a monopolistic setting]. However, when this status is not forthcoming, it moves more or less strongly, depending upon the historical circumstances and the relative strength of the other bodies with which it must contend, toward sectarianism" (54).

8. A handful of colorful wooden "peace churches" still stand in Poland today, legal through restricted Protestant churches in Catholic territories.

9. The archbishop of Canterbury is in the House of Lords, presides at coronations, and leads national days of mourning. The pastor of a large Pentecostal church in London has no such prominence or privilege.

10. Timothy L. Smith gives this vivid description:

> Gone was the material heritage of the European village—the cottages and garden plots, the dam and the mill, the oven and the threshing floor, the sheds and fences, roads and bridges which man and beast required. Even if the land had not lured tradesmen from their crafts, reconstructing the specialization of skills and the extensive division of labor that the colonists had known in Europe would have taken a generation. Nor had they found room about the ships for many of the tools and utensils they required. Homes had to be built at once, and crude furnishings—if possible, at least, a bed—fashioned out of materials found nearby. Fields must be cleared and planted and laboriously tended, and boats built by unaccustomed hands for fishing and trade. They must soon begin the arduous toil of making linen cloth, using spinning wheels and looms also constructed on the spot. ("Congregation, State, and Denomination: The Forming of the American Religious Structure," in Richey, *Denominationalism*, 50)

11. Ibid., 54.

12. Ibid., 59.

13. See Alan Heimert, *Religion and the American Mind* (Cambridge, MA: Harvard University Press, 1966).

14. Winthrop Hudson, "Denominationalism as a Basis for Ecumenicity," in Richey, *Denominationalism*, 23. See also Richey, "'Catholic' Protestantism and American Denominationalism," *Journal of Ecumenical Studies* 16 (1979): 213–31.

15. Quoted in Hudson, "Denominationalism," 24–25.

16. Quoted in ibid., 26.

17. Quoted in ibid., 29–30.

18. Quoted in ibid., 31–32.

19. Quoted in ibid., 32.

20. Quoted in ibid., 38.

21. Martin, "The Denomination," 5.

22. Robert Wuthnow, *Red State Religion: Faith and Politics in America's Heartland* (Princeton: Princeton University Press, 2011), 58–60. See also Wuthnow's discussion of the interdenominational features of international missions efforts in *Boundless Faith: The Global Outreach of American Churches* (Berkeley: University of California Press, 2010), 98–139. Not only congregations but also individuals have many contacts outside their denominational networks. "Network closure" is higher among parents and teens who attend religious services regularly; see Christian Smith, "Religious Participation and Network Closure among American Adolescents," *Journal for the Scientific Study of Religion* 42, no. 2 (2003): 259–67. Among adults, networks do follow denominational and religious lines, but not completely; interreligious associations are common. See Christopher Scheitle and Buster Smith, "A Note on the Frequency and Sources of Close Interreligious Ties," *Journal for the Scientific Study of Religion* 50, no. 2 (2011): 410–21.

23. Nancy Tatom Ammerman, *Pillars of Faith: American Congregations and Their Partners* (Berkeley: University of California Press, 2005), 160, 162. Ammerman discusses interdenominational benevolence at length (159–78). See the similar conclusions of Mark Chaves, *Congregations in America* (Cambridge, MA: Harvard University Press, 2004), 202–11.

24. Ammerman, *Pillars of Faith*, 163. See the similar conclusions of Ammerman's earlier study, *Congregation and Community* (New Brunswick, NJ: Rutgers University Press, 1997), 346–70.

25. This is the "heretical imperative," the imperative to choose, outlined by Peter Berger in a book of that title (*The Heretical Imperative: Contemporary Possibilities of Religious Affirmation* [Garden City, NY: Anchor/Doubleday, 1979]).

26. Robert D. Putnam and David E. Campbell, *American Grace: How Religion Divides and Unites Us* (New York: Simon & Schuster, 2012), 19.

27. Ibid., 21–22. See the similar results of Rodney Stark and his team in *What Americans Really Believe* (Waco: Baylor University Press, 2008).

28. Roger Finke and Rodney Stark, *The Churching of America, 1776–2005: Winners and Losers in Our Religious Economy* (New Brunswick, NJ: Rutgers University Press, 2005), 10.

29. Rational choice analyses that treat religious groups as competitors in a marketplace illuminate certain features of American religious life but miss others. Theorists argue that "religion flourishes under free-market conditions" and regard the separation of church and state "as a beneficial development for religion. Freed from state control, religion is able to develop in multiple ways that include organizations for minority populations." Rational choice theory attempts to explain the conservatism of American Christianity and is able to explain what secularization theory has trouble examining—the fact of religion's continuing potency in "late modernity." Answering Dean Kelley's question about "why conservative churches are growing," rational choice theory claims (in the words of Robert Wuthnow) that "small, conservative sects grow and flourish because they provide distinctive rewards for their members and institute strict moral practices that exclude free riders from becoming burdensome to the group." Wuthnow argues that rational choice theory misses critical factors: "Its emphasis on competition among religious organizations as the force propelling growth is too simple. It does little better than [secularization theory] in focusing attention on the relationships between blacks and whites or in specifying the conditions giving rise to competition among leaders within the same denomination or the reasons behind incidents of particular competition between Protestants and Catholics. The effects of population growth, changes in the economy, distance, and how people coped with the difficulties of daily existence have no place in the story. Nor is much attention

given to the relationships among churches and secular competitors or to religious entities' responses to political issues" (Robert Wuthnow, *Rough Country: How Texas Became America's Most Powerful Bible-Belt State* [Princeton: Princeton University Press, 2014], 452–53). R. Stephen Warner's "Work in Progress toward a New Paradigm for the Sociological Study of Religion in the United States," *American Journal of Sociology* 98, no. 5 (1993): 1044–93, is a defining essay on the development of the new paradigm in sociology of religion; see also Warner, "The World Is Not Flat: Theorizing Religion in Comparative and Historical Context," Association of Religion Data Archives, accessed September 25, 2015, http://www.thearda.com/rrh/papers/guidingpapers /ARDA_GuidingPapers_Warner.pdf.

30. Finke and Stark, *Churching of America*, 12.

31. David Martin makes many of the same points in a more measured way when he describes the advantages of fundamentally "Methodist" shape of American Christianity. He points out, for example, that even the "base communities" of Latin American liberation Catholicism were under the oversight of the hierarchy and were limited in their ability to respond to the needs they tried to address. Literal Methodists, by contrast, burned through the American frontier planting churches because they were not beholden to a conservative hierarchy.

32. On the differences between Anglo-American and Latin modes of modernization, see David Martin, *Tongues of Fire: The Explosion of Protestantism in Latin America* (London: Blackwell, 1990), chaps. 1–2. For a more theoretical discussion, see Wuthnow, *Rough Country*, 448–82. Roger Finke and Rodney Stark enthuse, somewhat immoderately, over the advantages of America's "free market" in religion; see *Churching of America*, 8–12. Their subtitle, *Winners and Losers in Our Religious Economy*, could have come from Donald Trump.

33. Nancy Tatom Ammerman, "Denominations: Who and What Are We Studying?" in Mullin and Richey, *Reimagining Denominationalism*, 115.

34. H. Richard Niebuhr, *The Social Sources of Denominationalism* (1929; repr., New York: Living Age Books, 1957), 214. See also Timothy L. Smith, "Religion and Ethnicity in America," *American Historical Review* 83, no. 5 (1978): 1155–85.

35. On the declining importance of ethnicity, see Ammerman, *Pillars of Faith*, 129, 138–39. Also Putnam and Campbell, *American Grace*, 289. Putnam and Campbell observe that cross-class fellowship is most common within evangelical churches (258).

36. Ammerman, "Denominations," 115. Ammerman offers a striking illustration of the professionalization of denominational life from the Southern Baptist Convention (SBC): "Long-standing tradition . . . has called for each church to send messengers to an annual meeting of the local association of churches bearing a letter of greeting. The churches all reported on the triumphs and struggles of their congregations during the year and perhaps even posed a perplexing theological or disciplinary question or two." In the SBC, that practice persists in a very different form: "What the church sends is now called a *Uniform* Church Letter (UCL, to the bureaucrats who handle them), and it resembles IRS form 1040 more than it does a friendly letter. It is full of technical language, with boxes to be filled in and columns to be added. It assumes that the programs in each church correspond to the plans and materials that have been formulated at headquarters, therefore making their outcomes reportable in uniform fashion. . . . It is the perfect example of the standardizing and quantifying Max Weber would have expected" (Ammerman, "Denominations," 116–17). The older practice is still carried on in some churches: one of the treasured moments of the meetings of the Presbyterian Church in America's Pacific Northwest Presbytery is the time devoted to church reports, delivered in person by a pastor or elder, followed by prayer. See Christopher R. Schlect, "Onward Christian Administrators" (PhD diss., Washington State University, 2015), who focuses on the Presbyterian schism.

37. Russell Richey, "Denominations and Denominationalism: An American Morphology," in Mullin and Richey, *Reimagining Denominationalism*, 77.

38. Ammerman, "Denominations," 120. Richey traces five stages in the history of American denominationalism: (1) "ethnic voluntarism or provincial voluntarism"; (2) "purposive mission-

ary association"; (3) a "churchly" style, inspired by Romanticism, that "took expressive form in both high-church and primitivist movements"; (4) a "corporate or managerial" stage at the beginning of the twentieth century; and (5) a form that combines "a number of contemporary cultural forms—the franchise, the regulatory agency, the caucus, the mall, the media" (Richey, "Denominations and Denominationalism," 77).

Chapter 6 The Case against Denominationalism

1. Sidney Mead, "Denominationalism: The Shape of Protestantism in America," in *Denominationalism*, ed. Russell E. Richey (1977; repr., Eugene, OR: Wipf & Stock, 2010), 75–76.

2. Ibid., 80.

3. C. Peter Wagner, *Our Kind of People: The Ethical Dimensions of Church Growth in America* (Atlanta: John Knox, 1979), 147, quoted in Michael O. Emerson and Christian Smith, *Divided by Faith: Evangelical Religion and the Problem of Race in America* (Oxford: Oxford University Press, 2001), 144. See the similar criticism of Charles Clayton Morrison, *The Unfinished Reformation* (New York: Harper & Brothers, 1953), 81–83. Wagner is summarizing the work of Dean Kelley, *Why Conservative Churches Are Growing: A Study in Sociology of Religion* (New York: Harper & Row, 1972).

4. Emerson and Smith, *Divided by Faith*, 142–43.

5. Ibid., 144.

6. Ibid., 145.

7. Ibid.

8. See Robert D. Putnam and David E. Campbell, *American Grace: How Religion Divides and Unites Us* (New York: Simon & Schuster, 2012), 288–91.

9. For an honest assessment of the intertwining of German ethnicity and eucharistic theology in the Lutheran Church–Missouri Synod, see David L. Carlson, "Fellowship and Communion in the Postmodern Era: The Case of the Lutheran Church–Missouri Synod," in *Church, Identity, and Change: Theology and Denominational Structures in Unsettled Times*, ed. David A. Roozen and James R. Nieman (Grand Rapids: Eerdmans, 2005), 263–93, esp. 266–77.

10. Carl E. Braaten and Robert W. Jenson, eds., *In One Body through the Cross: The Princeton Proposal for Christian Unity* (Grand Rapids: Eerdmans, 2003), 34.

11. Lesslie Newbigin, *The Reunion of the Church: A Defence of the South India Scheme*, rev. ed. (1960; repr., Eugene, OR: Wipf & Stock, 2011), 12. Personnel and resources are divvied up among denominations, which sometimes leads to poor use of resources. First Presbyterian sees a need in its local community and launches a ministry to address it. Third Baptist sees the same need and launches a ministry to address it. In the best of circumstances—in many situations—the two churches will know of one another and find ways to cooperate in ministry. The more denominationally minded the churches are, though, the less likely they are to cooperate, and the more likely they are to compete in the ministry. A hardcore Presbyterian church will want to address the issue in a peculiarly Presbyterian way, since that is, of course, the biblical way. Hardcore Baptists will address the need in a uniquely Baptist fashion, since that is, self-evidently, the biblical way. Weighty as such pragmatic arguments may be, they are not central to my purpose. Judging the church by standards of efficiency seems to be a systematic exercise in worldliness.

12. H. Richard Niebuhr, *The Social Sources of Denominationalism* (1929; repr., New York: Living Age Books, 1957), 21.

13. Newbigin, *Reunion of the Church*, 16.

14. Morrison, *Unfinished Reformation*, 46–47.

15. John Murray Cuddihy, *No Offense: Civil Religion and Protestant Taste* (New York: Seabury, 1978), 22.

16. J. Gresham Machen, *Christianity and Liberalism*, new ed. (Grand Rapids: Eerdmans, 2009). George Lindbeck, *The Nature of Doctrine: Religion and Theology in a Postliberal Age*

(Louisville: Westminster John Knox, 1984), describes liberalism as holding to an "experiential-expressive" view that treats doctrine as a symbolization of religious experience.

17. Machen himself helped found the Orthodox Presbyterian Church. Though the doctrinal issues were real and Machen entirely sincere, the story of the Presbyterian schism is of course complicated by other factors—personalities, turf wars, money. Theological differences were not as stark as has sometimes been portrayed. See Christopher R. Schlect, "Onward Christian Administrators" (PhD diss., Washington State University, 2015), who situates the fundamentalist-modernist controversy within an account of the organizational revolution of American denominationalism.

18. Braaten and Jenson, *In One Body*, 39, 43. See also Morrison, *Unfinished Reformation*, 84.

19. Sidney Mead argues that American denominationalism's "voluntaryism" works against deep theology. Denominations are defined by activity more than theology, and Mead thinks this encourages the idea that Christian faith itself is "an activity, a movement, which the group is engaged in promoting." This setting encourages the formation of certain kinds of leaders, and not ones who are profound theologians: "Whatever else top denominational leaders may be, they *must* be denominational politicians" (Mead, "Denominationalism," 75–102).

20. See Russell E. Richey, "Denominations and Denominationalism," in *Reimagining Denominationalism: Interpretive Essays*, ed. Robert Bruce Mullin and Russell E. Richey (Oxford: Oxford University Press, 1994), 83, concerning the division of churches over slavery:

> Whether . . . ecclesiastical issues of slavery divided the churches, historians debate and will doubtless continue to debate. What needs to be affirmed here is that slavery exposed important ecclesiastical issues and that after these divisions, if not before, each of the sectional churches found it important to construe its purposes in theological and ecclesiastical terms. So Old and New Schools, the Wesleyans, and both northern and southern Baptists and Methodists emerged from their respective division intensely committed to and defining themselves in terms of certain ecclesiological principles. A new quasi-confessionalism, then, derived from the slavery and sectional crises, from the divisions, and intensified itself greatly during and after the Civil War . . . as the churches fought each other altar to altar, laid blame on the other for the war, waved the bloody flag, and proclaimed themselves the true sons of the founder.

21. John Sutton and Mark Chaves, "Explaining Schism in American Protestant Denominations, 1890–1990," *Journal for the Scientific Study of Religion* 43, no. 2 (2004): 171. In this, they contest the analysis of Dean Hoge, *Division in the Protestant House: The Basic Reasons behind Intra-Church Conflicts* (Philadelphia: Westminster, 1976), who sees the theological issues as fundamental.

22. Sutton and Chaves, "Explaining Schism," 175.

23. Ibid., 185. This is a central argument of Schlect, "Onward Christian Administrators."

24. Sutton and Chaves, "Explaining Schism," 185. They recognize the irony of these findings: "At least since Niebuhr, ecumenically minded observers of American religion have presumed that large numbers of denominations represent the failure to bring together American Protestants under one organizational umbrella. By this light, denominational mergers were the organizational goals to be pursued, since each new merger would reduce the denominational Babel. The irony arises from our finding that denominational consolidation, including merger, has been a major source of schism" (188).

25. Roger Finke and Christopher P. Scheitle, "Understanding Schisms: Theoretical Explanations for their Origins," in *Sacred Schisms: How Religions Divide*, ed. James R. Lewis and Sarah M. Lewis (Cambridge: Cambridge University Press, 2014), 22, suggest that centralization will reduce the possibility of schism in the Southern Baptist Convention by increasing congregational dependency on the denomination. See also Nancy Tatom Ammerman, *Baptist Battles: Social Change and Religious Conflict in the Southern Baptist Convention* (New Brunswick, NJ: Rutgers University Press, 1995), 258–71, who argues that the chances of schism were low

because most congregations expected to carry on without much change. See also Michael I. Harrison and John K. Maniha, "Dynamics of Dissenting Movements within Established Organizations: Two Cases and a Theoretical Interpretation," *Journal for the Scientific Study of Religion* 17, no. 3 (1978): 207–24; the programmatic article by Fred Kniss and Mark Chaves, "Analyzing Intradenominational Conflict: New Directions," *Journal for the Scientific Study of Religion* 34, no. 2 (1995): 172–85; Mary Lou Steed, "Church Schism and Secession: A Necessary Sequence?," *Review of Religious Research* 27, no. 4 (1986): 344–55. For a careful study of a schism in the Serbian Orthodox Church, see Frank J. Fahey and Djuro J. Vrga, "The Anomic Character of a Schism: Differential Perception of Functions of the Serbian Orthodox Church by Two Feuding Factions," *Review of Religious Research* 12, no. 3 (1971): 177–85; Fahey and Vrga, "The Relationship of Religious Practices and Beliefs to Schism," *Sociological Analysis* 31, no. 1 (1970): 46–55. On the complications of church mergers over the century 1890–1990, see Mark Chaves and John Sutton, "Organizational Consolidation in American Protestant Denominations, 1890–1990," *Journal for the Scientific Study of Religion* 43, no. 1 (2004): 51–66.

26. Churches in the National or World Council of Churches were less likely to divide; membership in the National Association of Evangelicals (given their data) had a null effect on schism. Thus, while the congregations that result from dividing churches almost always retain their denominational affiliation (Methodist schisms produce two Methodist churches), "theology becomes relevant in the form of federation affiliation" (Sutton and Chaves, "Explaining Schism," 187). Robert C. Liebman, John R. Sutton, and Robert Wuthnow, "Exploring the Social Sources of Denominationalism: Schisms in American Protestant Denominations, 1890–1980," *American Sociological Review* 53 (1988): 351, agrees: "When the effect of size is controlled, linkage to a liberal denominational federation inhibits schism."

27. Finke and Scheitle, "Understanding Schisms," 22–23.

28. J. Gordon Melton, *Encyclopedia of American Religions*, 7th ed. (New York: Thomson Gale, 2003), 1.

29. Joseph M. Bryant, "Persecution and Schismogenesis," in Lewis and Lewis, *Sacred Schisms*, 154–55. The term "schismogenesis" comes from Gregory Bateson. See also Marshall Sahlins, *Culture in Practice: Selected Essays* (New York: Zone, 2000), 493–94.

30. Will Herberg, "Religion in a Secularized Society, II: Some Aspects of America's Three Religion Pluralism," *Review of Religious Research* 4 (1962): 36.

31. Ibid., 35.

32. See his classic exposition in *Protestant-Catholic-Jew: An Essay in American Religious Sociology* (1960; repr., Chicago: University of Chicago Press, 1983).

33. Herberg, "Religion in a Secularized Society," 39.

34. Melton, *Encyclopedia of American Religions*, 15–16.

35. Herberg, "Religion in a Secularized Society," 38.

36. David Sehat, *The Myth of American Religious Freedom* (Oxford: Oxford University Press, 2011).

37. Even churches that are used to functioning as *churches* adjust to the American scene: "Even American Catholics have come to think in such terms; theologically, the Catholic Church, of course, continues to regard itself as the one true church, but in their actual social attitudes American Catholics, hardly less than American Protestants or American Jews, tend to think of their church as a kind of denomination existing side by side with other denominations in a pluralistic harmony that is felt to be somehow of the texture of American life" (Herberg, "Religion in a Secularized Society," 35). For an overview of the Americanization of the Catholic Church, see José Casanova, *Public Religions in the Modern World* (Chicago: University of Chicago Press, 1994), 167–207.

38. Herberg, "Religion in a Secularized Society," 44–45. Civil religion has been a recurring theme in studies of American religion. See Robert Bellah, *The Broken Covenant: American Civil Religion in a Time of Trial* (Chicago: University of Chicago Press, 1992); Robert Bellah

and Phillip Hammond, *Varieties of Civil Religion* (1980; repr., Eugene, OR: Wipf & Stock, 2013); Sidney Mead, *The Nation with the Soul of a Church* (New York: Harper & Row, 1975). In a remarkable article, Fenggang Yang and Helen Rose Ebaugh drew on a study of eight immigrant religious groups in Houston to show how the groups reacted to their replanting in the American environment. In one way after another, each group adjusted to its American planting by becoming American, by being remade in the image of American Protestantism. See Yang and Ebaugh, "Transformations in New Immigrant Religions and Their Global Implications," *American Sociological Review* 66, no. 2 (2001): 269–88.

39. Mead, "Denominationalism," 83.

40. Cuddihy, *No Offense*, 31–43, offers Reinhold Niebuhr's transformation from Missouri Lutheran to urbane public theologian as a cautionary tale. Tolerance depends on "broken confidence in the finality of our own truth." Niebuhr's ultimate theological solution was to distinguish between faith and the expressions of faith; each religion proclaims its "highest insights" yet retains "an honorable and contrite recognition of the fact that all actual expressions of religious faith are subject to historical contingency and relativity." Niebuhr came to an Aristotelian moderation by insisting that we must operate with "some *decent* consciousness of the relativity of our own statement of even the most ultimate truth."

41. Niebuhr, *Social Sources*, 128. Roger Putnam makes the same point when he observes that Americans are not "true believers" (Putnam and Campbell, *American Grace*, 543–44). David Dockery hesitantly suggests that denominationalism "has resulted more in the Americanization of Christianity than the Christianization of America" ("So Many Denominations: The Rise, Decline, and Future of Denominationalism," in *Southern Baptists, Evangelicals, and the Future of Denominationalism*, ed. David Dockery [Nashville: B&H Academic, 2011], 13).

42. Cuddihy, *No Offense*, 42.

43. Ibid., 43.

44. Emerson and Smith, *Divided by Faith*, 162.

45. W. E. B. DuBois, "Will the Church Remove the Color Line?" *Christian Century*, December 9, 1931, quoted in ibid. Emerson and Smith offer one example: Does Christianity support economic inequality? Some Christians cite Christian reasons for answering yes; others cite Christian reasons for answering no. The two "compete ideologically against each other, fragmenting the religious voice." If there is an equality of power, the two voices neutralize each other. But power isn't equal, and so, Emerson and Smith argue, "at least in race relations, the dominant white religious voices, amid the vast variety, are nearly always those that are least prophetic, most supportive of the status quo. It is not just that the prophetic voice is fragmented; the prophetic voices that call for overcoming group divisions and inequalities are ghettoized" (Emerson and Smith, *Divided by Faith*, 162–64).

46. Emerson and Smith, *Divided by Faith*, 164–65.

47. Paul Murray, *Receptive Ecumenism and the Call to Catholic Learning: Exploring a Way for Contemporary Ecumenism* (Oxford: Oxford University Press, 2010).

Chapter 7 Denominationalism's Dividing Walls

1. Newman Smyth, *Passing Protestantism and Coming Catholicism* (New York: Scribner, 1908).

2. H. Richard Niebuhr, *The Social Sources of Denominationalism* (1929; repr., New York: Living Age Books, 1957), 240.

3. Ibid., 242.

4. Ibid., 247–49.

5. Ibid., 253.

6. Ibid., 261.

7. Ibid., 258–59, 263.

8. In *American Grace: How Religion Divides and Unites Us* (New York: Simon & Schuster, 2012), Robert D. Putnam and David E. Campbell treat black Protestantism as a distinct religious tradition, different from both evangelicalism and mainline Protestantism.

9. Charles Wilson Reagan, *Judgment and Grace in Dixie: Southern Faiths from Faulkner to Elvis* (Athens: University of Georgia Press, 1995).

10. Michael O. Emerson and Christian Smith, *Divided by Faith: Evangelical Religion and the Problem of Race in America* (Oxford: Oxford University Press, 2001), 74. For a brief summary of Emerson and Smith's argument, see Michael O. Emerson, "The Persistent Problem," Center for Christian Ethics at Baylor University, 2010, http://www.baylor.edu/content/services /document.php/110974.pdf.

11. Emerson and Smith, *Divided by Faith*, 76.

12. Ibid., 76–77.

13. Ibid., 77–78.

14. Ibid., 78–79.

15. Ibid., 89–90. Emerson and Smith speak of a "racialized," not a "racist," society, defining it as "a society wherein race matters profoundly for differences in life experiences, life opportunities, and social relationships" (7). It is not a society filled with racial hatreds but a society in which race matters *a lot*.

16. Robert Wuthnow, *Red State Religion: Faith and Politics in America's Heartland* (Princeton: Princeton University Press, 2014), 60.

17. Ibid., 209.

18. Ibid., 210–11.

19. Will Herberg, *Protestant-Catholic-Jew: An Essay in American Religious Sociology* (1960; repr., Chicago: University of Chicago Press, 1983), 155.

20. Ibid., 155–56.

21. "Pluralism, National Menace," *The Christian Century*, June 13, 1951, 701–3, quoted in ibid., 252.

22. Ibid., 160–61.

23. Some Catholics were remarkably eager to appear American. In an address to Congress in 1826, John England, bishop of Charleston, insisted that he was a big fan of the American system: "I would not allow to the Pope, or to any bishop of our church, outside the Union, the smallest interference with the humblest vote at our most insignificant balloting box. He has no right to such interference. You must, from the view which I have taken, see the plain distinction between spiritual authority and a right to interfere in the regulation of human government or civil concerns. You have in your constitution wisely kept them distinct and separate" (José Casanova, *Public Religions in the Modern World* [Chicago: University of Chicago Press, 1994], 171).

24. John Pinheiro, *Missionaries of Republicanism: A Religious History of the Mexican-American War* (New York: Oxford University Press, 2014), 25–26.

25. Ibid., 26.

26. Ibid., 27–28.

27. Ibid., 13.

28. David Sehat, *The Myth of American Religious Freedom* (Oxford: Oxford University Press, 2011), 189.

29. Ibid., 189–90.

Chapter 8 From Glory to Glory

1. As always, I am dependent on the work of James Jordan throughout this chapter. See especially *Through New Eyes: Developing a Biblical View of the World* (Eugene, OR: Wipf & Stock, 1999) and *Crisis, Opportunity, and the Christian Future* (Monroe, LA: Athanasius, 2009).

2. Eugen Rosenstock-Huessy, *The Christian Future: Or, the Modern Mind Outrun* (New York: Harper, 1946), 60.

3. The verb typically has a judicial sense (cf. Gen. 15:14; 30:6; 49:16; Deut. 32:36; 1 Sam. 2:10). As Paraclete (*parakletos*), the Spirit strives to convict the world of sin, righteousness, and judgment (see John 16:8). Prior to the flood, the human race is so thoroughly fleshly that its members do not respond to the striving of the Spirit.

4. On the connection between fleshliness and violence, see my *Delivered from the Elements of the World* (Downers Grove, IL: InterVarsity, 2016).

5. Both Cain and Abel bring *minchot*, "tribute offerings."

6. This is an indirect refutation of Satan's charge against God. Satan convinced Adam that Yahweh was greedily protecting his own privileges, his power to "know good and evil" and to pass judgment. That was never Yahweh's plan, and the gift of authority to Noah is proof that God intended to share his authority with his human sons and daughters. His generosity is evident when he gives Noah divine power, the authority to kill.

7. For further reflection on the significance of circumcision, see my *Delivered from the Elements of the World*.

8. When Moses returned to Egypt from Midian, he met Aaron, who assembled the "elders of the sons of Israel" to hear what Moses had to say (Exod. 4:27–31).

9. We arrive at this conclusion as follows: The battle of Aphek occurred in Samuel's youth. When he had full-grown sons, the people asked for a king (1 Sam. 8), which implies a passage of at least a couple of decades. To this we add the forty years of Saul's reign and the forty years of David's reign, and we arrive at approximately a century. Solomon began the temple in his fourth year (1 Kings 6:1) and finished in his eleventh year (1 Kings 6:37–38).

10. For more discussion of this Israel-among-gentiles arrangement, see my *Between Babel and Beast: America and Empires in Biblical Perspective* (Eugene, OR: Cascade Books, 2012).

Chapter 9 The Restructuring of Global Christianity

1. Philipp Blom, *Fracture: Life and Culture in the West, 1918–1938* (New York: Basic Books, 2015), 3–4. See Blom's earlier *The Vertigo Years: Change and Culture in the West, 1900–1914* (New York: Basic Books, 2010).

2. Blom, *Fracture*, 9.

3. Hugo Ball, *Schriften zum Theater, zur Kunst und Philosophie*, http://www.textlog .de/39027.html, quoted in ibid., vii.

4. The same, of course, could be said of every other major juncture in biblical history: Ahab was the worst of the kings of Israel, but it was during his reign that Elijah's ministry began; Nebuchadnezzar took Judah off into Babylonian exile, but that gave Jews their greatest opportunity for international influence ever. Because God is God, the worst of times are always also the best of times.

5. Scott W. Sunquist, *Understanding Christian Mission: Participation in Suffering and Glory* (Grand Rapids: Baker Academic, 2013), 118. On the epochal demographic shifts in world Christianity, see, briefly, 142–44, 370–95. More fully, see Philip Jenkins, *The Next Christendom: The Coming of Global Christianity*, 3rd ed. (Oxford: Oxford University Press, 2011); Jenkins, *The New Faces of Christianity: Believing the Bible in the Global South* (Oxford: Oxford University Press, 2008); Andrew Walls, *The Missionary Movement in Christian History: Studies in the Transmission of Faith* (Maryknoll, NY: Orbis Books, 1996); Walls, *The Cross-Cultural Process in Christian History: Studies in the Transmission and Appropriation of Faith* (Maryknoll, NY: Orbis Books, 2002); Walls, *Mission in the Twenty-First Century: Exploring the Five Marks of Global Mission* (Maryknoll, NY: Orbis Books, 2008).

6. Will Herberg, *Protestant-Catholic-Jew: An Essay in American Religious Sociology* (1960; repr., Chicago: University of Chicago Press, 1983).

7. For brief introductions to African Christianity and the African Independent Churches in particular, see Walls, *Missionary Movement*, 79–101, 111–18; Walls, *Cross-Cultural Process*, 85–115. See also Afe Adogame, Roswith Gerloff, and Klaus Hock, eds., *Christianity in Africa*

and the African Diaspora: The Appropriation of a Scattered Heritage (London: Continuum, 2008); Rufus Okikiolaolu Olubiyi Ositelu, *African Instituted Churches: Diversities, Growth, Gifts, Spirituality and Ecumenical Understanding of African Initiated Churches* (Münster: LIT Verlag, 2002).

8. Ogbu Kalu, *African Pentecostalism: An Introduction* (Oxford: Oxford University Press, 2008), 45. Kalu tells the same story more briefly in *Cambridge History of Christianity*, vol. 9, *World Christianities, c. 1914–2000*, ed. Hugh McLeod (Cambridge: Cambridge University Press, 2006), 211–12. A few more details are found at Médine Moussounga Keener, "Daniel Ndoundou," Dictionary of African Christian Biography, 2005, http://www.dacb.org/stories /congo/ndoundou_daniel.html. It is remarkably difficult to find information about Kibongi, and I am heavily reliant on Kalu's account. The main account is Carl Sundberg, *Conversion and Contextual Conceptions of Christ: A Missiological Study among Young Converts in Brazzaville, Republic of Congo* (Uppsala: Swedish Institute of Missionary Research, 2000), unfortunately unavailable to me.

9. Quoted in Kalu, *African Pentecostalism*, 46.

10. Ibid.

11. For overviews of Pentecostalism in various parts of the world, see David Martin, *Pentecostalism: The World Their Parish* (Oxford: Blackwell, 2002), 83–118 (for Latin America) and 132–52 (for Africa); Martin, *Tongues of Fire: The Explosion of Protestantism in Latin America* (Oxford: Blackwell, 1990), 49–109, for a country-by-country analysis of Latin America. See also chap. 10 below.

12. The most extensive description of the festival is found on the Aladura website, http://www.aladura.net/tabieorar.htm.

13. See Benjamin C. Ray, "Aladura Christianity: A Yoruba Religion," *Journal of Religion in Africa* 23, no. 3 (1993): 266–91. Though the Aladura sometimes make it sound as if prayer and fasting are "magical," Ray points out that they always acknowledge that God cannot be coerced and *chooses* to answer prayers. In terms made popular by Robin Horton, Aladura shares with traditional Yoruba religion an interest in "explanation, prediction, and control"; see Horton, "African Conversion," *Africa: Journal of International African Institute* 41, no. 2 (1971): 85–108. Christians renounce the means for prediction and control, especially divination, but Aladura Christianity has Christian ways to achieve the same ends.

14. "The Church of the Lord (Aladura)," *Ecumenical Review* 24, no. 2 (1972): 126.

15. Ibid., 126–27.

16. None is more chilling than Rufus Ositelu's prophecy about the United States, delivered at the festival in August 2000, a prediction concerning the year 2001: "Pray for forgiveness of sin in order to receive the grace of God not to allow less-powerful nation[s] to wage war against them." Quoted in "Tabieorar Festival," http://www.aladura.net/tabieorar.htm, citing *Divine Revelations from the Mount Tabieorar for the Year 2001* (Ogere, Nigeria: Grace Enterprises, 2001), 21.

17. Quoted in "Tabieorar Festival," http://www.aladura.net/tabieorar.htm.

18. This congregation, led by Mother Marie Cooper, is one of the subjects of Mark R. Gornik's *Word Made Global: Stories of African Christianity in New York City* (Grand Rapids: Eerdmans, 2011), a superb study of immigrant Christianity.

19. See Kofi Johnson, "Aladura: The Search for Authenticity, an Impetus for African Christianity," *Asian Journal of Pentecostal Studies* 14, no. 1 (2011): 149–65.

20. For overviews of Christianity in China, see Peter van der Veer, *The Modern Spirit of Asia: The Spiritual and the Secular in China and India* (Princeton: Princeton University Press, 2014), 100–113; Mark Noll, *From Every Tribe and Nation: A Historian's Discovery of the Global Christian Story* (Grand Rapids: Baker Academic, 2014), 156–64.

21. Joseph Tse-Hei Lee, "Christianity in Contemporary China: An Update," *Journal of Church and State* 49, no. 2 (2007): 277–304.

22. Grant Wacker, "China's Homegrown Protestants," *Christian Century*, February 6, 2013, 32. Wacker is reviewing Lian Xi's *Redeemed by Fire: The Rise of Popular Christianity in Modern China* (New Haven: Yale University Press, 2010). Daniel Bays claims that "a clear majority of rural churches" after 1980, in the places where the church was growing most rapidly, were "quasi-Pentecostal" in "style" (Bays, *A New History of Christianity in China* [London: Wiley-Blackwell, 2011], 194). Sunquist too claims that many Chinese churches are "Spirit churches" (*Understanding Christian Mission*, 165). Traditional Protestant denominations continue to have an important presence in China; see, for example, Bruce P. Baugus, ed., *China's Reforming Churches: Mission, Polity, and Ministry in the Next Christendom* (Grand Rapids: Reformation Heritage Books, 2014).

23. Bays, *New History*, 195.

24. Older, more established Pentecostal churches are ambivalent about the newer movements. See Kalu, *African Pentecostalism*, 75–82. On the violence of African Christianity, see the various essays in Emmanuel Katongole, *A Future for Africa: Critical Essays in Christian Social Imagination* (Scranton, PA: University of Scranton Press, 2005).

25. This needs to be qualified by the fact that some of these movements are directly inspired by movements that began in the United States. For an example, see the account of contacts between Ernest Angley and Zambian churches in Paul Gifford, *African Christianity: Its Public Role* (Bloomington: Indiana University Press, 1998), 202–3.

26. Sunquist (*Understanding Christian Mission*, 126) uses the phrase "Spirit churches" and defines them as "churches that identify themselves as led by the Spirit rather than schisms from the sixteenth century (Protestant churches), centered in Rome (Roman Catholic Church), or following a theology from the early church councils (Orthodox)." While these churches testify to "the success of Western missionary work," many were formed in express opposition to missionary churches rather than as continuations of them.

27. Quoted in Donald W. Norwood, *Reforming Rome: Karl Barth and Vatican II* (Grand Rapids: Eerdmans, 2015), 38.

28. Ibid., 39.

29. Ibid., 41.

30. Henri de Lubac and Yves Congar were two of the key figures in these developments. See de Lubac, *Catholicism: Christ and the Common Destiny of Man* (San Francisco: Ignatius, 1988). Of Congar's many works, *Lay People in the Church: A Study for a Theology of the Laity*, rev. ed. (Westminster, MD: Newman, 1965), and *True and False Reform in the Church*, rev. ed. (Collegeville, MN: Michael Glazier, 2011), are the most immediately relevant to the concerns of this book.

31. Paul D. Murray, ed., *Receptive Ecumenism and the Call to Catholic Learning: Exploring a Way for Contemporary Ecumenism* (Oxford: Oxford University Press, 2010).

32. Especially in Venice. See David M. Nicol, *Byzantium and Venice: A Study in Diplomatic and Cultural Relations* (Cambridge: Cambridge University Press, 2009).

33. See Paul L. Gavrilyuk, *Georges Florovsky and the Russian Religious Renaissance* (Oxford: Oxford University Press, 2014); Aidan Nichols, *Light from the East: Authors and Themes in Orthodox Theology* (London: Sheed & Ward, 1995).

34. Aidan Nichols, *Rome and the Eastern Churches*, 2nd ed. (San Francisco: Ignatius, 2010), 356.

35. Paul McPartlan, *The Eucharist Makes the Church: Henri de Lubac and John Zizioulas in Dialogue*, 2nd ed. (Fairfax, VA: Eastern Christian Publications, 2006).

36. See Christoph Schwöbel, "The Renaissance of Trinitarian Theology: Reasons, Problems and Tasks," in *Trinitarian Theology Today*, ed. Christoph Schwöbel (London: T&T Clark, 1995), 3–6.

37. Orthodoxy is still largely tied to ethnicity in America. See Alexey Krindatch, "Eastern Christianity in North American Religious Landscape: Ethnic Traditionalism versus Civic

Involvement and Social Transformations," accessed September 25, 2015, http://hirr.hartsem.edu/research/krindatch.pdf.

Chapter 10 American Denominationalism and the Global Church

1. See Philip Jenkins, *The Lost History of Christianity: The Thousand-Year Golden Age of the Church in the Middle East, Africa, and Asia—and How It Died* (San Francisco: Harper-One, 2009).

2. The following sources have been most helpful in getting a grasp on Pentecostal history and its current character: David Martin, *Tongues of Fire: The Explosion of Protestantism in Latin America* (Oxford: Blackwell, 1990); Martin, *Pentecostalism: The World Their Parish* (Oxford: Blackwell, 2002); Martin, "Pentecostalism: Transnational Voluntarism in the Global Religious Economy," in *The Future of Christianity: Reflections on Violence and Democracy, Religion and Secularization* (Surrey: Ashgate, 2011), 63–83; Richard Shaull and Waldo Cesar, *Pentecostalism and the Future of the Christian Churches: Promises, Limitations, Challenges* (Grand Rapids: Eerdmans, 2000). For Africa, see Ogbu Kalu, *African Pentecostalism: An Introduction* (Oxford: Oxford University Press, 2008). David Stoll, *Is Latin America Turning Protestant? The Politics of Evangelical Growth* (Berkeley: University of California Press, 1990), views Latin American Pentecostalism through the lens of US politics. Harvey Cox, *Fire from Heaven: The Rise of Pentecostal Spirituality and the Reshaping of Religion in the Twenty-First Century* (Cambridge, MA: Da Capo, 1995), is informative and lively but somehow contrives to turn the story of global Pentecostalism into a chapter in the story of Harvey Cox.

3. On the early history of the movement, see the vivid account of Cox, *Fire from Heaven*, 45–78.

4. Martin, "Pentecostalism," 67–68.

5. "Spirit and Power—A 10-Country Survey of Pentecostals," Pew Research Center, October 5, 2006, http://www.pewforum.org/2006/10/05/spirit-and-power/.

6. This argument is *not* intended as a criticism of Pentecostalism. I am not trying to deny them entry into the Protestant club; the cocktails are bad, and Pentecostals wouldn't drink them anyway. My point is simply to highlight the novelty of Pentecostalism and to suggest that its sheer existence demands more theological and practical attention, and a more sympathetic assessment, from classic Protestants than we have given it.

7. Martin stresses the analogies between Pentecostalism and Methodism. He traces the genealogy of Pentecostalism back to Wesleyan holiness movements and argues that the Pentecostal churches have an effect on individual members and on their cultures that is similar to the effect of Methodism on converts and on English culture during the eighteenth century. Pentecostalism reenacted the Halévy thesis for Latin America, Africa, and parts of Asia. For this argument, see Martin, *Tongues of Fire*, 27–46, and *Pentecostalism*, 7–11.

8. Both Cox (*Fire from Heaven*, 139–57) and Martin emphasize the role of music in Pentecostalism. Martin regularly cites Élie Halévy's claim that Methodism "saved England from the type of revolutionary upheaval that constantly overtook France" and gives it a musical spin: Pentecostalism forges new forms of sociality in its music; it is "a form of popular culture, and it partly spreads through catchy tunes" ("Pentecostalism," 80).

9. "What Willow Believes," Willow Creek Community Church, accessed August 22, 2015, http://www.willowcreek.org/aboutwillow/what-willow-believes.

10. William Seymour, "Precious Atonement," reprinted in Vinson Synan and Charles R. Fox Jr., *William J. Seymour: Pioneer of the Azusa Street Revival* (Alachua, FL: Bridge Logos Foundation, 2012).

11. Don Williams, "Theological Perspective and Reflection on the Vineyard Christian Fellowship," in *Church, Identity, and Change: Theology and Denominational Structures in Unsettled Times*, ed. David A. Roozen and James R. Nieman (Grand Rapids: Eerdmans, 2005), 181–82.

12. Martin, *Pentecostalism*, 4.

13. Cox, *Fire from Heaven*, 58.

14. "Assemblies of God 2014 Statistics Released, Reveals Ethnic Transformation," Flower Pentecostal Heritage Center, June 18, 2015, https://ifphc.wordpress.com/2015/06/18/assemblies -of-god-2014-statistics-released-reveals-ethnic-transformation/.

15. P. A. Hardiment, "Confessing the Apostolic Faith from the Perspective of the Pentecostal Movement," *One In Christ* 23, nos. 1–2 (1987): 67.

16. Shaull and Cesar, *Pentecostalism and the Future of the Christian Churches*, 105–7.

17. Murl Owen Dirksen, "Pentecostal Healing" (PhD diss., University of Tennessee, Knoxville, 1984), quoted in Martin, *Tongues of Fire*, 165.

18. Martin, *Tongues of Fire*, 165.

19. For various dimensions of this development, see Afe Adogame and James V. Spickard, eds., *Religion Crossing Boundaries: Transnational Religious and Social Dynamics in Africa and the New African Diaspora* (Leiden: Brill, 2010); Fred Kniss and Paul D. Numrich, *Sacred Assemblies and Civic Engagement: How Religion Matters for America's Newest Immigrants* (New Brunswick, NJ: Rutgers University Press, 2007); Manuel Vasquez and Marie Friedman Marquardt, *Globalizing the Sacred: Religion across the Americas* (New Brunswick, NJ: Rutgers University Press, 2003); R. Stephen Warner and Judith Wittner, eds., *Gatherings in Diaspora: Religious Communities and the New Immigration* (Philadelphia: Temple University Press, 1998); R. Stephen Warner, "Religion, Boundaries, and Bridges," *Sociology of Religion* 58, no. 3 (1997): 217–38; Janel Kragt Bakker, "The Sister Church Phenomenon: A Case Study of the Restructuring of American Christianity against the Backdrop of Globalization," *International Bulletin of Missionary Research* 36, no. 3 (2012): 129–34. On the development of transnational migration studies in general, see Peggy Levitt and B. Nadya Jaworsky, "Transnational Migration Studies: Past Developments and Future Trends," *Annual Review of Sociology* 33 (2007): 129–56; Levitt, *The Transnational Villagers* (Berkeley: University of California Press, 2001).

20. Peggy Levitt, *God Needs No Passport: Immigrants and the Changing American Religious Landscape* (New York: New Press, 2007), 11. Levitt speaks of the "new religious architecture" evident in America (chap. 5). See also Martin, *Pentecostalism*, 37–38, who refers to Lux del Mundo as one of the Latin American movements that has made a significant impact on North America. Martin points out (47) that Swedish immigrants to the United States were responsible for establishing the first Pentecostal church in Brazil. Many have noted that the Embassy of God, the largest church in Kiev, Ukraine, is pastored by a Nigerian, Sunday Adelaja. See Michael W. Foley and Dean R. Hoge, *Religion and the New Immigrants: How Faith Communities Form Our Newest Citizens* (Oxford: Oxford University Press, 2007); Levitt, "Between God, Ethnicity, and Country: An Approach to the Study of Transnational Religion" (paper presented at Princeton University, 2001), http://www.transcomm.ox.ac.uk/working%20papers/Levitt.pdf.

21. Helen Rose Ebaugh, "Transnationality and Religion in Immigrant Congregations: The Global Impact," *Nordic Journal of Religion and Society* 23, no. 2 (2010): 111. Religion has been unjustly neglected in studies of globalization and immigration. For a summary of recent literature, see Wendy Cadge and Elaine Howard Ecklund, "Immigration and Religion," *Annual Review of Sociology* 33 (2007): 359–79. See also Jacqueline Hagan and Helen Rose Ebaugh, "Calling upon the Sacred: Migrants' Use of Religion in the Migration Process," *International Migration Review* 37, no. 4 (2003): 1145–62.

22. Chinese immigrants living in the United States nearly doubled between 1980 and 1990, from 299,000 to 536,000 (Kate Hooper and Jeanne Batalova, "Chinese Immigrants in the United States," Migration Policy Institute, January 28, 2015, http://www.migrationpolicy.org /article/chinese-immigrants-united-states). In the year 2000 it was estimated that there were 200,000 Chinese nationals in Europe (Frank Laczko, "Europe Attracts More Migrants from China," Migration Policy Institute, July 1, 2003, http://www.migrationpolicy.org/article /europe-attracts-more-migrants-china).

23. Ruth Gledhill, "Church Attendance Has Been Propped Up by Immigrants, Says Study," *Guardian*, June 3, 2014, http://www.theguardian.com/world/2014/jun/03/church-attendance -propped-immigrants-study.

24. Jehu J. Hanciles, *Beyond Christendom: Globalization, African Migration, and the Transformation of the West* (Maryknoll, NY: Orbis Books, 2008), 306–7. Similar movements are evident among Chinese, Hispanics, and Koreans: "According to the best available estimates, there are over 3,500 Catholic parishes [in the United States] where Mass is celebrated in Spanish, and 7,000 Hispanic/Latino Protestant congregations, most of them Pentecostal or Evangelical churches, and many of them nondenominational. . . . In 1988, the last count available, there were 2,018 Korean-American churches in the United States" (Fenggang Yang and Helen Rose Ebaugh, "Transformations in New Immigrant Religions and their Global Implications," *American Sociological Review* 66, no. 2 [2001]: 271). Already in 1998 there were seven hundred Chinese Protestant churches in the United States (Hanciles, *Beyond Christendom*, 297), and there are Chinese congregations in nearly every state. More than three hundred Chinese congregations exist in Canada; Chinese church leaders meet every month in the cross-denominational Greater Vancouver Chinese Ministerial, and a similar group meets in Toronto (Bruce L. Guenther, "Ethnicity and Evangelical Protestants in Canada," in *Christianity and Ethnicity in Canada*, ed. Paul Bramadat and David Seljak [Toronto: University of Toronto Press, 2008], 379–80). We can only imagine what kind of chemical reaction—religious, political, economic—is going to be catalyzed by the growing Chinese presence in sub-Saharan Africa (Howard French, *China's Second Continent: How a Million Migrants Are Building a New Empire in Africa* [New York: Vintage, 2015]).

25. Hanciles, *Beyond Christendom*, 324.

26. Hanciles (ibid., 297) notes the disparity between the percentage of Christians in South Korea, Taiwan, and China and the large proportion of Christians among migrants. For example, "only 2 percent of the Taiwanese population is Christian; yet 25 to 30 percent of Taiwanese immigrants in the United States are Christians, and as many as two-thirds of the members of the Taiwanese Christian congregations are converts."

27. I have not focused on the most obvious migration, that of Hispanics. Hispanic immigration has already revived the Catholic Church, and in many cities Hispanic churches have been planted from a home base in Latin America. For a brief overview of Hispanic immigration to the United States and its impact on the churches, see M. Daniel Carroll R., *Christians at the Border: Immigration, the Church, and the Bible*, 2nd ed. (Grand Rapids: Brazos, 2013), 1–42. See also the Pew Research Center report "Changing Faiths: Latinos and the Transformation of American Religion," April 25, 2007, http://www.pewhispanic.org/2007/04/25 /changing-faiths-latinos-and-the-transformation-of-american-religion/.

28. Paul Gifford, *African Christianity: Its Public Role* (Bloomington: Indiana University Press, 1998), 221.

29. Ibid., 183, 307.

30. My evidence is anecdotal, coming from a conversation with a Zimbabwean pastor who now serves a church in Anniston, Alabama.

31. Hanciles, *Beyond Christendom*, 320–21.

32. Ibid., 328–33.

33. Ibid., 337. As Peggy Levitt makes clear, not every Christian option in the States originated in the States. See Levitt, *God Needs No Passport*.

34. The classic study of the social origins of American denominationalism is H. Richard Niebuhr, *The Social Sources of Denominationalism* (1929; repr., New York: Living Age Books, 1957).

35. Yang and Ebaugh, "Transformations," 279.

36. Ibid.

37. Ibid., 279–80.

38. Ibid., 271.

39. Hanciles, *Beyond Christendom*, 293–96.

40. Fred J. Hood's study of the "evolution" of denominationalism among the Reformed churches of the middle Atlantic and Southern states is highly illuminating on this and other points. See Hood, "Evolution of the Denomination among the Reformed of the Middle and Southern States, 1780–1840," in *Denominationalism*, ed. Russell E. Richey (1977; repr., Eugene, OR: Wipf & Stock, 2010). Early on, denominations were understood as having to do with the internal government of the church. Missions, and especially the patriotic mission of Christianizing America, were carried out not through denominational structures but through the myriad voluntary societies that came into existence in the early nineteenth century: "In the wake of the fragmentation of Protestantism and the retreat of civil government from jurisdiction in matters of religion, the societies seemed to be the most efficient way to encourage religion and therefore promote the national welfare" (148). These societies claimed to be, and in some ways were, ecumenical efforts, but Hood argues that most of them were guided by some sectarian vision. The American Sunday School Union was controlled by middle-state and Southern Reformed churches, and the United Domestic Missionary Society was primarily funded and run by Reformed groups (153). See also William Swatos, "Beyond Denominationalism? Community and Culture in American Religion," *Journal for the Scientific Study of Religion* 20, no. 3 (1981): 217–27.

41. For details of the hypocrisies involved and the controversies the declaration provoked, see Gifford, *African Christianity*, 197–219. At the time President Chiluba said, "On behalf of the nation, I have now entered into covenant with the living God. . . . I submit the Government and the entire nation of Zambia to the Lordship of Jesus Christ. I further declare that Zambia is a Christian nation that will seek to be governed by the righteous principles of the Word of God" (quoted in ibid., 198). These are words that have not been uttered by a Western political leader since the seventeenth century.

42. Hanciles, *Beyond Christendom*, 350–56.

43. Peggy Levitt has made a similar argument with respect to Latinos in the United States. Since, she writes, "we live in an increasingly differentiated society," Latinos bring "their own versions of Judeo-Christian norms and practices that may challenge the existing value consensus." This means that "America's civil religious fabric is being irrevocably rewoven in the process of incorporating new Latino immigrants" and that "civil religion no longer stops at our borders but, rather, that increasingly it is a set of values and beliefs that is transnationally defined" ("Two Nations Under God? Latino Religious Life in the United States," in *Latinos: Remaking America*, ed. Marcelo M. Suarez-Orozco and Mariela Paez [Berkeley: University of California Press, 2002], 161). Levitt attributes this in part to the role of John Paul II in forming a "global civil society" (the phrase is from José Casanova), a "vision of community in which nation-state boundaries recede and a religious transnational civil society takes center stage. He [offered] an alternative membership that also empowers, protects, and speaks out for its members" (158). See also Levitt's discussion of "religious global citizens" as critical examples of cosmopolitan globalization (*God Needs No Passport*, 83–88).

44. Mark R. Gornik, *Word Made Global: Stories of African Christianity in New York City* (Grand Rapids: Eerdmans, 2011), 266–67.

45. Dean S. Gilliland, "How 'Christian' Are African Independent Churches?" *Missiology* 14, no. 3 (1986): 259–72. The divide was not merely between missionary and indigenous churches. The independent churches themselves have little connection with one another, sometimes because of a history of schism and battle.

46. A handful of majority-world evangelicals have been recognized as theological peers, not only explaining their traditions to the rest of us, but also making constructive contributions to evangelical theology. Simon Chan, who teaches at Trinity Theological College in Singapore, has written on Pentecostal theology, but his *Liturgical Theology: The Church as Worshiping*

Community (Downers Grove, IL: IVP Academic, 2006) has contributed to the renewal of interest in liturgy among evangelicals. Amos Yong has been president of the Society for Pentecostal Studies, but he has the stature to offer a meditation on the future of evangelical theology from an Asian American, Pentecostal perspective. Ugandan Catholic Emmanuel Katongole writes mainly on Africa and African theology (e.g., *The Sacrifice of Africa: A Political Theology for Africa* [Grand Rapids: Eerdmans, 2010]), but he has done so from prominent positions at Duke and Notre Dame.

47. Emmanuel Katongole, "A Tale of Many Stories," in *Shaping a Global Theological Mind*, ed. Darren Marks (Aldershot, UK: Ashgate, 2008), 89, quoted in Gornik, *Word Made Global*, 264.

48. Andrew Walls, *The Cross-Cultural Process in Christian History: Studies in the Transmission and Appropriation of Faith* (Maryknoll, NY: Orbis Books, 2002), 79.

Chapter 11 American Denominationalism in the Twenty-First Century

1. Charles Clayton Morrison, *The Unfinished Reformation* (New York: Harper & Brothers, 1953), was already announcing the collapse of denominations in the middle of the last century. Nineteenth-century observers like Philip Schaff anticipated that sectarianism would eventually run its course and give way to unity. Historians have been more cautious, noting the various transformations that denominations have undergone during the course of their history (see the arguments and literature above in chap. 5). David A. Roozen and James R. Nieman, as editors of *Church, Identity, and Change: Theology and Denominational Structures in Unsettled Times* (Grand Rapids: Eerdmans, 2005), do not ignore the challenges of denominations but highlight various strands of evidence to support their view that denominations are changing but not dying:

- Many people are investing considerable energy in the future of their denominations. . . .
- Many denominations, particularly within oldline Protestantism, face serious problems and may never regain the numerical, missiological, or cultural prominence they once enjoyed. Yet . . . neither social analysts nor denominational leaders actually believed that even the more challenged denominations were in imminent danger of collapse. . . . In denominations beyond the oldline, images of steadfast purpose and high energy predominate. . . .
- Historians have noted that during the roughly 350 years of Protestantism in North America, there have been several distinct transitions in the nature of denominations. . . . As Russell Richey succinctly remarked . . . , "Radical change is not a new experience."
- Scholars have reminded us that denominations, in addition to being organizations, are also traditions and cultures. As such, they typically have a more foundational and adaptable permanence than their organizational carriers, enabling a greater durability than appearances might first suggest. (1–2)

Roozen and Nieman conclude that "the issue facing denominations as they enter the new millennium is not death but instead how they can and do bear their particular legacies faithfully and effectively into a changing future" (3).

2. Willow Creek describes baptism as "an outward expression of an inward commitment to a personal relationship with Jesus Christ. Willow believes the decision to be baptized is up to the individual." The church celebrates the Lord's Supper "regularly" to "remember our Savior, who sacrificed Himself for our sins" ("What Willow Believes," Willow Creek Community Church, accessed August 21, 2015, http://www.willowcreek.org/aboutwillow/what-willow-believes).

3. Donald E. Miller, *Reinventing American Protestantism: Christianity in the New Millennium* (Berkeley: University of California Press, 1997), 19. Miller gives a vivid, sympathetic portrait of Calvary Chapel, Hope Chapel, and the Vineyard movement but overenthuses when he describes these churches as harbingers of a second reformation.

4. Wade Clark Roof and William McKinney, *American Mainline Religion: Its Changing Shape and Future* (New Brunswick, NJ: Rutgers University Press, 1987), 68–71. In his later *Spiritual Marketplace: Baby Boomers and the Remaking of American Religion* (Princeton: Princeton

University Press, 1999), Roof reiterates the argument that boundaries are being blurred, religious identities are becoming plastic, and traditions are merging and overlapping. John Dever, "Fading Denominationalism: New Concepts of Church," *Review and Expositor* 90 (1993): 501–15, provides a good popular overview of the argument.

5. Roof and McKinney, *American Mainline Religion*, 145. One of the main indexes of the porousness of denominational boundaries is the increase in the incidence of "mixed" or interdenominational marriages. See Robert Putnam and David E. Campbell, *American Grace: How Religion Divides and Unites Us* (New York: Simon & Schuster, 2012), 148–53.

6. For a brief account, see Roof and McKinney, *American Mainline Religion*, 172–81. David Dockery writes, "In 1955 . . . one of twenty-five churchgoing Americans tended over a lifetime to change denominations. In 1985, one in three Americans during their lifetimes changed denominations. Today, in 2009, that number is about 60 percent, which means that nearly everyone will make a denominational change in the twenty-first century" ("So Many Denominations: The Rise, Decline, and Future of Denominationalism," in *Southern Baptists, Evangelicals, and the Future of Denominationalism*, ed. David S. Dockery [Nashville: B&H Academic, 2011], 22). See also Putnam and Campbell, *American Grace*, 159–60.

7. Douglas Wilson, *Mother Kirk: Essays and Forays in Practical Ecclesiology* (Moscow, ID: Canon, 2001), 88.

8. For all the energy that this lends, it is not always welcomed by cradle Catholics. A prominent theologian once remarked to me that he is all for the First Amendment, with one qualification: conversion from one Christian tradition to another should be banned.

9. See D. Oliver Herbel, *Turning to Tradition: Converts and the Making of an American Orthodox Church* (Oxford: Oxford University Press, 2013).

10. Dean Kelley, *Why Conservative Churches Are Growing: A Study in Sociology of Religion* (New York: Harper & Row, 1972).

11. Dean R. Hoge, Benton Johnson, and Donald A. Luidens, *Vanishing Boundaries: The Religion of Mainline Protestant Baby Boomers* (Louisville: Westminster John Knox, 1994), 192.

12. Ibid., 192–94.

13. Ibid., 194.

14. Ibid., 198.

15. Ibid., 200.

16. Putnam and Campbell, *American Grace*, 17.

17. Roof and McKinney, *American Mainline Religion*, 225.

18. Ibid., 245.

19. Ibid., 247. Christian Smith is getting at a similar phenomenon in his claim that "moralistic therapeutic deism" has become the de facto established religion in America (*Soul Searching: The Religious and Spiritual Lives of American Teenagers*, with Melinda Lundquist Denton [New York: Oxford University Press, 2005]).

20. The key studies of this phenomenon are Robert Wuthnow, *The Restructuring of American Religion* (Princeton: Princeton University Press, 1990); James Davison Hunter, *Culture Wars: The Struggle to Control the Family, Art, Education and Politics in America* (New York: Basic Books, 1992). Putnam and Campbell (*American Grace*) make the culture war central to recent American religious history, a story of two contrary aftershocks. The religious right was a conservative response to the 1960s but had spent its force by the 1990s. We are in the midst of a second aftershock, a reaction to the reactionaries and a rejection of the "bigotry" of the religious right on sexual questions (see their summary on p. 80). While I do not discount this plotting, Putnam and Campbell exaggerate the role of the culture wars. Other factors have been equally or even more important in the current rearrangement of American Christianity.

21. Timothy George, "Charles Colson's 'Ecumenism of the Trenches,'" *National Catholic Register*, April 25, 2012. On the effect of culture-war restructuring on the sectarian Lutherans of the Missouri Synod, see David L. Carlson, "Fellowship and Communion in the Postmodern

Era: The Case of the Lutheran Church–Missouri Synod," in Roozen and Nieman, *Church, Identity, and Change*, 284–85, 289.

22. Wuthnow, *Restructuring of American Religion*.

23. The Presbyterian Church in America and the Orthodox Presbyterian Church are, after all, almost completely united on abortion and sodomy.

24. Robert Wuthnow has measured generational changes in scores on a "Civil Religion Index." He found that

almost four people in five (79 percent) agree that the United States was founded on Christian principles, with 51 percent agreeing strongly, and only 18 percent disagreeing. Similarly, 80 percent agree that America has been strong because of its faith in God (54 percent agree strongly). However, younger adults are much less likely to hold these views than older adults are. Only 37 percent of adults age 21 through 29 agree strongly that the United States was founded on Christian principles, whereas 71 percent of adults age 65 and older agree strongly. . . . Thus, 39 percent of adults age 21 through 29 agree strongly that America has been strong because of its faith in God, compared with 69 percent of those age 65 and older who say this.

Measured by the Civil Religion Index, 31 percent of adults in their twenties scored high, but the proportion was 70 percent among the 65-and-older crowd. See Wuthnow, *After the Baby Boomers: How Twenty- and Thirty-Somethings Are Shaping the Future of American Religion* (Princeton: Princeton University Press, 2010), 164–65.

25. One of the most insightful treatments of this trend is Joseph Bottum's recent *An Anxious Age: The Post-Protestant Ethic and the Spirit of America* (New York: Image, 2014). In Bottum's view, the collapse of mainline Protestantism is the central event of recent American political history. We now live in an age of anxiety because we can't answer the question, What replaces the mainline's soft establishment? Evangelicalism is too ecclesially weightless; Catholicism is too complex and now too ridden by scandal. What has emerged is a post-Protestant elite, which Bottum brands the "elect." The elite are not made up of the 1 percent or inhabitants of DC. Many of the elite do not think of themselves as elite at all, though their educational, economic, and social standing places them on the top of the American heap. Bottum's conclusion is somber. Absent a religious vocabulary and religious institutions that cultivate and sustain civic virtues, including the virtues of the family, what's left is "the consumer society, which is about choice, and the nanny state, which forbids and penalizes bad choices" (288). Bottum puts in a good word for the civility, the *niceness*, that even anemic American civil religion promotes, but argues that "American civil religion . . . appears derived from, even parasitical on, American Protestantism." The residual niceness that still characterizes one-on-one relationships among Americans "seems a thin reed on which to rest the future of national character," not strong enough to stand against the Manichean re-enchantment of public discourse (293–94). What, he wonders, might keep the new elites from legislating traditional believers out of the public square altogether?

Chapter 12 A Way Forward

1. See the very honest, sobering accounts assembled in André Birmelé, ed., *Local Ecumenism: How Church Unity Is Seen and Practiced by Congregations* (Strasbourg, France: Institute for Ecumenical Research, 1984).

2. John Williamson Nevin, "Catholic Unity," Theologia, accessed September 24, 2015, http://www.hornes.org/theologia/john-nevin/catholic-unity.

3. For a discussion of the federative model and its limitations, see Harding Meyer, *That All May Be One: Perceptions and Models of Ecumenicity* (Grand Rapids: Eerdmans, 1999), 81–88. Meyer discusses facts that might limit cooperation on pp. 77–79.

4. Meyer (ibid., 94–101) describes this as the "model of organic union."

5. See Walter Kasper, *A Handbook of Spiritual Ecumenism* (Hyde Park, NY: New City Press, 2007), 10.

6. Ibid., 11.

7. Paul D. Murray, *Receptive Ecumenism and the Call to Catholic Learning: Exploring a Way for Contemporary Ecumenism* (Oxford: Oxford University Press, 2010). For a brief statement of his program, see Murray, "Vatican II: On Celebrating Vatican II as Catholic and Ecumenical," in *The Second Vatican Council: Celebrating Its Achievements and the Future*, ed. Gavin D'Costa and Emma Jane Harris (London: Bloomsbury, 2013), 85–103.

8. Carl E. Braaten and Robert W. Jenson, *In One Body through the Cross: The Princeton Proposal for Christian Unity* (Grand Rapids: Eerdmans, 2003), 44–45.

9. Murray, *Receptive Ecumenism*, ix–x.

10. Eugen Rosenstock-Huessy, *I Am an Impure Thinker* (West Haven, VT: Argo Books, 2001), 12.

11. Murray, *Receptive Ecumenism*, 14.

12. Orthodox Christians sometimes claim that they hold only to the doctrine of the ecumenical councils. Even where that is true in a sense, it cannot be reasonably denied that the Orthodox churches, like all churches, have undergone doctrinal development.

13. This has been the claim of the new perspective on Paul. Contrary to some caricatures, the advocates of this program do not denounce the Reformation but argue that Paul is simply addressing a different set of questions. I believe the analogy between first-century Judaizing and the Reformation is stronger than is sometimes thought. Drawing on some of the new perspective literature, and also on apocalyptic interpretations of Paul, I argue for an alternative framework in *Delivered from the Elements of the World* (Downers Grove, IL: InterVarsity, 2016).

14. For a more substantive set of suggestions, see my programmatic "Signs of the Eschatological *Ecclesia*," in *The Oxford Handbook of Sacramental Theology*, ed. Hans Boersma and Matthew Levering (Oxford: Oxford University Press, 2015).

15. I have been accused, for instance, of holding to "Lutheran" views of baptism. To which the proper response is: What does that have to do with the truth of my views on baptism? Perhaps Lutherans are more biblical at some points than we Reformed. Suggestions of that sort, though, are the kinds of things that made me a target for a theological trial in the first place. See, for this suggestion, Braaten and Jenson, *In One Body*, 45–46.

16. Ironically, the very resistance to liturgical changes shows how important liturgy is in nonliturgical churches.

17. There are no easy ways to overcome centuries of hostility to ritual and liturgy, but a few guidelines might be useful. First, pastors must convince their churches that liturgical forms are *biblical*. This is not hard to do if you start with Leviticus; but then, second, pastors must convince their churches that liturgical forms are necessary to the *church*, not just to Old Testament Israel. Pointing to the simple fact that Jesus *commanded* two rituals—baptism and the Supper—may go some way to answering this. It may also be useful for pastors to show how liturgically and ritually structured life is in general. God created the world ritualistically, speaking and acting according to the same pattern again and again for six days. Liturgy is written into the warp and woof of the world. Finally, pastors must learn to read Scripture sacramentally, recognizing that the whole story of the Bible—from Adam's fall through the Mosaic feasts and the visions of the prophets to Jesus's ministry and the marriage supper of the Lamb—is about food and feasting. Pastors must learn to see baptism in the waters of creation, the rivers flowing from Eden, the flood and the splitting of the sea and the Jordan River. When it becomes clear that the washing and the meal are fundamental themes of Scripture, it will be easier to make the case that the church ought to give more attention to practicing these rituals. Many will object to weekly Communion on pragmatic grounds: It makes the service too long! It makes us look Catholic! It is logistically difficult to serve Communion every week in such a large church! The Lord's Supper will no longer be special! There are resources available to pastors who want to

convince their congregations to make this major liturgical change, and I will not attempt to address all the objections in depth here. The logistical issue is a real one in some large churches, and it needs to be worked through with some care. The fact that weekly Communion makes a church more closely resemble a Catholic Church is, in my book, an advantage, since in this respect the Catholic Church maintains the catholic practice of the church throughout the ages. To the objection that weekly Communion makes the Supper less special, I have three responses: first, that the church eating together *ought* to be normal and common; second, that nearly everyone I know who attends a weekly-Communion church says that the Supper takes on more meaning by being done weekly; and, third, that if we really believed infrequency enhanced the special-ness of a ritual, we would advise newlyweds to limit their kisses to one a month and agree to make love annually. Every now and again, you will find someone giving biblical and theological arguments for *in*frequent Communion. That is very rare. Virtually none of the objections to weekly Communion are theological or biblical, and that is, in my judgment, because there are no plausible biblical or theological reasons to have it less frequently.

18. Instituting weekly celebration of Communion is the fundamental liturgical reform, but the bare performance of the rite is not enough. Especially in churches where frequent Com-munion is a new practice, pastors need to continuously remind members of the reasons for the practice. Doing the Supper is critical, but as a church does the Supper, it ought also to be growing in the depth of its understanding of the Supper. And of course none of this should weaken the prophetic-evangelical stress on the necessary connection of liturgy and life. God *hates* flawless worship offered from oppressive hands and lying lips.

After weekly Communion, reinstituting the Psalter as the songbook of the church is the next most important liturgical reform. Before the rise of revivalist and gospel hymnody, the psalms had always been central to the church's worship. Medieval monks sang the Psalter each week. Luther's chorales were based on psalms ("A Mighty Fortress" is linked to Psalm 45), and Luther also wrote psalm settings both for liturgy and as congregational hymns. In Geneva the pastors produced the Genevan Psalter with its lively Geneva jigs, still in use in some churches today; Anglican churches chanted psalms; and Scottish Presbyterians also produced metrical psalms. The psalms inculcate a very different kind of piety than the piety of revival hymns. Many of the psalms, of course, come from David, a warrior and a king, a man of action. His passionate, sometimes desperate prayers are uttered in the context of conflict, battle, flight, loss, persecution, deprivation. They are militant, sometimes raw. The psalms are public hymns. When David dreams of retreat and safety, he does not think of retreating to the garden alone, but of joining the throngs of worshipers at Yahweh's temple. A congregation trained to live out of and in the Psalter is a congregation prepared for battle. It is a congregation prepared for public witness. No congregation trained in the psalms will be surprised when fiery trials hit.

19. Braaten and Jenson, *In One Body*, 48: "Until leaders of local churches see their members as baptized into the whole people of God, there will be no visible unity of all in each place."

20. One area where we need to come up with creative institutional structures is marriage. With marriage law in flux, rapidly abandoning a Christian outlook regarding marriage, we need to consider the possibility that the church will need to take a more active role in overseeing marriage, divorce, custody, etc. A state monopoly of marriage law is not a permanent given, and churches need to be considering seriously what it will take to set up marriage courts.

21. This is evident, for instance, in the reaction of some Protestants to the rise of Pente-costalism. See Harvey Cox, *Fire from Heaven: The Rise of Pentecostal Spirituality and the Reshaping of Religion in the Twenty-First Century* (Cambridge, MA: Da Capo, 1995), 74–75.

22. See Mark R. Gornik, *Word Made Global: Stories of African Christianity in New York City* (Grand Rapids: Eerdmans, 2011), 264–68.

23. Though Catholic and Orthodox traditions have taken a secondary place in this book, much the same can be said with regard to both. A Protestantism that aims only to reunite Protestantism will fail, both at being genuinely Protestant (= biblical) and at being genuinely

united. Strengthening one's tribe is not a way to overcome tribalism. Tribal enclaves are opened only by invasion and hospitality, only by the giving and receiving of gifts.

24. Rev. Stu Kerns made a pastors' group in Lincoln, Nebraska, the subject of his DMin dissertation, "Diverse Clergy in Mutually Supportive Friendships" (Covenant Theological Seminary, 2009). Kerns isolated several factors that made this group of nine pastors function well as a support network: a baseline of common beliefs, similar job descriptions, personal connection, and structure.

25. As laid out by Lesslie Newbigin, this involved the following four points:
(1) All members and ministers of the uniting Churches are accepted as members and ministers respectively of the united Church. . . . Bishops of the four dioceses are accepted as bishops of the united church, and all the other ministers of the uniting Churches who have been ordained as ministers of the Word and Sacraments are acknowledged as such in the united Church and have the status of Presbyters therein. . . . (2) In the united Church every ordination of presbyters will be performed by the laying on of hands of the bishop and presbyters, and all consecrations of bishops by the laying on of hands at least of three bishops. . . . (3) The uniting Churches pledge themselves that the union will not be used to over-ride conscientiously held convictions and to impose on congregations either forms of worship or a ministry to which they conscientiously object. . . . (4) . . . It is agreed that the intention and expectation of the uniting Churches is that eventually every minister exercising a permanent ministry in the united Church will be an episcopally ordained minister. (*The Reunion of the Church: A Defence of the South India Scheme*, rev. ed. [1960; repr., Eugene, OR: Wipf & Stock, 2011], 107)

26. Ibid., 115.

27. For this distinction, see Braaten and Jenson, *In One Body*, 53–54. In 1953, Charles Clayton Morrison identified the episcopate, along with baptism and congregational polity, as the most difficult issue in ecumenical discussion (*The Unfinished Reformation* [New York: Harper, 1953], chap. 7).

28. My friend has now written a book on his experience in Boulder: Richard Bledsoe, *The Metropolitan Manifesto* (Monroe, LA: Athanasius Press, 2015).

29. Russell Working, "Aurora Murders at Lowest Level Since 1987," *Chicago Tribune*, December 30, 2008.

30. Randy Shoof, "National Day of Prayer—Prayer Walk across Aurora," Mission America Coalition, http://community.elevatorup.com/Brix?pageID=23833.

31. Braaten and Jenson, *In One Body*, 49.

32. One of the great "catholic" achievements of American evangelicalism has been the formulation of gospel presentations that can be used across denominational lines. Whatever the problems of the Four Spiritual Laws or Evangelism Explosion, these presentations give lay Christians from many different Protestant churches an easily mastered way to present the gospel clearly and truthfully.

Index

Abram, 106
Adam, 102–5
African immigrant churches, 142–43, 146
African Independent Church, 122, 127
Aladura, the, 124
Allen, Richard, 90
Americanism, 91–95, 146
angels, 34
Anglicans, 47–48
anti-Catholicism, 49, 94–95
  and labor, 97
  and the Mexican-American War, 96–97
  See also Catholicism, Roman
anti-creedalism, 182
Aphek, battle of, 121
Apologetical Narration, An, 61
Assemblies of God, 139
Aurora, Illinois, 186
Azusa Street revival, 138

Babel, 12, 105–6
Ball, Hugo, 120
baptism, 18, 47, 176–77, 199n40
Beza, Theodore, 46
Boulder, Colorado, 185–86
Bucer, Martin, 40, 46
Buddhism, 144
bureaucracy, 32–33
Burroughs, Jeremiah, 62–63

Calvin, John, 40, 42, 129, 174, 199n31
Catholicism, Reformational. *See* Reformational
  Catholicism
Catholicism, Roman, 38, 41, 47–48, 130. *See*
  also anti-Catholicism

Cesar, Waldo, 140
Chaves, Mark, 80
China, 126–27
church, true, 42, 47–48
church discipline and Communion, 181
Church of South India, 25, 27, 185
Clark, Tom, 183–84
Communion, 18, 31, 41, 80, 130, 176–77, 180–
  81, 196n16, 220–21nn17–18
communio sanctorum, 40–41, 43, 46
consumerism, religious, 65–66, 74, 79, 86
Contarini, Gasparo, 129
Corinthians, divisions among the, 17, 18, 38,
  195n10
Cuddihy, John, 78, 85
culture wars, 158, 218n20

Dawkins, Robby, 186
denominationalism, 3–4, 75–79, 201n2,
  216n40
  in America, 60–65, 85–86, 93, 98
  and culture, 67–68
  and doctrine, 77–79
  and homogeneity, 74–77
  and immigration, 146
  and meta-governmental structures, 57–59
  and schismogenesis, 81–82
  and unity, 184–85
  virtues of, 55–56, 59, 62, 66, 69
  and war, 86–87
  See also pluralism, religious
doctrine, 2, 67, 168, 173, 178, 182
  and denominationalism, 77–79
DuBois, W. E. B., 86

Ebaugh, Helen Rose, 144
ecumenicism, 77, 144–45
  federative, 166
  receptive, 167–69
  spiritual, 167
Elliott, Stephen, 90
Emerson, Michael, 73, 86, 91, 208n45
Engbarth, David, 186
"Ephesian moment" (Walls), 148
Ephesians, unity in the book of, 15–17
Eucharist. See Communion
Evangelical Church of Congo, The, 123
evangelicals, 22, 137
  and individualism, 92–93
  and race, 92–93
exodus, the, 107–9

Finke, Roger, 66

Galatian church, 14, 20
Genesis
  creation and fall in, 11–12, 101–5
  postdiluvian world in, 105–7
George, Timothy, 160
Gilliland, Dean, 147
Goodman, Godfrey, 47
Gornik, Mark, 147
grace, 62, 174

Haas, Dan, 186
Hall, Joseph, 48
Hanciles, Jehu, 142, 146
Herberg, Will, 82–84, 94
Hoge, Dean, 155
Hollenweger, Walter, 141
Hooft, Willem Visser 't, 193n3
Hutchinson, Anne, 60

idolatry, 42–46, 199n31
immigrant churches, 141–46, 214n19, 215n24,
  215n27
immigration, 141–42, 145, 216n43
  and catholicity, 144, 183
  and denominationalism, 145–46
individualism, 157–58

James, justification in the book of, 175
Jenkins, Philip, 134–35
Jenson, Robert, 195n16
Johnson, Darlingston, 143
Jones, Samuel Porter, 63

Jordan, James, 31
justification, 45–46, 174–75

Kalu, Ogbu, 123
Kasper, Walter, 167
Katongole, Emmanuel, 147–48
Kelley, Dean, 155, 205n3
Ketcham, Nathan, 184
Kibongi, Raymond Buana, 123
koinonia, 195n16

Latimer, Hugh, 42
Levitt, Peggy, 216n43
liberalism, 78, 160, 178
liturgy, 30, 114, 220n17
Lord's Supper, the. See Communion
Lumen Gentium, 130
Luther, Martin, 41, 43–46, 176, 190

Machen, J. Gresham, 78
McNeill, John T., 40–42, 48, 198n13
Magnusson, John, 123
Martin, David, 63, 134–35, 138, 140
Mead, Sidney, 72, 85
Melanchthon, Philipp, 46
micro-Christendoms, 185–87
missions, 68, 122, 126, 143, 147, 153
Montagu, Richard, 47
Murray, Paul, 167

Nephilim, 104
Nevin, John Williamson, 166
Newbigin, Lesslie, 193n6, 222n25
Niebuhr, H. Richard, 67, 75, 85–86, 90–91, 154,
  197n2
Noah, 104–5
nondenominationalism, 152–53

Orthodoxy, 38, 131, 170
Ositelu, Josiah Olunowo, 125
Ositelu, Rufus, 125

Pastorius, Francis Daniel, 60
pastors, 33–34, 148, 178–84, 187
Pentecostalism, 123, 125–27, 134–35, 137, 141
  and class, 139–40
  and race, 138–39
  and the Spirit, 136
Philippians, unity in the book of, 17, 20
pluralism, religious, 58–59, 66. See also
  denominationalism
postmodernism, 120
prayer, 31–32, 165, 167, 178, 186, 188
Prayer Coalition for Reconciliation, 186

Princeton Proposal for Christian Unity, 168
Protestantism, 37–39
   American, 93–94, 97
   and church-state relations, 114
   and confessionalization, 48–49, 200n46
   death of, 190–91
   and grace, 174
   history of, 48–49
   mainline, 156, 219n25
   and nondenominationalism, 152
   and Pentecostalism, 135, 139
   and Reformational Catholicism, 51, 190–91
Protestant Reformation. *See* Reformation,
   Protestant
Psalms, 31–32, 221n18
Psalter, the, 31–32, 221n18

race
   and denominationalism, 89–91
   and economic inequality, 208n45
   and evangelicals, 92–93
   See also segregation
Radner, Ephraim, 5
receptivity, 167–69
Reformation, English, 42
Reformation, Protestant, 4, 39–42
   and confessionalization, 49–51
   and idolatry, 42–46, 199n31
Reformational Catholicism, 6, 39, 50, 190–91
   and the Bible, 28–30, 179–80
   and church discipline, 33
   vs. denominational Christianity, 55–57, 77–78
   ecclesiological vision of, 28–36
   and lay Christians, 187–89
   and music, 31–32
religion
   civil, 219n24
   operational, 82–83
Roe v. Wade, 159
Roman Catholicism. *See* Catholicism, Roman
Rosenstock-Huessy, Eugen, 14–15, 103, 168–69

sacraments, 45–47, 171, 176, 196n6
saints, 32
Sayler, David, 184
schismogenesis, 81–82
sectarianism, 58, 73
secularism, 65
   and denominationalism, 82–84
segregation
   church, 74–76
   and denominationalism, 91
   See also race

Sehat, David, 84, 97
Seymour, William, 136–38
slavery, 206n20
Smith, Christian, 73, 86, 91, 208n45
Smith, Timothy L., 202n10
Smyth, Newman, 89
soteriology, 174
Stark, Rodney, 66
Sutton, John, 80
Swatos, William, 57–58

Tabieorar, 124–25
theosis, 195n16
tribalism, 172

unity
   and biblical interpretation, 179–80
   of the church, 165–72
   and church discipline, 182–83
   and denominational identity, 184–85
   doctrinal and theological, 168, 172–78
   in Ephesians, 15–17
   evangelical, 195n16
   lay Christians and, 187–90
   liturgical, 180–81
   in the New Testament, 194–95n10
   organizational, 32–33
   in Philippians, 17, 20

Vatican II, 129–30
Vineyard, the, 138

Walls, Andrew, 148
war and denominationalism, 86–87
Westminster Confession, 136, 174
Williams, Roger, 60
Willow Creek Community Church, 136
Wilson, Douglas, 154
Wimber, John, 137
Wittenberg Concord, 46
World Council of Churches (WCC), 22, 32
   Assembly at New Delhi (1961), 21, 36
World War I, 119–20
Wright, N. T., 14
Wuthnow, Robert, 94, 160
Yahweh, 102, 104–5
Yang, Fenggang, 144
Yeago, David, 43, 44

Zwingli, Ulrich, 39, 176